The Rich Get Richer and the Poor Get Prison

The Rich Get Richer and the Poor Get Prison

Ideology, Class, and Criminal Justice

FOURTH EDITION

JEFFREY REIMAN

The American University, Washington, D.C.

Allyn & Bacon
Boston London Toronto Sydney Tokyo Singapore

Library of Congress Cataloging-in-Publication Data

Reiman, Jeffrey H.

The rich get richer and the poor get prison : ideology, class, and criminal justice / Jeffrey Reiman. —4th ed.

p. cm.

Includes index.

ISBN 0-02-399252-2

1. Criminal justice, Administration of—United States. 2. Social classes—United States. 3. United States—Social policy. I. Title.

HV9950.R46 1995

364.973—dc20 94-17222 CIP

Editor: Karen Hanson
Production Supervisor: Jane O'Neil
Production Manager: Francesca Drago
Interior Design: Robert Freese
Cover Design: Curtis Tow Graphics

Allyn & Bacon
A Simon & Schuster Company
160 Gould Street
Needham Heights, Massachusetts 02/94

Printed in the United States of America

10 9 8 7 6 5 4 3 2 1 99 98 97 96 95 94

For John Wildeman

Preface to the Fourth Edition

The Clinton administration and the Congress are currently wailing about the worsening problem of street crime and putting together legislation to build more prisons and hire more police officers, even though most experts are telling them that street crime has not really worsened all that much, that neither more cops nor more prisons will reduce it anyway, and that we already have the largest percentage of our citizens behind bars of any modern nation! Meanwhile, though the crimes involve thefts of millions of dollars, prosecutions in the savings and loan scandal are proceeding at a snail's pace, prison sentences when handed out are averaging 18 months to two years, and only pennies of each dollar fined are being collected. Could this difference in response have anything to do with the fact that street crime is the work of poor youngsters, and bank defrauders are a higher class of crook?

As this question suggests, recent events continue to bear out the main theses of the original edition of this book: It is still true that the well-off folks who are guilty of white-collar crimes are treated more gently than the poor ones who are guilty of nonviolent property crimes. It is still true that better-off offenders are less likely to end up behind bars than poor offenders, even when they have committed the same offense. It is still true that acts, such as those that result in occupational death and disease, are not treated as crimes (or if treated as crimes, not treated as serious crimes) though they pose at least as great a danger to the public as the acts that are treated as (serious) crimes—and often a significantly greater danger. In short, it is still true that *the rich get richer and the poor get prison.*

In revising the book for this fourth edition, I have mainly tried to show that this is true by updating the statistics on criminal and noncriminal harms and incorporating the results of the relevant research that has appeared since the last edition. I have tried to introduce these updates with as little violation of the original edition's style and argument as possible, though in some cases I have revised and expanded arguments based on what teachers who have used the book in class have told me about student responses to certain parts of the book.

This edition reports findings of studies published as recently as 1993. However, where I compare the relative danger of criminal versus noncriminal harms (such as occupational and environmental hazards), I generally use figures for 1992 or 1991, because these were the latest years for which I could find adequate statistics on both types of harm. When new statistics were not available, I have, where it seemed plausible, assumed that earlier statistics reflect continuing trends and enable projections from the past into the present. In all cases, I have tried to keep my assumptions as conservative as possible to keep the argument on the firmest ground.

Those interested in the relationship between politics and research should find the following facts intriguing. This is the fourth time I have tried to arrive at estimates of the amount and cost of white-collar crime in the United States. I am increasingly struck by the fact that, though we are literally inundated with statistics on "common" crimes and have been since the federal government began collecting and publishing them in the 1930s, and though everyone agrees that white-collar crime costs the nation far more than the common crimes, no public or private agency regularly collects statistics on white-collar crime. Furthermore, this is also the fourth time that I have reviewed the scholarly sociology and criminology journals looking for studies on the relationship between socioeconomic status and arrest, conviction, and sentencing. When the first edition of *The Rich Get Richer* appeared, there was a substantial number of such studies, largely stimulated by President Johnson's establishment in 1965 of the President's Commission on Law Enforcement and the Administration of Justice. Almost universally, these studies showed the presence of significant bias against lower-class suspects at every stage of criminal justice processing from arrest on. With each subsequent edition of *The Rich Get Richer,* the number of new studies on this topic has decreased, so that now, having looked at virtually every major (and many not-so-major) journal in the field between 1988 and 1993, I find that the number of new studies has dwindled to a trickle. It seems to me that a young criminologist could make a name for him- or herself by trying to replicate some of the studies done in the wake of the President's Commission, but no one seems to be biting. It's worth wondering why this is happening. Has the Reagan-era "get tough on crooks" attitude made the question of economic deprivation and bias taboo? Perhaps, but social scientists have a profound obligation not to give in to such pressure. What we don't know will hurt us.

In the last edition, I introduced two changes aimed at making the book more useful for classroom teachers. First, summaries and study questions were added to the chapters after the Introduction. The study questions require students both to recall what they have read and to think critically about it. The questions can be used by instructors for testing and review and by students as a way of making sure they have covered and thought about the most important issues in each chapter. Second, a short essay on Marxian theory and criminal justice was added as an appendix. The essay covers the ground from a general statement of Marxian theories of capitalism, ideology, and law, to a Marxian theory of criminal justice. Many instructors have found this a handy and economical way of introducing their students to Marxian theory and its relation to criminal law and criminology. The essay addresses some of the same issues discussed in the main text of *The Rich Get Richer* and thus offers an alternative theoretical framework for understanding those issues. Although this framework is compatible with that developed in the main text, the argument of *The Rich Get Richer* stands alone without it. I have continued these two changes in this edition and added a third, a list of additional readings at the end of each chapter so that students stimulated by the material in the chapter could read further on particular topics. Moreover, the additional readings should help instructors when they assign outside reading or research on the topics touched upon in the book

Because I have revised rather that rewritten *The Rich Get Richer,* I am still indebted to those who helped me with the original edition. They are thanked in the following section, *Acknowledgments for the First Edition.* I thank also Marcia Trick who helped me so much on the second and third editions, and Jean Landis who pitched in on the third. For this fourth edition, I have been assisted by an exceptional graduate student in criminal justice and sociology, Paul Leighton. I thank Paul not only for his hard work and good judgment in gathering the data, statistics and studies, that I used in updating the book; but also for his excellent suggestions, many of which I have incorporated in the book and which I think have improved it.

As before, I am grateful to The American University for providing me with a supportive and lively intellectual environment, not to mention a recent sabbatical during which I could do the lion's share of the work of revision. I thank also Chris Cardone, my editor at Macmillan, for her support, her good counsel, and her good cheer. I am grateful for the comments of Peter J. Benekos of Mercyhurst College in Pennsylvania and Barry Truchil of Ryder College in New Jersey. I thank also my wife, Sue Headlee, who has delighted and inspired me for more than 18 years.

Finally, while this edition was being prepared, John Wildeman, Professor of Sociology at Hofstra University, died at the age of 56. John was a close friend for 25 years. I owe him much. It was due to him that the process was set in motion that led to my joining the faculty of The American University, where I have spent virtually all my professional life. It was John who introduced me to the work of Richard Quinney, which both excited and frustrated me into writing this book. John was an outrageous guy, a lover of freedom and justice, a hater of conformity and hypocrisy, a loyal friend who died too young. I dedicate this edition to his memory.

Jeffrey Reiman

Acknowledgments for the First Edition

This book is the product of seven years of teaching in the School of Justice (formerly, the Center for the Administration of Justice), a multidisciplinary criminal justice education program at The American University in Washington, D.C. I have had the benefit of the school's lively and diverse faculty and student body. And, although they will surely not agree with all that I have to say, I have drawn heavily on what I have learned from my colleagues over the years and stand in their debt. In addition, more than is ordinarily recognized, a teacher receives guidance from students as they test, confirm, reject, and expand what they learn in class in the light of their own experience. Here, too, I am deeply in debt. My thanks go to the hundreds of students who have shared some part of their world with me as they passed through The American University, and in particular to three students whose encouragement, loyalty, and wisdom are very much a part of the development of the ideas in this book: Elizabeth Crimi, Bernard Demczuk, and Lloyd Raines.

I express my gratitude to The American University for providing me with a summer research grant that enabled me to devote full time to the book in the summer of 1976 when most of the actual writing was done. I am also grateful to Bernard Demczuk who was my research assistant during the academic year 1975 to 1976 and who gathered much of the research data. I owe thanks as well to Cathy Sacks for ably and carefully typing the final manuscript.

Drafts of the manuscript for this book were read in whole or in part by (or at) Bernard Demczuk, Sue Hollis, Richard Myren, Lloyd Raines, Phillip Scribner, I. F. Stone, and John Wildeman. I am grateful for their many comments and I incorporate many of their recommendations in the final version. I have made my mistakes in spite of them.

Finally, for teaching me about artichokes, the meaning of history, and countless other mysteries, this book is dedicated to Sue Headlee Hollis.

J. R.

Contents

Tables

The Rich Get Richer and the Poor Get Prison

FREE COPY

Introduction: Criminal Justice Through the Looking Glass, or Winning by Losing

The inescapable conclusion is that society secretly wants crime, needs crime, and gains definite satisfactions from the present mishandling of it.

Karl Menninger, *The Crime of Punishment*

A criminal justice system is a mirror in which a whole society can see the darker outlines of its face. Our ideas of justice and evil take on visible form in it, and thus we see ourselves in deep relief. Step through this looking glass to view the American criminal justice system—and ultimately the whole society it reflects—from a radically different angle of vision.

In particular, entertain the idea that the goal of our criminal justice system is not to reduce crime or to achieve justice but to project to the American public a visible image of the threat of crime. To do this, it must maintain the existence of a sizable population of criminals. To do this, it must fail in the struggle to reduce crime. Crime may, of course, occasionally decline, as it has from time to time in recent years—but not because of criminal justice policies.

You will rightly demand to know how and why a society such as ours would tolerate a criminal justice system designed to fail in the fight against crime. A considerable portion of this book is devoted to answering this question. Right now, however, a short explanation of how this upside-down idea of criminal justice was born will best introduce it, and me.

Some years ago, I taught a seminar for graduate students titled "The Philosophy of Punishment and Rehabilitation." Many of the students were already working in the field of corrections as probation officers or prison guards or halfway-house counselors. First we examined the various philosophical justifications for legal punishment, and then we directed our attention to the actual functioning of our correctional system. For much of the semester we talked about the myriad inconsistencies and cruelties and overall irrationality of the system. We discussed the arbitrariness with which offenders are sentenced to prison and the arbitrariness with which they are treated once there. We discussed the lack of privacy and the deprivation of sources of personal identity and dignity, the ever-present physical violence, as well as the lack of meaningful counseling or job training within prison walls. We discussed the harassment of parolees, the inescapability of the "ex-con" stigma, the refusal of society to let a person finish paying his or her "debt to society," and the nearly total absence of meaningful noncriminal opportunities for the ex-prisoner. We confronted time and again the bald irrationality of a society that builds prisons to prevent crime knowing full well that they do not and that does not even seriously try to rid its prisons and postrelease practices of those features that guarantee a high rate of *recidivism*: the return to crime by prison alumni. How could we fail so miserably? We are neither an evil nor a stupid nor an impoverished people. How could we continue to bend our energies and spend our hard-earned tax dollars on cures we know are not working?

Toward the end of the semester I asked the students to imagine that, instead of designing a correctional system to reduce and prevent crime, we had to design one that would maintain and encourage a stable and visible  "class" of criminals. What would it look like? The response was electrifying. In briefer and somewhat more orderly form, here is a sample of the proposals that emerged in our discussion:

First. It would be helpful to have laws on the books against drug use or prostitution or gambling—laws that prohibit acts that have no unwilling victim. This would make many people "criminals" for what they regard as normal behavior and would increase their need to engage in *secondary* crime (the drug addict's need to steal to pay for drugs, the prostitute's need for a pimp, because police protection is unavailable, and so on).

Second. It would be good to give police, prosecutors, and judges broad discretion to decide who got arrested, who got charged, and who got sentenced to prison. This would mean that almost anyone who got as far as prison would know of others who committed the same crime but who either were not arrested or were not charged or were not sentenced to prison. This would assure us that a good portion of the prison population would experience their confinement as arbitrary and unjust and thus respond with rage, which would make them more "antisocial," rather than respond with remorse, which would make them feel more bound by social norms.

Third. The prison experience should be not only painful but also demeaning. The pain of loss of liberty might deter future crime. But demeaning and emasculating prisoners by placing them in an enforced childhood characterized by no privacy and no control over their time and actions, as well as by the constant threat of rape or assault, is sure to overcome any deterrent effect by weakening whatever capacities a prisoner had for self-control. Indeed, by humiliating and brutalizing prisoners we can be sure to increase their potential for aggressive violence.[1]

Fourth. It goes almost without saying that prisoners should neither be trained in a marketable skill nor provided with a job after release. Of course, their prison records should stand as a perpetual stigma to discourage employers from hiring them. Otherwise, they might be tempted *not* to return to crime after release.

Fifth. The ex-offenders' sense that they will always be different from "decent citizens," that they can never finally settle their debt to society, should be reinforced by the following means. They should be deprived for the rest of their lives of rights, such as the right to vote. They should be harassed by police as "likely suspects" and be subject to the whims of parole officers who can at any time threaten to send them back to prison for things no ordinary citizens could be arrested for, such as going out of town or drinking or fraternizing with the "wrong people."

And so on.

In short, *asked to design a system that would maintain and encourage the existence of a stable and visible "class of criminals," we "constructed" the American criminal justice system!*

What is to be made of this? First, it is, of course, only part of the truth. Some steps have been taken to reduce sentencing discretion. And some prison officials do try to treat their inmates with dignity and to respect their privacy and self-determination to the greatest extent possible within an institution dedicated to involuntary confinement. Minimum security prisons and halfway houses are certainly moves in this direction. Some prisons do provide meaningful job training, and some parole officers are not only fair but go out of their way to help their "clients" find jobs and make it "legally." And plenty of people are arrested for doing things that no society ought to tolerate, such as rape, murder, assault, or armed robbery, and many are in prison who might be preying on their fellow citizens if they were not. *All of this is true.* Complex social practices are just that: *complex.* They are neither all good nor all bad. For all that, though, the "successes" of the system, the "good" prisons, the halfway houses that really help offenders make it, are still the exceptions. They are not even prevalent enough to be called the beginning of the trend of the future. *On the whole, most of the system's practices make more sense if we look at them as ingredients in an attempt to maintain rather than to reduce crime!*

This statement calls for an explanation. The one I will offer is that the practices of the criminal justice system keep before the public the *real* threat of crime and the *distorted* image that crime is primarily the work of the poor. The value of this *to those in positions of power* is that it deflects the discontent and potential hostility of Middle America away from the classes above them and toward the classes below them. If this explanation is hard to swallow, it should be noted in its favor that it not only explains our dismal failure to reduce crime but also explains why the criminal justice system functions in a way that is biased against the poor at every stage from arrest to conviction. Indeed, even at the earlier stage, when crimes are defined in law, the system primarily concentrates on the predatory acts of the poor and tends to exclude or deemphasize the equally or more dangerous predatory acts of those who are well off. In sum, I will argue that *the criminal justice system fails to reduce crime while making it look as if crime is the work of the poor*. It does this in a way that conveys the image that the real danger to decent, law-abiding Americans comes from below them, rather than from above them, on the economic ladder. This image sanctifies the status quo with its disparities of wealth, privilege, and opportunity and thus serves the interests of the rich and powerful in America—the very ones who could change criminal justice policy if they were really unhappy with it.

Therefore, it seems appropriate to ask you to look at criminal justice "through the looking glass." On the one hand, this suggests a reversal of common expectations. Reverse your expectations about criminal justice and entertain the notion that the system's real goal is the very reverse of its announced goal. On the other hand, the figure of the looking glass suggests the prevalence of image over reality. My argument is that the system functions the way it does *because it creates a particular image of crime: the image that it is a threat from the poor.* Of course, for this image to be believable there must be a reality to back it up. The system must actually fight crime—or at least some crime—but only enough to keep it from getting out of hand and to keep the struggle against crime vividly and dramatically in the public's view—never enough to substantially reduce or eliminate crime.

I call this outrageous way of looking at criminal justice policy the *Pyrrhic defeat* theory. A "Pyrrhic victory" is a military victory purchased at such a cost in troops and treasure that it amounts to a defeat. The Pyrrhic defeat theory argues that the failure of the criminal justice system yields such benefits to those in positions of power that it amounts to success. In what follows, I will try to explain the failure of the criminal justice system to reduce crime by showing the benefits that accrue to the powerful in America from this failure. I will argue that from the standpoint of those with the power to make criminal justice policy in America: *Nothing succeeds like failure.* I challenge you to keep an open mind and determine for yourself whether the Pyrrhic defeat theory does not make more sense out of criminal justice policy and practice than the old-fashioned idea that the goal of the system is to reduce crime.

The Pyrrhic defeat theory has several components. Above all, it must provide an explanation of *how* the failure to reduce crime could benefit anyone—anyone other than criminals, that is. This is the task of Chapter 4, "To the Vanquished Belong the Spoils: Who Is Winning the Losing War Against Crime?" I argue there that the failure to reduce crime broadcasts a potent *ideological* message to the American people, a message that benefits and protects the powerful and privileged in our society by legitimating the present social order with its disparities of wealth and privilege and by diverting public discontent and opposition away from the rich and powerful and onto the poor and powerless.

To provide this benefit, however, not just any failure will do. It is necessary that the failure of the criminal justice system take a particular shape. *It must take a dive in the fight against crime while making it look as if serious crime and thus the real danger to society is the work of the poor.* The system accomplishes this both by what it does and by what it refuses to do. In Chapter 2, "A Crime by Any Other Name … ," I argue that the criminal justice system refuses to label and treat as crime a large number of acts that produce as much or more damage to life and limb as the so-called crimes of the poor. In Chapter 3, "… and the Poor Get Prison," I show how, even among the acts treated as crimes, the criminal justice system is biased from start to finish in a way that guarantees that *for the same crimes* members of the lower classes are much more likely than members of the middle and upper classes to be arrested, convicted, and imprisoned—thus providing living "proof" that crime is a threat from the poor. (A statement of the main propositions that form the core of the Pyrrhic defeat theory is found in Chapter 2 in the section titled "Criminal Justice as Creative Art.")

One caution is in order: The argument in Chapters 1 through 4 is not a "conspiracy theory." It is the task of social analysis to find patterns in social behavior and then explain them. Naturally, when we find patterns, particularly patterns that serve some people's interests, we are inclined to think of these patterns as *intended* by those whose interests are served, as somehow brought into being *because* they serve those interests. This way of thinking is generally called a "conspiracy theory." Later I will say more about the shortcomings of this way of thinking, and I will explain in detail how the Pyrrhic defeat theory differs from it. For the present, however, note that although I speak of the criminal justice system as "not wanting" to reduce crime and of the failure to reduce crime as resulting in benefits to the rich and powerful in our society, *I am not maintaining that the rich and powerful intentionally make the system fail to gather up the resulting benefits.* My view is rather that the system has grown up piecemeal over time and usually with the best of intentions. The unplanned and unintended overall result is a system that not only fails to reduce crime but does so in a way that serves the interests of the rich and powerful. One consequence of this fact is that those who could change the system feel no need to do so. And thus it keeps on rolling along.

Our criminal justice system is characterized by beliefs about what is criminal, and beliefs about how to deal with crime, that predate industrial society. Rather than being anyone's conscious plan, the system reflects attitudes so deeply embedded in tradition as to appear natural. To understand why it persists even though it fails to protect us, all that is necessary is to recognize that, on the one hand, those who are the most victimized by crime are not those in positions to make and implement policy. Crime falls more frequently and more harshly on the poor than on the better off (see Chapter 4). On the other hand, there are enough benefits to the wealthy from the identification of crime with the poor and the system's failure to reduce crime (see Chapter 4, the section "The Poverty of Criminals and the Crime of Poverty") that those with the power to make profound changes in the system feel no compulsion nor see any incentive to make them. In short, the criminal justice system came into existence in an earlier epoch and persists in the present because, even though it is failing, indeed because of the way it fails, it generates no effective demand for change. When I speak of the criminal justice system as "designed to fail," I mean no more than this. I call this explanation of the existence and persistence of our failing criminal justice system the *historical inertia* explanation. In Chapter 4, I shall spell out this explanation in greater detail.

In the concluding chapter, I present an argument that the conditions described in Chapters 1, 2, and 3 (whether or not one accepts my explanation for them in Chapter 4) undermine the essential moral difference between criminal justice and crime itself. In this chapter, called "*Criminal* Justice or Criminal *Justice*," I make some recommendations for reform of the system. However, these are not offered as ways to "improve" the system but as the minimal conditions necessary to establish the moral superiority of that system to crime itself.

It will prevent confusion later if the reader remembers that when I speak of the criminal justice system, I mean more than the familiar institutions of police, courts, and prisons. I mean the entire system that runs from the decisions of lawmakers about what acts are criminal all the way to the decisions of judges and parole boards about who will be in prison to pay for these acts.

I claim no particular originality for the Pyrrhic defeat theory. It is a child of the marriage of several streams of Western social theory. Although this is discussed at greater length in what follows, it will serve clarity to indicate from the start the parents and the grandparents of this child. The idea that crime serves important functions for a society comes from Émile Durkheim. The notion that public policy can be best understood as serving the interests of the rich and powerful in a society stems from Karl Marx. From Kai Erikson is derived the notion that the institutions designed to fight crime instead contribute to its existence. From Richard Quinney comes the concept of the "reality" of crime as *created* in the process that runs from the definition of some acts as "criminal" in the law to the treatment of some persons as "criminals" by the agents of the law. The Pyrrhic defeat theory combines these ideas into the view that the failure of criminal justice policy becomes intelligible when we see that it creates the "reality" of crime as the work of the poor and thus projects an image that serves the interests of the rich and powerful in American society.

Though the Pyrrhic defeat theory draws on the ideas just mentioned, it changes them in the process. For example, the theory veers away from traditional Marxist accounts of legal institutions insofar as such accounts generally emphasize the *repressive* function of the criminal justice system, whereas my view emphasizes its *ideological* function. On the whole, Marxists see the criminal justice system as serving the powerful by *successfully* repressing the poor. My view is that the system serves the powerful by its *failure* to reduce crime, not by its success. Needless to add, insofar as the system fails in some respects and succeeds in others, these approaches are not necessarily incompatible. Nevertheless, in looking at the ideological rather than the repressive function of criminal justice, I will focus primarily on the image its *failure* conveys rather than on what it actually *succeeds* in repressing.[2] (The Appendix contains a general statement of the relationship between Marxian theory and criminal justice. One point I make there that is worth mentioning here is that it is not necessary to be a socialist to profit from Marx's insights into capitalism and its legal system. This is important to note because many people think the recent demise of socialism in eastern Europe and the former Soviet Union amounts to a refutation of Marxism. Actually, Marx had very little to say about socialism or communism. Most of his writings are about capitalism, and one might agree with his analysis of capitalism even if one thought that socialism was awful or impossible.)

Having located the Pyrrhic defeat theory in its family tree, I wish to say a word about the relationship between crime and economics. It is my view that the social order (shaped decisively by the economic system) causes or promotes most of the crime that troubles us. This is true of all classes in the society, because a competitive economy that refuses to guarantee its members a decent living places pressures on all members to enhance their economic position by whatever means available. It degrades and humiliates the poor while encouraging the greed of the well off.[3] Nevertheless, these economic pressures work with particular harshness on the poor because their condition of extreme need and their relative lack of access to opportunities for lawful economic advancement vastly intensify for them the pressures toward crime that exist at all levels of our society.

These views lead to others that, if not taken in their proper context, may strike you as paradoxical. Evidence will be presented showing that there is a considerable amount of crime in our society at all socioeconomic levels. At the same time, it will be argued that poverty is a *source* of crime—I say "source" rather than "cause" because the link between poverty and crime is not like a physical relationship between cause and effect. Many, perhaps most, poor people do not commit serious crimes. Nevertheless, there is evidence suggesting that the particular pressures of poverty lead poor people to commit a higher proportion of the crimes that people fear (such as homicide, burglary, and assault) than their number in the population. There is no contradiction between this and the recognition that those who are well off commit many more crimes than is generally acknowledged, both the crimes widely feared and those not widely feared (such as white-collar crimes). There is no contradiction here, because, as will be shown, the poor are arrested far more frequently than those who are well off when they have committed the same crimes; and the well-to-do are only rarely arrested for white-collar crimes. Thus, if arrest records were brought in line with the real incidence of crime, it is likely that those who are well off would appear in the records far more than they do at present, even though the poor would still probably appear in numbers greater than their proportion of the population in arrests for the crimes people fear. In addition to this, I will argue that those who are well off commit dangerous acts that are not defined as crimes and yet that are as or more harmful than the crimes people fear. Thus, if we had an accurate picture of who is really dangerous to society, there is reason to believe that those who are well off would receive still greater representation. On this basis, the following propositions will be put forth, which may appear contradictory if these various levels of analysis are not kept distinct.

1. Society fails to protect people from the crimes they fear by refusing to alleviate the poverty that breeds them (among other things, documented in Chapter 1).
2. The criminal justice system fails to protect people from the most serious dangers by failing to define the dangerous acts of those who

are well off as crimes (documented in Chapter 2) and by failing to enforce the law vigorously against the well-to-do when they commit acts that are defined as crimes (documented in Chapter 3).

3. By virtue of these and other failures, the criminal justice system succeeds in creating the image that crime is almost exclusively the work of the poor, an image that serves the interests of the powerful (argued in Chapter 4).

The view that the social order is responsible for crime does not mean that individuals are wholly blameless for their criminal acts or that we ought not have a criminal justice system able to protect us against them. To borrow an analogy from Ernest van den Haag, it would be foolhardy to refuse to fight a fire because its causes were suspect. The fact that society produces criminals is no reason to avoid facing the realization that these criminals are dangerous and must be dealt with. Also, although blaming society for crime may require that we tone down our blame of individual criminals, it does not require that we eliminate blame entirely or deny that they are responsible for their crimes. This is particularly important to remember because so many of the victims of the crimes of the poor are poor themselves. To point to the unique social pressures that lead the poor to prey on one another is to point to a mitigating, not an excusing, factor. Even the victims of exploitation and oppression have moral obligations not to harm those who do not exploit them or who share their oppression.

Abbreviations Used in the Notes

Challenge	*The Challenge of Crime in a Free Society: A Report by the President's Commission on Law Enforcement and Administration of Justice* (Washington, D.C.: U.S. Government Printing Office, February 1967).
Sourcebook-1992	Kathleen Maguire, Ann L. Pastore, and Timothy J. Flanagan, eds., *Sourcebook of Criminal Justice Statistics—1992.* U.S. Department of Justice, Office of Justice Programs, Bureau of Justice Statistics (Washington, D.C.: U.S. Government Printing Office, 1993). References to other editions of this annual publication will be indicated by *Sourcebook,* followed by the year in the title. Other editions may have different editors.
StatAbst-1992	U.S. Bureau of the Census, *Statistical Abstract of the United States: 1992,* 112th ed. (Washington, D.C.: U.S. Government Printing Office, 1992). References to other editions of this annual publication will be indicated by *StatAbst,* followed by the year in the title.

UCR-1992 U.S. Department of Justice, Federal Bureau of Investigation, *Uniform Crime Reports for the United States: 1992* (Washington, D.C.: U.S Government Printing Office, 1993). References to other editions of this annual report will be indicated by *UCR* followed by the year for which the statistics are reported. In general, these reports are published in the fall of the year following the year they cover.

BJS Bureau of Justice Statistics, a source of many reports cited in this book. The Bureau of Justice Statistics is an agency of the U.S. Department of Justice. It is part of the Justice Department's Office of Justice Programs, which also includes the Bureau of Justice Assistance, the National Institute of Justice, the Office of Juvenile Justice and Delinquency Prevention, and the Office for Victims of Crime. Reports of the Bureau of Justice Statistics are published by the U.S. Government Printing Office in Washington, D.C., normally in the year following the year in the title of the report.

Notes to the Introduction

1. I recently came upon the following account:

> *Dr. Meredith Bombar, a social psychologist and ... associate professor of psychology at Elmira College, notes that it would be difficult intentionally to shape a more effective breeding ground for aggression than that which already exists in the average prison. In personal correspondence, Dr. Bombar writes, "When I teach Social Psychology class, I spend a week or so going over the social/learned causes of aggression (e.g., provocation, modeling, punishment, extreme frustration, roles and social norms calling for aggression, physical discomfort, crowding, presence of guns and other objects associated with aggression, etc.). After the students have digested that, I ask them to imagine a horrible fantasy world which would put together all of these known social/environmental causes of aggression. What would it be? A typical prison."* Lee Griffith, *The Fall of the Prison: Biblical Perspectives on Prison Abolition* (Grand Rapids: Eerdmans, 1993), p. 65n.

2. To these remarks should be added the recognition that since the 1960s, a new generation of Marxist theorists, primarily French, has begun to look specifically at the ideological functions performed by the institutions of the state. Most noteworthy in this respect is the work of Louis Althusser and Nicos Poulantzas. See, especially, Louis Althusser, "Ideology and Ideological State Apparatuses," in *Lenin and Philosophy and Other Essays* (London: New Left Books, 1971), pp. 121–73; and Nicos Poulantzas, *Fascism and Dictatorship* (London: New Left Books, 1974), pp. 299–309. These writers refer to the pioneering insights of

Antonio Gramsci into the ideological functions of state institutions. See Quintin Hoare and Geoffrey Nowell-Smith, eds., *Selections from the Prison Notebooks of Antonio Gramsci* (London: Lawrence and Wishart, 1971); and Carl Boggs, *Gramsci's Marxism* (London: Pluto Press, 1976). For other contemporary analyses of the relationship between the state and ideology, see Ralph Miliband, *The State in Capitalist Society* (New York: Basic Books, 1969), pp. 179–264; and Jürgen Habermas, *Legitimation Crisis* (Boston: Beacon Press, 1975). The Frankfurt School of social theory, of which Jürgen Habermas and Herbert Marcuse are probably the best-known representatives, is distinguished by the application of Marxism as well as Freudian theory to the analysis of ideology. See Martin Jay, *The Dialectical Imagination: The Frankfurt School of Social Theory, 1930–1950* (Boston: Little Brown, 1973).

3. See, for example, John Braithwaite, "Poverty, Power, and White-Collar Crime: Sutherland and the Paradoxes of Criminological Theory," in Kip Schlegel and David Weisburd, eds., *White-Collar Crime Revisited* (Boston: Northeastern University Press, 1992), pp. 78–107.

1

Crime Control in America: Nothing Succeeds Like Failure

My love she speaks softly
She knows there's no success like failure
And that failure's no success at all.

Bob Dylan, *Love Minus Zero/No Limit*

Designed to Fail

Something in the American grain keeps us from admitting defeat both to ourselves and to others. Perhaps it is the heady air of the long-closed frontier trapped in our lungs; whatever it is, it keeps us from confessing to anything more serious than the temporary elusiveness of victory. Americans never confess to having lost a war, although we do admit there are a few we did not win. Domestically, no public policy ever fails, although some do not succeed. Hence former President Ronald Reagan's remarks about crime control in America can be read only as a confession of failure, *American style:*

> *The frightening reality—for all of the speeches of those of us in government, for all of the surveys, studies, and blue ribbon panels, for all of the 14-point programs and the declarations of war on crime, crime has advanced and advanced steadily in its upward climb, and our citizens have grown more and more frustrated, frightened, and angry.*[1]

Former President George Bush continued in the same vein in his 1992 State of the Union Message:

> *We must do something about crime and drugs.... It is time for a major, renewed investment in fighting violent street crime.*[2]

And so too, President Bill Clinton, in his 1994 State of the Union Message, tells us that

> *while Americans are more secure from threats from abroad, I think we all know that in many ways we are less secure from threats here at home.... Violent crime and the fear it provokes are crippling our society, limiting personal freedom and fraying the ties that bind us.*[3]

This follows the even more explicit admission of failure made by Clinton and his running mate, Al Gore, in their campaign agenda, *Putting People First.* Listen to their arrangement of this old familiar tune:

> *Despite all the tough talk we hear from Washington, crime and drug use are expanding dramatically in America. Today more people are victims of violent crime and more addicted to drugs than ever before. We have a national problem on our hands that requires a tough national response. The Clinton-Gore national crime strategy will use the powers of the White House to prevent and punish crime.*
>
> *We need to put more police on the streets and more criminals behind bars.*[4]

Needless to say, we've been putting more police on the streets and more criminals behind bars for the past 20 years, the very period during which crime and drug use have expanded dramatically, according to our newest leaders. But we do not need a presidential announcement to learn that our assaults on the crime problem are a failure. Everyone knows that for all our efforts, intelligence, and money, serious crime remains an enormous social problem. Although rates for some crimes do occasionally decrease from one year to the next, our crime rates remain very high compared with other advanced nations, and they are usually going *up*.

In 1960, the average citizen had less than a 1-in-50 chance of being a victim of one of the crimes on the FBI Index (murder, forcible rape, robbery, aggravated assault, burglary, larceny, or auto theft). In 1970, that chance grew to 1-in-25. In 1986, the FBI reported nearly 5,500 Index crimes per 100,000 citizens, a further increase in the likelihood of victimization to a 1-in-18 chance. And by 1991, this rate was approaching 6,000 Index crimes (5,897.8 to be exact) per 100,000 citizens—a better than one-in-seventeen chance. (The FBI reports a slight decline to 5,660.2 per 100,000 citizens in 1992, almost all of it accounted for by a small drop in the number of property crimes; the rate for violent crimes remained virtually identical to that for 1991).[5] The FBI, however, counts only the crimes that are *reported.* Using "victimization studies" (asking randomly selected citizens whether or not they had been a victim of a crime reported to the police), experts estimate that *unreported* crime is at least double the number of reported crimes, and in some cases as much as six times as great. For example, the FBI reported 1,029,580 crimes of violence in 1977, 1,488,140 in 1986, and 1,911,767 in 1991 (1,932,270 in 1992). Victimization surveys, however, reported 5,902,000 crimes of violence in 1977, 5,515,000 in 1986, and 6,424,000 in 1991.[6]

There is a divergence between the crime trends portrayed in the FBI's *Uniform Crime Reports* (UCR) and the picture presented by the Bureau of Justice's *National Crime Victimization Survey* (NCVS)—previously called the *National Crime Survey* (NCS). The UCR's figures reflect crimes reported to the police and are thus subject to the vagaries of victims' and police departments' reporting practices. The NCVS probably gets a fuller picture of crime incidence overall because it is mainly a telephone survey asking recipients about victimization experiences whether reported or not. On the other hand, NCVS does not include crimes against children under 12 or against businesses. The UCR is thought to overstate violent crime because inner-city police departments tend to report more fully than rural or small-town departments. The NCVS is thought to understate violent crime because its victims are often in the hospital or otherwise unreachable by a telephone survey. For obvious reasons, the NCVS does not include information about murder and nonnegligent homicide. I have generally used the UCR figures rather than the NCVS figures because the former are more accurate for assessing *trends* in violent crimes. Violent crimes have a high and generally stable rate of being reported to the police, thus making the UCR figures a reasonably accurate indicator of the trends in their occurrence, even if it somewhat overstates their rate per inhabitant nationwide.[7] Moreover, it is the FBI's UCR that gets the most publicity and thus that plays the key role in creating our image of crime—a central concern in this book.

Through 1991, the UCR shows a rapidly increasing amount of crime, while victimization reports show a stable, even occasionally slightly declining, but much larger amount of crime persisting through the period of intense criminal justice activity and expenditure. According to the FBI, there was more violent crime in 1992 than in 1991, and violent crime in 1991 "was the highest ever recorded, up 5 percent over 1990, 29 percent over 1987, and 45 percent over 1982." By contrast, the NCVS says that violent crime in 1991 does "not differ measurably from that estimated for 1981"—when, however, they already depicted a number of violent crimes higher than the FBI has ever reported.[8] Whichever way you take it—a smaller amount of crime rapidly increasing or a larger amount remaining stable or even occasionally dipping slightly—criminal justice policy is failing to make our lives substantially safer.

How are we to comprehend this failure? It appears that our government is failing to fulfill the most fundamental task of governance: keeping our streets and homes safe, assuring us of what the Founding Fathers called "domestic tranquility," providing us with the minimal requirement of civilized society. It appears that our new centurions with all their modern equipment and know-how are no more able than the old Roman centurions to hold the line against the forces of barbarism and chaos.

One way to understand this failure is to look at the *excuses* that are offered for it. This we will do—but mainly to show that they do not hold up!

One commonly heard excuse is that we can't reduce crime because our laws and our courts are too lenient. *Translation:* We are failing to reduce crime because we don't have the heart to do what has to be done.

Another excuse points to some feature of modern life, such as urbanization or population growth (particularly the increase in the number of individuals in the crime-prone ages of 15 to 24), and says that this feature is responsible for the growth in crime. This means that crime cannot be reduced unless we are prepared to return to horse-and-buggy days or to abolish adolescence. *Translation:* We are failing to reduce crime because it is impossible to reduce crime.

Some try to excuse our failure by claiming that we simply do not know how to reduce crime. *Translation:* Even though we are doing our best, we are failing to reduce crime because our knowledge of the causes of crime is still too primitive to make our best good enough.

These excuses simply do not pass muster. There is no evidence that we are too lenient on crime, though the belief is widely held and regularly exploited by politicians seeking votes. Our rates of incarceration are as high as or higher than those of other modern nations, and we are the only one still to impose the death penalty.

Moreover, although increasing urbanization and a growing youth population account for some of the increase in crime, they by no means account for all the increase, and certainly not for the impossibility of reducing crime. Crime rates vary widely (and wildly) when we compare cities of similar population size and density. Some very large and densely populated cities have lower crime rates than small and sparsely populated ones. Some cities are high in one type of crime and low in another, and so on. This means that growing crime is not a simple, unavoidable consequence of increasing urbanization. If crime rates vary between large cities, urbanization cannot explain away our inability to reduce crime *at least* to the *lowest* rates prevalent in large cities. Similarly, the crime rate has increased far more rapidly than the youth population, both in absolute numbers and as a fraction of the total population. This means that growing crime is not a simple, unavoidable consequence of a growing youth population. If crime rates increase faster than the young themselves are, then increasing youth itself is not the cause of increasing crime. We have to know why young people are committing

more crimes now than they did in the past, and it is no answer to point to their youth. A growing youth population cannot explain away our inability to reduce crime *at least* down to the rate at which the young are increasing (or decreasing) in our population.

On the other hand, the excuse that we do not know how to reduce crime also does not hold up. The bald truth is that we *do* know some of the sources of crime and *we obstinately refuse to remedy them!* We know that poverty increases the pressures to commit crimes in pursuit of property, and that crimes to obtain property account for about 90 percent of the crime rate—and yet we do little to improve the conditions of our impoverished inner-city neighborhoods beyond clicking our tongues over the strange coincidence that these are also the neighborhoods with the highest crime rates. We know that our prisons undermine human dignity and that the ex-con stigma closes the door to many lawful occupations—and yet we do little to improve these conditions beyond shaking our heads over the fact that so much crime is committed by *recidivists:* people who have already enjoyed the hospitality of our jails and penitentiaries. We know that heroin addiction "forces" people into crime *because* of the high prices of illegal heroin—and yet we refuse to make cheap heroin legally available. We know that guns figure in most murders and make possible many thefts—and yet we refuse to adopt effective gun control. In other words, we may not know how to eliminate crime, but we certainly know how to reduce crime and the suffering it produces. The simple truth is that, as with crime, so with crime reduction, *ignorance is no excuse.*

Later in this chapter, I look at these excuses in greater detail and show that they do not explain our failure to reduce crime. And I present evidence to support my claim that we could reduce crime and the harm it causes, if we wanted to. So the question "How are we to comprehend our failure to reduce crime?" still stares us in the face. Examination of the excuses and then of policies that could reduce crime suggest that our failure is avoidable. What has to be explained is not why *we cannot* reduce crime but why *we will not!* Oddly enough, this parodoxical result points us in the direction of an answer to our question.

Failure is, after all, in the eye of the beholder. The last runner across the finish line has failed in the race only if he or she wanted to win. If the runner wanted to lose, the "failure" is, in fact, a success. Here, I think lies the key to understanding our criminal justice system.

If we look at the system as "wanting" to reduce crime, it is an abysmal failure—and we cannot understand it. If we look at it as *not* wanting to reduce crime, it's a howling success—and all we need to understand is why the goal of the criminal justice system is to fail to reduce crime. If we can understand this, then the system's "failure," as well as its obstinate refusal to implement the policies that could remedy that "failure," becomes perfectly understandable.

In other words, I propose that we can make more sense out of criminal justice policy by assuming that its goal is to maintain crime than by assuming that its goal is to reduce crime!

In the remainder of this chapter, I explore in greater detail the excuses for the failure to reduce crime and offer evidence to back up my assertion that there are policies that could reduce crime that we refuse to implement. I then briefly outline the relationship between the Pyrrhic defeat theory and the criminological theory of Kai Erikson and Émile Durkheim, to which it is akin.

Four Excuses That Will Not Wash, Or How We Could Reduce Crime If We Wanted To

On July 23, 1965, President Lyndon Johnson signed an executive order establishing the President's Commission on Law Enforcement and Administration of Justice to investigate the causes and nature of crime, to collect existing knowledge about our criminal justice system, and to make recommendations about how that system might better meet "the challenge of crime in a free society." The commission presented its report to the president early in 1967, thick with data and recommendations. Because we are a nation higher on commissions than on commitments, it should come as no surprise that for all the light cast on the crime problem by the President's Commission, little heat has been generated and virtually no profound changes in criminal justice policy have taken place in the nearly 30 years since the report was issued.

During this period, however, more and more money has been poured into crime control with the bleak results I have already outlined. When the commission wrote, it estimated that more than $4 billion was being spent annually at the national, state, and local levels to pay for police, courts, and correctional facilities in the fight against crime.[9] Since that time the total number of reported Index crimes grew from 4,710,000 in 1965 to a staggering 14,872,883 in 1991.[10] The annual cost to the public of this brand of domestic tranquility reached $74,249,120,000 for fiscal year 1990, with over 1.7 million persons (1,658,366 full-time equivalents) employed by the criminal justice system.[11] Taking inflation into account, we note that this represents real growth of 360 percent in criminal justice spending since 1965. Dollar-for-dollar, crime control is hardly an impressive investment.

Multiplying almost as fast as crime and anticrime dollars are excuses for our failure to stem the rapid growth of crime (not to say the failure to actually reduce it) in the face of increased expenditure, personnel, research, and knowledge. Four excuses (or, more charitably, "explanations") have sufficient currency to make them worthy of consideration as well as to set in relief the Pyrrhic defeat thesis, which I propose in their place.

First Excuse

One excuse is that we are too soft on crime.[12] This view is widespread among laypersons (in 1991, 80 percent of people polled thought courts were not harsh enough) and conservative critics of criminal justice policy (Ernest van den Haag, for example, claims that "non-punishment is the major 'social' cause of crime").[13] This view is hard to disprove because, no matter how harsh we are, one can always say we should have been harsher. Nonetheless, the evidence is that we are quite harsh, in general harsher than other modern industrial nations, and that we have gotten strikingly harsher in recent years with little effect on the crime rate. In 1988, the U.S. rate of incarceration (in jails and prisons) was 388 prisoners per 100,000 people in the national population. For the same year, the rate for the United Kingdom was 97.4 per 100,000, for West Germany it was 84.9, for Belgium it was 65.4. The rate for Canada, with a society in many ways much like our own, was about 110 persons for every 100,000 inhabitants.[14] Some have argued that our incarceration rates are not so different from those of other countries when compared with our higher crime rates. This finding is based on comparing our incarceration rates for serious crimes with those of other countries for those same crimes. We are still incarcerating more people than those other countries, owing to the fact that we criminalize acts, such as prostitution and other victimless crimes, that other countries do not.[15] But even if our incarceration rates stand in the same proportion to our crime rates as those of other countries, that still indicates that we are no more lenient than other modern nations. Nor, of course, should it be forgotten that we are the only Western industrialized nation still to have the death penalty, let alone to execute people who have committed crimes while under the age of 18. And the recently passed crime bill expands the federal death penalty to cover 52 offenses.[16]

Moreover, we have become markedly harsher during the last decade. Recall the dramatic increases in criminal justice personnel and expenditures, mentioned above. Here's what we got for this investment: Where we used to have the third-highest rate of incarceration in the world, behind the Union of South Africa and the (now former) Soviet Union, we have now pulled ahead of these two models of justice to lead the world in the percentage of inhabitants behind bars.[17] The recent growth in crime comes in the face of this toughening of sentencing and thus suggests that crime persists even though we have a harsh criminal justice system, leading one criminologist to characterize the get-tough approach to crime as a conservative social experiment that has been tested and shown to fail.[18]

This hasn't deterred our new liberal president from calling for locking up more criminals, as we saw above. Nor has it deterred the U.S. Senate from passing a new $23 billion crime bill aimed at adding "100,000 police officers to the nation's streets [and building] a network of high-security regional prisons."[19] And the National Rifle Association (NRA) has recently announced that it will be opening a new publicity campaign calling for tougher sentencing and more prisons.[20]

Second Excuse

Another excuse is that crime is an inescapable companion of any complex, populous, industrialized society. As we become more complex, more populous, more industrialized, and particularly more *urbanized,* we will have more crime as inevitably as we will have more ulcers and more traffic. These are the costs of modern life, the benefits of which abound and clearly outweigh the costs. Growing crime, then, takes its place alongside death and taxes. We can fight it, but we cannot win, and we should not tear our hair out about it.

It takes little reflection to see that this is less an explanation than a recipe for resignation. Furthermore, it does not account for the fact that other complex, populous, and highly industrialized nations such as Japan have crime rates that are not only lower than ours but that do not accelerate as quickly as ours. In 1990, the total number of criminal offenses known to the police in Japan was 1,726,188 (a little under 1,400 offenses for every 100,000 inhabitants).[21] In other words, about *one-eighth* the number of serious offenses known to the police in America that year occurred in a country with *half* the population of the United States crowded onto a land less than *one-twentieth* the size of the United States.

Reporting the results of her study of the relationship between crime and modernization around the world, Louise Shelley writes,

> *Although both societies have undergone urbanization and industrialization, Japan and Switzerland have been exempt from many of the crime problems that currently plague the other developed countries. Most other developed countries have considerably higher rates of crime commission than these two societies, but few developed countries have as high rates of crime commission as the United States.*[22]

This generalization is borne out strikingly by comparing homicide rates in the United States with those in other modern nations. In 1990, Japan had a homicide rate of 1 per 100,000 inhabitants, England and Wales had a rate of

2.26, Belgium had a rate of 2.2, Switzerland 3.17, and West Germany 3.9. For 1990, the U.S. homicide rate was 9.4 per 100,000 inhabitants.[23] New York City alone has more killings a year than all of Japan!

Moreover, the "costs of modern life" or urbanization excuse does not account for the striking differences in the crime rates *within* our own modern complex, populous, and urbanized nation. Within the United States in 1991, the homicide rate ranged from 1.1 per 100,000 inhabitants in North Dakota to 15.3 in Texas and 16.9 in Louisiana.[24] In 1968, *Time* magazine reported that

> *Texas, home of the shoot-out and divorce-by-pistol, leads the U.S. with about 1000 homicides a year, more than 14 other states combined. Houston is the U.S. murder capital: 244 last year, more than in England, which has 45 million more people.*[25]

By 1991, however, Texas (with 2,652 homicides) was in second place behind California (with 3,859). New York (with 2,571) was close behind Texas—and Houston's glory as the murder capital had clearly faded. Houston reported 608 homicides in 1991, roundly outdone by Los Angeles with 1,027 and Chicago with 925 and left far behind by New York City, which captured the 1991 murder title for a city with an astounding 2,154 (40 killings a week!).[26]

Such variations are not limited to murder. A comparison of crime rates (incidence of FBI Index crimes per 100,000 inhabitants) for standard metropolitan statistical areas (areas "made up of a core city with a population of 50,000 or more inhabitants and the surrounding county or counties which share certain metropolitan characteristics") reveals a striking *lack* of correlation between crime rate and population size (which we can take as a reasonable, though rough, index of urbanization and the other marks of modernity, such as complexity and industrialization, that are offered as explanations for the intractability of crime). Citizens of the New York City metropolitan area (population 8,578,871) have about the same chance of being victimized by an Index crime (8,484 per 100,000 inhabitants) as citizens living in and around Waco, Texas, where the population is 193,150 and the crime rate is 8,535 per 100,000, and a slightly smaller chance than citizens living in and around New Orleans, where the population is 1,248,294 and the crime rate is 8,840 per 100,000, and an even smaller chance than citizens in the area of Little Rock, Arkansas, where the population is 517,844 and the crime rate is 9,352 per 100,000.[27]

It might reasonably be thought that population *density* (number of persons per square mile) is a better indicator of urbanization than population as such. Thus, if crime is an ineluctable product of urbanization, we should see a clear correlation between population density and crime rates. The facts, however, do not bear this out. Instead, they indicate a striking lack of correlation between cities' population densities and their crime rates. (See Table 1, in which ten large cities are ranked by population density and then by their crime rates.)[28]

In other words, classifying crime with death and taxes and saying that it is an inevitable companion of modernity or urbanization just will not explain our failure to reduce it. Even if death and taxes are inevitable (unfortunately not in that order), some die prematurely and some die suspiciously and some pay too much in taxes and some pay none at all. None

TABLE 1

Large Cities by Population Density and Crime Rates (per 100,000 population)

City and Population per Square Mile	*Overall Crime Rank and Rate*	*Violent Crime Rank and Rate*	*Property Crime Rank and Rate*
New York City (23,701)	7th 9,236	6th 2,318	9th 6,918
Philadelphia (11,734)	10th 6,835	8th 1,408	10th 5,427
Miami (10,080)	1st 18,394	1st 4,252	1st 14,142
Washington, D.C. (9,883)	4th 10,756	5th 2,452	5th 8,303
Detroit (7,410)	3rd 12,263	3rd 2,727	3rd 9,536
Los Angeles (7,428)	6th 9,730	4th 2,526	7th 7,204
Cleveland (6,537)	9th 8,945	7th 1,832	8th 7,113
Milwaukee (6,537)	8th 9,044	10th 979	6th 8,065
Phoenix (2,342)	5th 9,958	9th 1,106	4th 8,853
Kansas City (Mo.) (1,397)	2nd 13,198	2nd 2,833	2nd 10,366

SOURCE: *StatAbst-1992*, Table 38, pp. 35–37; *UCR 1991*, pp. 84–105

NOTE: The rates and rankings are calculated by using UCR data for the cities themselves, not the metropolitan areas.

of these variations is inevitable or unimportant. So too with crime. Even if crime is inevitable in modern societies, its rates and types vary extensively—and this is neither inevitable nor unimportant. Indeed, the variations in crime rates between modern cities and nations is proof that the *extent* of crime is not a simple consequence of urbanization. Other factors must explain the differences. It is these differences that suggest that although some crime may be an ineradicable consequence of urbanization, this in no way excuses our failure to reduce crime at least to the lowest rates reported in modern cities and nations.

Third Excuse

A third excuse takes the form of attributing crime to young people—particularly young men between the ages of 14 or 15 or 16 and 24 or 25. This explanation goes as follows: Young people in our society, especially males, find themselves emerging from the security of childhood into the frightening chaos of adult responsibility. Little is or can be done by the adult society to ease the transition by providing meaningful outlets for the newly bursting youthful energy aroused in still immature and irresponsible youngsters. Hence, these youngsters both mimic the power of manhood and attack the society that frightens and ignores them by resorting to violent crime. Add to this the rapid increase of people in this age group since the baby boom of the 1940s (only tapering off as we entered the 1980s), and we have another explanation that amounts to a recipe for resignation: We can no more expect to reduce crime than we can hope to eradicate adolescence. We can fight crime, but it will be with us until we figure out a way for people to get from childhood to adulthood without passing through their teens.

There can be no doubt that youngsters show up disproportionately in crime statistics. In 1975, *Time* reported that "forty-four percent of the nation's murderers are 25 or younger, and 10 percent are under 18. Of those arrested for street crimes, excluding murder, fully 75 percent are under 25 and 45 percent are under 18."[29] In 1991, persons between the ages of 16 and 24 constituted 13 percent of the nation's population. They represented, however, about 40 percent of those arrested for the Index crimes of willful homicide, rape, robbery, aggravated assault, larceny, burglary, motor vehicle theft, and arson.[30]

However, there are problems with attributing crime to youth. The most important is that crime rates have grown faster than either the absolute number of young people or their percentage of the population. (See Table 2, comparing national crime rates in recent years with the percent of the population represented by people aged 14 to 24.)

Notice that while there is a rough parallel between the rise and fall of crime rates and percentage of young people in the population, there are also impor-

TABLE 2

Crime Rates Compared with Youth Population

Year	*Crime Rate (Index Crimes per 100,000 Persons)*	*14- to 24-year-olds (Percent of Population)*
1960	1,123	15.1
1970	2,741	19.9
1975	5,282	20.8
1980	5,950	20.4
1985	5,207	18.2
1990	5,820	16.1

SOURCE: *UCR-1990,* p. 50; *UCR-1985,* p. 41; *UCR-1980,* p. 41; *UCR-1970,* p. 65; *StatAbst-1992,* pp. 14–15; *StatAbst-1987,* p. 14. (Note: Owing to changes in categories, the percent of 14- to 24-year-olds for 1990 is based on the percent of 15- to 24-year-olds in 1990 plus the percent of 14-year-olds in 1991.)

tant divergences: The percentage of young people in the population in 1990 was only slightly higher than that in 1960, and yet the crime rate in 1990 was *five times higher* than that of 1960. Obviously, this growth in crime cannot be attributed to youth. The same can be said of the years 1970 and 1975, when young people's percentage in the population grew slightly, and crime rates doubled. Or compare 1980 and 1990, when the youth percentage dropped almost 5 points and the crime rate dropped only slightly. In that same period, the number of 15- to 24-year-olds decreased absolutely by 5,660,000, while the absolute number of Index crimes rose by over 1 million.[31]

Similar discrepancies show up when the *National Crime Victimization Survey* is used. Compare, for example, 1981 with 1973, the first year for which we have NCV survey results. In 1973, the number of people aged 16 to 24 was 34,967,000, and in 1981, their number had increased 10 percent to 38,591,000. As a percentage of the national population they went from 16.5 to 16.8—an increase of slightly under 2 percent in their percentage of the population (16.8 – 16.5 = .3; .3 is 1.8 percent of 16.5). During that same period, the NCVS shows an increase in reported violent victimizations of 23 *percent,* from 5,351,000 to 6,582,000—more than twice the increase in the absolute number of 16- to 24-year-olds, more than ten times the increase in their fraction of the population. Or compare 1975 and 1984, years in which the number of 16- to 24-year-olds are nearly the same (36,544,000 and 36,677,000, respectively). The NCVS reports an increase in violent victimizations of *8 percent* from 1975 (5,573,000 victimizations) to 1984 (6,582,000). In 1984, there were 133,000 more 16- to 24-year-olds than there were in 1975 but 448,000 more violent victimizations.[32]

There are 5 million fewer 16- to 24-year-olds now than there were in the first years of the eighties, yet the FBI says violent crime (as of 1992) is up 53.6 percent over 1983, and the NCVS says that violent crime (as of 1991) is the same as 1981.[33] Moreover, the period of decline in the youth population coincided with an increase in serious crime in New York City, and even when crime rates recently went down, they never returned to the levels of the 1940s when the percentage of young people 16 to 24 years old was about 14, roughly comparable to what it is now.[34]

Note that I am not denying that a large number of crimes are committed by young people. I think it is true that much of the decrease in crime rates that we were experiencing up until a few years ago can be attributed to the end of the baby boom and the resultant decrease in the number of persons in the 16- to 24-year-old group.[35] But that youngsters commit a lot of crime is no basis for treating crime as the inevitable result of youth. One reason is that, while the propensity to commit crimes against persons and property declines with age, it declines much more slowly for crimes of violence than for property crimes: "Age-specific arrest rates peak in the 16 to 18 year age range for all Index crimes, then drop quickly to half the peak by age 21 for the property crimes and slowly to age 35 for person crimes."[36] Thus property crime is more directly attributable to youth than crimes against the person, which are fewer in number but more generally feared.

The facts suggest that, although the number of youngsters in the populace has an important effect on the crime rates, it cannot fully explain them or explain them away. When this group declined, crime went down but not in proportion to the decline in the youth population. When this group was growing, the crime rates were growing faster than it was. And after a brief decline, this is now happening again. If crime increases faster (or decreases slower) than the youth population, then that increase (or decrease) cannot be explained by the increase (or decrease) in youths.

If crime *among* these youngsters increases, then this certainly is not explained by their youth. Something other than their youth or their numbers must explain why they are committing more crimes than people their age did in other periods. For example, some observers have suggested that increased youth population increases crime exponentially by, among other things, increasing the competition for jobs. This in turn increases unemployment, which predictably leads to crime.[37] But from this it doesn't follow that the increased crime results from the increased youth population, because at least part of the responsibility must be ascribed to the failure of the economy to provide jobs for the new youthful candidates. In any case, the greater likelihood of young people committing crime provides no excuse for failing to reduce the growth of crime at least to the rate at which the number of young people is growing (or shrinking). Moreover, this remains a failure even when a declining youth population leads to declining crime rates, because neither decline can be credited to criminal justice policies. So another excuse for our failure fails to excuse.

Fourth Excuse

The fourth excuse is that we don't know how to reduce crime. After all, I have just suggested, and many studies bear out, that all the new prisons and longer sentences of the Reagan era have had little impact on crime rates. We have seen that crime is on the rise even after an enormous increase in the number and percentage of Americans behind bars. What decreases we have seen are largely attributable to the shrinking of the youth population. After adjusting crime rates in the 1980s to reflect the decline in number of young people in the population, Steffensmeier and Harer observe:

> *Imprisonment rates rose far more sharply in the eighties than in any previous decade in the nation's history. In spite of their record-setting pace, there was no discernible drop in either the nation's Crime Rate as a whole or in the "serious" street crime rate.... [T]he fact that tougher enforcement and bulging prisons have not led to the expected reduction in crime ... suggests that the criminal justice system does not contain the solution to the nation's crime problem, and that no law enforcement strategy can be confidently recommended to remedy it.*[38]

This idea is, of course, not new. Although the nation's leaders are still in the grips of the fantasy that more police and prisons will reduce crime, the fact is that the futility of this approach was already recognized before the hardening of the Reagan years. A 1975 article by Joel D. Weisman, titled "Chicago Reflects Police Frustration in Fight Against Crime," in the *Washington Post* gives a good sampling of this view among experts in and outside of police departments.

> *Boston Police Commissioner Robert J. diGrazia claims police can only displace crime—not reduce or eliminate it. "It's like squeezing a balloon," said [David] Fogel [executive director of the Illinois Law Enforcement Commission]. "You push the air away from where you're squeezing but it expands the rest of the balloon."*
>
> *James Q. Wilson, a professor of political science at Harvard University and author of the book* Thinking About Crime, *said police can contribute to reducing crime but it is unclear by how much. The data are too unreliable, he contended.*[39]

An article by Leroy Aarons, also from 1975, titled, "U.S. Penal System 'Truths' Questioned," reflects similar bewilderment among correctional officials. Reporting the conclusions of a "recent issue of *Corrections* magazine," which "devoted 27 pages to an article on the current ferment in the field," Aarons writes:

> *The article concluded, based on interviews with wardens, administrators and students of corrections around the country that:*
>
> - *There is little or no evidence that correctional "treatment" programs work.*
> - *The gradual restructuring of the correctional system over the last 50 years around the notion of individualized and enforced treatment for all offenders was a mistake.*

Aarons concludes his own article with an observation drawn from current doubts among corrections experts but applicable to the whole criminal justice system:

> *It seems clear that, in the long run, solutions to the age-old problem of what to do with those individuals deemed law-breakers still elude society.*[40]

In fact, in his sweeping history of the American criminal justice system from colonial times to the present, *Crime and Punishment in American History*, Stanford's Lawrence Friedman recounts the striking number of "wars on crime" that we have fought and lost, and argues that the criminal

justice system can do little about crime.[41] In October 1993, the *Washington Post* ran an article on what to do about violence in the nation's capital. All the experts agreed with FBI director, Louis J. Freeh, who said:

> *The crime and disorder which flow from hopeless poverty, unloved children, and drug abuse can't be solved merely by bottomless prisons, mandatory sentencing minimums or more police.*[42]

Less than a month later, the U.S. Senate passed a tough federal crime bill calling for more prisons, longer sentences, more cops, and nothing for crime prevention.[43]

This excuse for our failure is as interesting for what it says as for what it doesn't say. It doesn't say that we cannot reduce crime. What it says is that our criminal justice system—cops, courts, prisons—does not reduce crime. This supports the suggestion that I made at the start, namely, that we should stop trying to understand our criminal justice system as a mechanism aimed at reducing crime. We shall still want to know why we maintain such a criminal justice system, and indeed, why we keep feeding it more money and labor power in the face of the enduring knowledge of its enduring failure. But what the excuse doesn't say raises even more questions. Because it doesn't say that we, the American people, acting through our government and legal system, cannot reduce crime and the harm it causes. It doesn't say that the criminal justice system, understood—in the broad terms I suggested in the Introduction—to include the legal system that defines crime and that determines general policy toward actual and potential criminals, cannot reduce crime. In the rest of this section, I point to some policies that are likely to reduce crime. Then, we shall want to know why we maintain a criminal justice system that doesn't reduce crime and why we don't implement policies that might.

There are many things that we do know about the sources of crime. Note that I have said "sources" rather than "causes," because the kind of knowledge we have is far from the precise knowledge that a physicist has about how some event *causes* another. We know that poverty, slums, and unemployment are *sources* of street crime. We do not fully understand how they *cause* crime, because we know as well that many, if not most, poor, unemployed slum dwellers do not engage in street crime. Yet to say that this means we do not know that such conditions increase the likelihood of an individual resorting to violent crime is like saying that we do not know that a bullet in the head is deadly because some people survive or because we do not fully understand the physiological process that links the wound with the termination of life.

Known Sources of Crime

Those youngsters who figure so prominently in arrest statistics are not drawn equally from all economic strata. Although there is much reported and even more unreported crime among middle-class youngsters, the street crime attributed to this age group that makes our city streets a perpetual war zone is largely the work of poor ghetto youth. This is the group at the lowest end of the economic spectrum. This is a group among whom unemployment approaches 50 percent, with underemployment (the rate of persons either jobless or with part-time, low-wage jobs) still higher. This is a group with no realistic chance (for any but a rare individual) to enter college or amass sufficient capital (legally) to start a business or to get into the union-protected, high-wage, skilled job markets. We know that poverty is a *source* of crime, even if we do not know how it *causes* crime—and yet we do virtually nothing to improve the life chances of the vast majority of the inner-city poor. They are as poor as ever and are facing cuts in welfare and other services.

The gap between rich and poor worsened during the eighties. Says *Economist,* "For all the talk of the fragmentation of America, there is only one division that is dangerously getting worse, and that is the gap between rich and poor."[44] In 1980, the poorest fifth of the nation's families received 5.2 percent of the aggregate income, and the richest fifth received 41.5 percent.

By 1990, the share of the poorest fifth had declined to 4.6 percent while that of the richest fifth had risen to 44.3 percent. During this same period, the share of the top 5 percent rose from 15.3 to 17.4 percent.[45] The Census Bureau reports that the number of poor Americans rose for the third year in a row in 1992, to 36.9 million.[46]

That poverty is a source of crime is not refuted by the large and growing amount of white-collar crime that I shall document later. In fact, poverty contributes to crime by creating need, while—at the other end of the spectrum—wealth can contribute to crime by unleashing greed. Some criminologists have argued that economic inequality itself worsens crimes of the poor and of the well off by increasing the opportunities for the well off and increasing the humiliation of the poor.[47] And inequality has worsened in recent years.

Moreover, this was the predictable outcome of the Reagan administration's strategy of fighting inflation by cutting services to the poor while reducing the taxes of the wealthy. In September 1982, a group of 34 prominent economists sharply criticized Reagan's economic policy as "extremely regressive in its impact on our society, redistributing wealth and power from the middle class and the poor to the rich, and shifting more of the tax burden away from business and onto low- and middle-income consumers."[48] In that same month, a study released by the Urban Institute concluded that "the Reagan administration's policies are not only aiding upper-income families at the expense of the working poor, but also are widening the gulf between affluent and poorer regions of the country."[49] The study maintained that Reagan's tax cuts required sacrifices of low-income families, while yielding small gains for middle-income families and large gains for the upper-income families; and that the combined effect of the administration's tax and social service spending cuts was "to penalize working families near the poverty line who receive some federal benefits ... creating 'major work disincentives.'"

Almost a decade later, an article in *Business Week*, looking back at the 1980s, confirms the charge in retrospect: "At the uppermost end of the income scale, tax cuts made aftertax income surge even higher than pretax income. And at the low end of the distribution scale, cuts in income transfers hurt the poor." The article notes also "the extraordinarily high level of child poverty in America today. One in five children under the age of 15 lives in poverty, and a staggering 50% of all black children under the age of six live in poverty."[50]

Moreover, as unemployment has gone up and down over the past decades, unemployment at the bottom of society remains strikingly worse than the national average. For example, over the past 25 years black unemployment has remained slightly more than twice the rate of white unemployment. In 1967, when 3.4 percent of white workers were unemployed,

7.4 percent of black workers were jobless. By 1991, 6 percent of white workers were unemployed and 12.4 percent of blacks were. Among those in the crime-prone ages of 16 to 19, 16.4 percent of white youngsters and 36.3 (more than one of every three) black youngsters were jobless.[51]

Writes Todd Clear, professor of criminal justice at Rutgers University, "Let's start investing in things that really reduce crime: good schools, jobs and a future for young parents and their children."[52] Why don't we?

There is more. We know that prison produces more criminals than it cures. We know that more than 70 percent of the inmates in the nation's prisons or jails are not there for the first time. We know that prison inmates are denied autonomy and privacy and subjected to indignities, mortifications, and acts of violence as regular features of their confinement—all of which is heightened by overcrowding. State and federal prisons were at 123.3 percent of design capacity in 1990.[53] The predictable result, as delineated by Robert Johnson and Hans Toch in *The Pains of Imprisonment,* "is that the prison's survivors become tougher, more pugnacious, and less able to feel for themselves and others, while its nonsurvivors become weaker, more susceptible, and less able to control their lives."[54] Prisoners are thus bereft of both training and capacity to handle daily problems in competent and socially constructive ways, inside or outside of prison. Once on the outside, burdened with the stigma of a prison record and rarely trained in a marketable skill, they find few opportunities for noncriminal employment open to them.

Should we then really pretend that we do not *know* why they turn to crime? Can we honestly act as if we do not know that our prison system (combined with our failure to ensure a meaningful postrelease noncriminal alternative for the ex-con) is a *source* of crime? Recidivism does not happen because ex-cons miss their alma mater. In fact, if prisons are built to deter people from crime, one would expect that ex-prisoners would be the most deterred because the deprivations of prison are more real to them than to the rest of us. Recidivism is thus a doubly poignant testimony to the job that prison does in preparing its graduates for crime—and yet we do little to change the nature of prisons or to provide real services to ex-convicts.

We know that it is about as difficult to obtain a handgun in the United States as a candy bar. In 1968 Franklin Zimring tried to estimate the numbers of guns (not only handguns) in civilian hands by using both the results of public opinion polls and the available figures on domestic production, as well as foreign import of firearms for civilian use. He concluded:

> *Survey results thus indicate ownership of approximately 80 million firearms, while production and import totals indicate approximately 100 million. We can do no better than average these two figures and conservatively estimate the number of firearms now in civilian hands in this country ... 35 million rifles, 31 million shotguns, and 24 million handguns—in 60 million households.*[55]

That was in 1968. Using similar sources of information, Gary Kleck estimates that, by 1990, the civilian stock of guns in the United States had passed the 200 million mark.[56] Nearly one-half of American households have at least one gun. And about a quarter have at least one handgun. Half of handgun owners surveyed said that their guns were currently loaded.[57]

The President's Crime Commission reported that in 1965, "5,600 murders, 34,700 aggravated assaults and the vast majority of the 68,400 armed robberies were committed by means of firearms. All but 10 of 278 law enforcement officers murdered during the period 1960–65 were killed with firearms." The commission concluded almost 30 years ago that

> *more than one-half of all willful homicides and armed robberies, and almost one-fifth of all aggravated assaults, involve use of firearms. As long as there is no effective gun-control legislation, violent crimes and the injuries they inflict will be harder to reduce than they might otherwise be.*[58]

The situation has worsened since the commission's warning. The FBI reported that the "proportion of violent crimes committed with firearms has increased in recent years"—from being employed in the commission of 26 percent of violent offenses in 1987 to 31 percent in 1991. The FBI writes: "As in previous years, firearms were the weapons used in approximately 7 of every 10 murders committed in the United States. Of those murders for which weapons were reported, 55 percent were by handguns, 5 percent by shotguns, and 4 percent by rifles."[59] Moreover, guns kill and maim outside of crime as well. "Every 14 minutes someone in America dies from a gunshot wound. Slightly more than half of those deaths are suicides, about 44 percent are homicides and 4 percent are unintentional shootings."[60] The Centers for Disease Control reports that there were 240,000 nonfatal shootings in 1989.[61] A study published in the *New England Journal of Medicine* in October 1993 found that people in households with guns were almost three times more likely to experience a homicide than people in homes without guns.[62] Guns also take a grave and worsening toll among our children. In 1985, there were 13.3 gun deaths among 15- to 24-year-olds for every 100,000 persons in that age group. By 1990, the rate had risen to 23.5 per 100,000 in the age group.[63] According to a report from the Children's Defense Fund, nearly 50,000 children were killed by guns between 1979 and 1991.[64]

In the face of facts like these—indeed, in the face of his own nearly fatal shooting by a would-be assassin—President Reagan refused to support any legislative attempts to control the sale of handguns.[65] His successor, President Bush, followed suit.[66] On Thanksgiving Day, 1993, Bush's successor, Bill Clinton, signed into law the so-called Brady Bill, which goes only so far as imposing a five-day waiting period for gun purchases, to enable checks to see whether would-be gun purchasers have criminal records. The Brady Bill leaves it to the states to enforce the waiting period and to get their police to make a "reasonable effort" to conduct the background checks. However, the bill provides no sanctions for states that do not comply, and it leaves it effectively up to states to provide funding for the checks and to determine what is a "reasonable effort."[67] It remains to be seen whether the Brady Bill will make a difference.

Can we believe that our leaders sincerely want to cut down on violent crime and the injuries it produces when they oppose even as much as *registering* guns or *licensing* gun owners, much less actually restricting the sale and movement of guns as a matter of national policy? (President Clinton has expressed some support for the idea of registering gun owners; but the difficulty of getting even the mild Brady Bill provisions into law gives little reason for optimism that anything will come of the idea.) Are we to believe that the availability of guns does not contribute to our soaring crime rate? Zimring's study indicates that areas with a high number of privately owned guns have more crimes involving guns than do areas with lower numbers of privately owned firearms. His data also indicate that cities that experience an increase in legal gun sales also experience an increase in gun-related suicides, accidents, and crimes.[68]

This is hardly more than what common sense would lead us to expect. Can we really believe that if guns were less readily available, violent criminals would simply switch to other weapons to commit the same amount of crimes and do the same amount of damage? Is there a weapon other than the handgun that works as quickly, that allows its user so safe a distance, or that makes the criminal's physical strength (or speed or courage for that matter) as irrelevant? Could a bank robber hold a row of tellers at bay with a switchblade? Would an escaping felon protect himself from a pursuing police officer with a hand grenade? Zimring's studies also indicate that if gun users switched to the next deadliest weapon—the knife—and attempted the same number of crimes, we could still expect *80 percent fewer fatalities* because the fatality rate of the knife is roughly one-fifth that of the gun. Another researcher found that family and intimate assaults involving firearms were 12 times more likely to result in death than those that did not.[69] In other words, even if guns were eliminated and crimes not reduced, we could expect to save as many as four out of every five persons who are now the victims of firearm homicide, and maybe more!

Finally, the United States has an enormous drug abuse and addiction problem. There is considerable evidence, however, that our attempts to cure it are worse than the disease itself. Consider first heroin. Some people think this drug is out of fashion and no longer widely used. Far from it! It's use is widespread and persistent. The number of heroin users is hard to estimate because we only know of the ones who get caught and because there are a large but unknown number of individuals who (contrary to popular mythology) shoot up occasionally without becoming addicts—a practice known as "chipping." In his book *The Heroin Solution,* Arnold Trebach suggests that this number may be as high as 3.5 million.[70] A survey carried out in 1991 by the National Institute for Drug Abuse found that 701,000 people admitted to using heroin in the last year. This was a telephone survey and, because heroin users are less likely to have or answer phones or admit their practices to unknown callers, it surely undercounted the number of users.[71] A recent study suggests that there are between 500,000 and a million heroin addicts.[72]

As shocking as these numbers may be, it must be at least as shocking to discover that there is little evidence proving that heroin is a *dangerous* drug. There is no evidence conclusively establishing a link between heroin and disease or tissue degeneration such as that established for tobacco and alcohol. James Q. Wilson, a defender of the prohibition on heroin and other drugs, admits that "there are apparently no specific pathologies—serious illnesses or physiological deterioration—that are known to result from heroin use per se."[73] On the basis of available scientific evidence, there is every reason to suspect that we do our bodies more damage, more *irreversible* damage, by smoking cigarettes and drinking liquor than by using heroin. Most of the physical damage associated with heroin use is probably attributable to the trauma of withdrawal—and this is a product not so much of heroin but of its unavailability.

It might be said that the evil of heroin is that it is *addicting,* because this is a bad thing even if the addicting substance is not itself harmful. It is hard to deny that the image of a person enslaved to a chemical is rather ugly and is repugnant to our sense that the dignity of human beings lies in their capacity to control their destinies. More questionable, however, is whether this is, in the case of adults, anybody's business but their own. Even so, suppose we agree that addiction is an evil worthy of prevention. Doesn't that make us hypocrites? What about all our other addictions? What about cigarette smoking, which, unlike heroin, contributes to cancer and heart disease? Nicotine's addictiveness—according to former Surgeon General C. Everett Koop—is similar to that of heroin. (By the way, cigarettes appear to be *more addicting than cocaine,* more likely to addict the new user and more difficult to quit once addicted.)[74] What about the roughly 15 million alcoholics in the nation working their way through their livers and into their graves? What about the people who cannot get started without a caffeine fix in the morning and those who, once started, cannot slow down without their alcohol fix in the evening? What of the folks who can't face daily life without their Valium? Are they not all addicts?[75]

Suffice it to say, then, at the very least, our attitudes about heroin are inconsistent and irrational, and there is reason to believe they are outrageous and hypocritical. Even if this were not so, even if we could be much more certain that heroin addiction was a disease worth preventing, the fact would remain that the "cure" we have chosen is worse than the disease. We *know* that treating the possession of heroin as a criminal offense produces more crime than it prevents.

The key to this process is that the legal prohibition on heroin drives its price up, because only people willing to risk punishment will sell it. The heroin for which an addict may be paying $100 or more a day could be produced legally for small change (as it is in Great Britain, where heroin is dispensed to addicts by government-controlled clinics). Moreover, once deprived, a heroin addict begins to experience a painful physical need for the drug. Thus a powerful demand exists for the high-priced supply of heroin. Considering that most heroin addicts don't have high-paying jobs if they have regular employment at all, this means they will be driven by physical need to rob to get the money to pay for their drugs. Add to that the fact that to get $100 for stolen goods, one has to rob several times that amount, because fences don't pay list price.

Says former Washington, D.C. police chief Maurice Turner, "If you see an addict going through withdrawal, he's in some kind of damn pain. . . . When they get pretty well strung out, they have about a $100 to $120-a-day habit. When they get that type of habit, they're going to have to steal approximately six times that much."[76] The result is a recipe for large-scale and continual robbery and burglary, which would not exist if the drug were available legally. A recent study by Anglin and Speckart of the relationship between narcotics use and crime concludes that there is "strong evidence that there is a strong causal relationship, at least in the United States, between addiction to narcotics and property crime levels."[77]

Do a little arithmetic. Imagine that there are half a million addicts with $100-a-day habits. And let's make some conservative assumptions about these addicts. Suppose that they fill their habits only 250 days a year (sometimes they're in jail, or in the hospital). Suppose that they have to steal for half their drug needs, and that they must steal three times the dollar value of what they need, because they must convert their booty into cash through a fence. (These conservative assumptions are similar to those made in a report of the U.S. Department of Health, Education and Welfare, entitled *Social Cost of Drug Abuse,* estimating the amount of theft heroin addicts had to engage in to support their habits in 1974.)[78] If you've done your arithmetic, you have seen that our half million addicts will need to steal $18,750,000,000 a year to support their habits. This is more than the $15.2 billion that the FBI estimates as the loss due to property crimes during

1992[79]—and it doesn't even take into consideration theft by those addicted to other drugs, such as crack (a potent cocaine derivative).

Even if you think that this $18.75 billion in theft is an improbable figure, and even if you also assume that the FBI's estimate of the value of stolen property would increase dramatically if we knew the value of unreported theft, you cannot escape the conclusion that theft by drug addicts—who have no other means of supporting their habit—accounts for an astounding amount of property crime. The Bureau of Justice reports, "Almost a third of those convicted of robbery and burglary [admitted to having] committed their crime to obtain money for drugs, as had about a quarter of those in jail for larceny and fraud."[80] How many more did so as well but wouldn't admit it?

Looking at heroin, we must recognize it is not the "disease" of heroin addiction that leads to property crime. There is, writes Trebach, "nothing in the pharmacology, or physical and psychological impact, of the drug that would propel a user to crime."[81] Nor is there anything about heroin itself that makes it extremely costly. The heroin that an addict pays $100 or more a day for could be legally produced at a cost of a few cents for a day's supply. Thus, it is not the "disease" of heroin addiction but its "cure" that leads to property crime. *It is our steadfast refusal to provide heroin through legal sources that, for approximately a half a million individuals on the streets, translates a physical need for a drug into a physical need to steal billions of dollars worth of property a year.*

Prior to 1914, when anyone could go into a drugstore and purchase heroin and other opiates the way we buy aspirin today, hundreds of thousands of upstanding, law-abiding citizens were hooked.[82] Opiate addiction is not in itself a *cause* of crime—if anything, it is a pacifier.[83] However, once sale or possession of heroin is made a serious criminal offense, a number of consequences follow. First, as already mentioned, the prices go up, because those who supply it face grave penalties, and those who want it want it bad. Second, because the supply (and the quality) of the drug fluctuates, depending on how vigorously the agents of the law try to prevent it, the addict's life is continuously unstable. Addicts live in constant uncertainty about the next fix and must devote much of their wit and energy to getting it and to getting enough money to pay for it. They do not, then, fit easily into the routines of a nine-to-five job, even if they could get one that would pay enough to support their habit. Finally, all the difficulties of securing the drug add up to an incentive to be not merely a user of heroin but a dealer as well because this both earns money and makes one's own supply more certain. Addicts thus have an incentive to find and encourage new addicts, which they would not have if heroin were legally and cheaply available. If we add to this the fact that heroin addiction has remained widespread and possibly even increased in spite of all our law enforcement efforts, can we doubt that the cure is worse than the disease? Can we doubt that the cure is a *source* of crime?

Against this conclusion, it is sometimes countered that studies show that a large proportion of criminal heroin addicts were criminals before they were addicts. Such studies would only refute the claim that the illegality of heroin is a source of crime if the claim was that heroin addiction turns otherwise law-abiding citizens into thieves. Rather, the claim is that the illegality of heroin (and thus its limited availability and almost unlimited price) places addicts in situations in which they *must* engage in theft continually and at a high level to keep a step ahead of the pains of withdrawal. Anglin and Speckart affirm that "while involvement in property crime activities generally precedes the addiction career, after addiction occurs the highly elevated property crime levels demonstrated by addicts appear to be regulated by similarly high narcotics use levels."[84] Thus, even for addicts who already were criminals, heroin addiction increases the amount they need to steal and works to make them virtually immune to attempts to wean them from a life of crime. Consequently, even if all criminal heroin addicts were criminals before they were addicts, the illegality of heroin would still be a source of crime because of the increased pressure it places on the addict to steal a lot and often. And much the same applies to other illegal addictive drugs.

Recently, attention has shifted from heroin to "crack," a highly addictive derivative of cocaine. Some 3 million Americans are said to use cocaine regularly, about 336,000 daily.[85] Having learned nothing from our experience with heroin, we have applied to cocaine and crack the same policy that failed with heroin—with predictable results: First of all, our large-scale attempts to reduce the flow of cocaine into the country have failed. Says Trebach,

> *After seven years of a multi-billion dollar drug war, our prisons are filled to record levels, violent drug traffickers pollute our cities, and drug abuse is rampant. Despite the most aggressive drug war campaign in history, so much cocaine has been imported since 1981 that the price has dropped to one-third its former level. While some of our children now find it more difficult to buy marijuana, many find it much easier to buy crack and cocaine.*[86]

According to law enforcement officials, "the amount of cocaine coming into the country has soared from 1,872 kilograms in fiscal year 1981 to 35,970 in fiscal 1987."[87] The General Accounting Office reports that U.S. efforts to reduce cultivation of drug crops in Bolivia and Columbia "have been almost entirely ineffective and the cultivation of drug crops has increased dramatically in both countries."[88] This caps a long history of failure starting with Nixon's (successful) attempt to pressure Turkey into eradicating local cultivation of poppies (source of opium and thus of heroin) in 1971 and continuing with both Reagan and Bush's attempts to pressure foreign countries to reduce domestic production of narcotic substances. Though Nixon was successful with Turkey, the result was just to move production elsewhere. In spite of three U.S.-led international drug wars since then, worldwide illicit opium production rose from 990 tons in 1971 to 4,200 tons in 1989, and Andean coca leaf (source of cocaine and thus of crack) production grew from 291,100 tons in 1987 to 337,100 tons in 1991.[89] (Total world opium production in 1991 was up 8 percent from the year prior, and nearly double the level of the mid-1980s.[90]) Likewise, attempts to use the coast guard and navy to interdict cocaine coming into the United States by sea have failed to put a dent in the traffic—after all, America has over 88,000 miles of coastline.[91] The *Wall Street Journal* reports that a kilogram of cocaine that cost between $55,000 and $65,000 in 1981 cost between $20,000 and $40,000 in 1987. They even report a "rock-bottom" price in Miami of $14,000 for a kilo.[92] The Bureau of Justice Statistics indicates that this is still the rock-bottom wholesale price of 80-percent-pure powdered Colombian cocaine in Miami.[93] The National Institute on Drug Abuse estimates that the number of daily users of cocaine rose from 292,000 in 1988 to 336,000 in 1990.[94]

In 1988, the *National Law Journal* surveyed 181 chief prosecutors or their top drug deputies throughout the United States and reported that "nearly two-thirds of the country's top state and local prosecutors say they are having little to no impact in the fight against illegal narcotics."[95] This failing drug war is now costing federal, state, and local governments approximately $16 billion a year.[96] To that must be added the *nonfinancial* costs, such as increased violence among competing drug traffickers and increased corruption among law enforcement officials on the front line in the drug war. The year 1988 saw the nation's capital reach and overtake its annual homicide record, with all experts attributing the surge in murders to the struggle to capture the lucrative drug market.[97] The *New York Times* reports that "researchers say there are now more than 100 cases each year in state and Federal courts in which law enforcement officials are charged or implicated in drug corruption."[98] Says William Green, assistant commissioner for internal affairs at the U.S. Customs Service, "The money that's being offered by the drug dealers is so big it is just hard to visualize."[99]

Though many who would call for the legalization of heroin (and less dangerous drugs, such as marijuana) hesitate to call for legalization of crack, it seems clear that our efforts to fight crack are also failing and costing us more than the drug itself. Moreover, as Trebach suggests, there is reason to believe that our policy is contributing to the popularity of crack. The crackdown on importation of marijuana has given drug traffickers an incentive to shift to cocaine because much smaller amounts of it are needed for intoxication and thus much smaller amounts are needed to make big money. It remains the case that most drug arrests are for marijuana use or possession, and that marijuana is a relatively safe drug.[100]

The 1988 surgeon general's report lists tobacco as a more dangerous drug than marijuana.[101] According to the findings and conclusions of Francis Young, administrative law judge for the Drug Enforcement Administration, there are no documented marijuana user fatalities ("despite [its 5,000 year-] long history of use and the extraordinarily high numbers of social smokers, there is simply no credible medical reports to suggest that consuming marijuana has caused a single death"!), and no amount of marijuana that a person could possibly eat or smoke would constitute a lethal dose. By contrast, even aspirin overdose causes hundreds of deaths a year.[102]

With the drugs that can cause death from overdose, the dangers have been blown wildly out of proportion. Trebach points out that although federal authorities documented 2,177 deaths from the most popular illicit drugs in 1985, between 400,000 and 500,000 people died from alcohol and tobacco during that same year. He adds that 59 children aged 17 and under died from drug overdoses in 1987, while "408 American children (from infants through the age of 14) were murdered by their parents in 1983"![103]

In sum, we have an antidrug policy that is failing at its own goals and succeeding only in adding to crime. First, there are the heroin and crack addicts, who must steal to support their habit. Then, there are the drug merchants who are offered fabulous incentives to provide illicit substances to a willing body of consumers. This in turn contributes to the high rate of inner-city murders and other violence as drug gangs battle for the enormous sums of money available. Next, there are the law enforcement officials who, after risking their lives for low salaries, are corrupted by nearly irresistible amounts of money. Finally, there are the otherwise law-abiding citizens who are made criminals because they use cocaine, a drug less harmful than tobacco, and those who are made criminals because they use marijuana, a drug that is safer than alcohol and less deadly than aspirin. Much of the recent dramatic growth in our prison population (documented above) is the result of the hardening of drug enforcement policy in the Reagan years: In 1968, there were 162,000 drug arrests nationwide, in 1977 there were 569,000, and in 1989 there were 1,150,000 million drug arrests.[104] Drug offenders amounted to 58 percent of all inmates sent to federal prison in 1991.[105]

And all this is occurring at a time when there is increasing evidence that what does work to reduce substance abuse is public education. Because this has succeeded in reducing alcohol and tobacco consumption and, in some cases, marijuana and cocaine consumption as well, it's time that we take the money we are wasting in the "war on drugs" and spend it on public education instead. Because that would be far less costly than the "war," this would leave over money to fight a more effective war against muggers and rapists rather than recreational drug users. Evidence from the 11 states that decriminalized marijuana possession in the 1970s suggests that decriminalization does not lead to increased use. And President Clinton's recently appointed surgeon general, Joycelyn Elders, has recommended that we study seriously the possibility of decriminalizing drugs as a means to reducing violence, noting that "other countries had decriminalized drug use and had reduced their crime rates without increasing the use of narcotics."[106] Baltimore Mayor Kurt Schmoke has called for consideration of decriminalization, and so has Jerry Wilson, former chief of police for Washington, D.C. (where 42 percent of murders were drug-related in 1990).[107] Some form of decriminalization of marijuana, heroin, and cocaine would reduce the criminalization of law-abiding users, would reduce the need for addicts to steal, would reduce incentives to drug traffickers and smugglers, and would free up personnel and resources for a more effective war against the crimes that people most fear.

In the face of all this, it is hard to believe that we do not know how to reduce crime at all. It is hard not to share the frustration expressed by Norval Morris, dean of the University of Chicago Law School: "It is trite but it remains true that the main causes of crime are social and economic. The question arises whether people really care. The solutions are so obvious. *It's almost as if America wished for a high crime rate.*"[108] If this is so, then the *system's failure is only in the eye of the victim: For those in control, it is a roaring success!*

How Crime Pays: Erikson and Durkheim

Kai T. Erikson has suggested in his book *Wayward Puritans* that societies derive benefit from the existence of crime and thus there is reason to believe that social institutions work to maintain rather than to eliminate crime. Because the Pyrrhic defeat theory draws heavily upon this insight, it will serve to clarify my own view if we compare it with Erikson's.

Professor Erikson's theory is based on the view of crime that finds expression in one of the classic works of sociological theory, *The Division of Labor in Society,* by Émile Durkheim. Writing toward the end of the nineteenth century, Durkheim

> *had suggested that crime (and by extension other forms of deviation) may actually perform a needed service to society by drawing people together in a common posture of anger and indignation. The deviant individual violates rules of conduct which the rest of the community holds in high respect; and when these people come together to express their outrage over the offense and to bear witness against the offender, they develop a tighter bond of solidarity than existed earlier.*[109]

The solidarity that holds a community together, in this view, is a function of the intensity with which the members of the community share a living sense of the group's cultural identity, of the boundary between acceptable and unacceptable behavior that gives the group its distinctive character. It is necessary, then, for the existence of a community as a *community* that its members learn and constantly relearn the location of its "boundaries." Erikson writes that these boundaries are learned in dramatic confrontations with

> *policing agents whose special business it is to guard the cultural integrity of the community. Whether these confrontations take the form of criminal trials, excommunication hearings, courts-martial, or even case conferences, they act as boundary-maintaining devices in the sense that they demonstrate to whatever audience is concerned where the line is drawn between behavior that belongs in the special universe of the group and behavior that does not.*[110]

In brief, this means not only that a community makes good use of unacceptable behavior *but that it positively needs unacceptable behavior*. Not only does unacceptable behavior cast in relief the terrain of behavior acceptable to the community; it also reinforces the intensity with which the members of the community identify that terrain as their shared territory. On this view, *deviant behavior is an ingredient in the glue that holds a community together.* "This," Erikson continues,

> *raises a delicate theoretical issue. If we grant that human groups often derive benefit from deviant behavior, can we then assume that they are organized in such a way as to promote this resource? Can we assume, in other words, that forces operate in the social structure to recruit offenders and to commit them to long periods of service in the deviant ranks?* ...
>
> *Looking at the matter from a long-range historical perspective, it is fair to conclude that prisons have done a conspicuously poor job of reforming the convicts placed in their custody; but the very consistency of this failure may have a peculiar logic of its own. Perhaps we find it difficult to change the worst of our penal practices because we* expect *the prison to harden the inmate's commitment to deviant forms of behavior and draw him more deeply into the deviant ranks.*[111]

Drawing on Durkheim's recognition that societies benefit from the existence of deviants, Erikson entertains the view that societies have institutions whose unannounced function is to recruit and maintain a reliable supply of deviants. Modified for our purposes, Erikson's view would become the hypothesis that the American criminal justice system fails to reduce crime because a visible criminal population is essential to maintaining the "boundaries" that mark the cultural identity of American society and to maintaining the solidarity among those who share that identity. In other words, in its failure, the criminal justice system succeeds in providing some of the cement necessary to hold American society together as a society.

As I said in the Introduction, this is one of the ideas that contributes to the Pyrrhic defeat theory, but it is also transformed in the process. Here, then, my aim is to acknowledge my debt to the Durkheim-Erikson thesis and to state the difference between it and the view that I will defend. The debt is to the insight that societies may promote behavior that they seem to desire to stamp out, that failure to eliminate deviance may be a success of some sort.

The difference, on the other hand, is this: Both Durkheim and Erikson jump from the *general* proposition that the failure to eliminate deviance promotes social solidarity to the *specific* conclusion that the form in which this failure occurs in a particular society can be explained by the contribution the failure makes to promoting consensus on shared beliefs and thus feelings of social solidarity. This is a "jump" because it leaves out the important question of how a social group forms its particular consensus around one set of shared beliefs rather than another; that is, Durkheim and Erikson implicitly assume that a consensus already exists (at least virtually) and that deviance is promoted to manifest and reinforce it. This leads to the view that social institutions reflect beliefs already in people's heads and already largely and spontaneously shared by all of them.

In my view, even if it is granted that societies work to strengthen feelings of social solidarity, the set of beliefs about the world around which those feelings will crystallize are by no means already in people's heads and spontaneously shared. A consensus is made, not born, although, again, I do not mean that it is made intentionally. It is created, not just reflected, by social institutions. Thus, the failure to stamp out deviance does not simply reinforce a consensus that already exists; it is part of the process by which a very particular consensus is created. In developing the Pyrrhic defeat theory, I try to show how the failure of criminal justice works to create and reinforce a very particular set of beliefs about the world, about what is dangerous and what is not, who is a threat and who is not. This does not merely shore up general feelings of social solidarity; it allows those feelings to be attached to a social order characterized by striking disparities of wealth, power, and privilege, and considerable injustice.

Summary

In this chapter, I have tried to establish the first part of the Pyrrhic defeat theory, namely, that the war on crime is a failure and an avoidable one: The American criminal justice system—by which I mean the entire process from lawmaking to law enforcing—has done little or nothing to reduce the enormous amount of crime that characterizes our society and threatens our citizens. Over the last several decades, crime has generally risen, although in recent years it has occasionally declined. No doubt demographic changes, most significantly the growth followed by the decrease in the number of youngsters in the crime-prone years, have played a role in this. This in itself suggests that criminal justice policy and practice cannot be credited with the recent occasional declines. At the same time, however, neither can it be thought on this basis that public policy cannot reduce the crime we have. To support this, I have shown that crime is neither a simple and unavoidable consequence of the number of youngsters nor of the degree of urbanization. I have suggested that there are a number of things we have good reason to believe would succeed in reducing crime—effective gun control, decriminalization of illicit drugs, and, of course, amelioration of poverty—that we refuse to do. I concluded the chapter by showing that the Pyrrhic defeat theory shares, with the Durkheim-Erikson view of the functional nature of crime, the idea that societies may promote behavior that they seem to want to eliminate. My theory differs from their view in insisting that the failure to stamp out crime doesn't simply reflect an existing consensus but contributes to creating one, one that is functional for only a certain part of our society.

Study Questions

1. Why do crime rates rise and fall?

2. What causes crime? What conditions make crime more likely?

3. What excuses have been given for our inability to reduce the amount of crime we have? How do you evaluate these excuses?

4. How do you think we could reduce the amount of crime?

5. What does it mean to say that "crime is functional for a society"? How does the Pyrrhic defeat theory differ on this from the Durkheim-Erikson theory?

6. List the costs and benefits of our current war on drugs. Is it worth it? Do you think that legalizing all or some illicit drugs would reduce crime? If so, would you agree to legalization?

7. What is meant by saying that the criminal justice system is "designed to fail"?

Additional Readings

BOUZA, ANTHONY (Chief, Ret). *How to Stop Crime.* New York: Plenum Press, 1993.

CHRISTIE, NILS. *Crime Control as Industry: Toward Gulags, Western Style?* London: Routledge, 1993.

HAGAN, JOHN. *Structural Criminology.* New Brunswick: Rutgers University Press, 1989.

IRWIN, JOHN AND JAMES AUSTIN. *It's About Time: America's Imprisonment Binge.* Belmont, Calif.: Wadsworth, 1994.

MESSERSCHMIDT, J. *Capitalism, Patriarchy and Crime.* Totowa, N.J.: Rowman and Littlefield, 1985.

QUINNEY, RICHARD. *Class, State and Crime.* New York: Longman, 1977.

SCHEINGOLD, STUART. *The Politics of Street Crime: Criminal Process and Cultural Obsession.* Philadelphia: Temple University Press, 1991.

Notes to Chapter 1

1. Speech of the president to the International Association of Chiefs of Police, New Orleans, Louisiana, September 28, 1981, reported in Weekly Compilation of Presidential Documents (July-September 1981), pp. 1039ff.
2. Quoted in *BJS National Update* 1, no. 4, April 1992, p. 1.
3. State of the Union Message (January 25, 1994), as reported in the *Washington Post,* January 26, 1994, p. A13.
4. Governor Bill Clinton and Senator Al Gore, *Putting People First: How We Can All Change America* (New York: Times Books, 1992), p. 71.
5. *UCR-1992,* p. 58.
6. *UCR-1986,* p. 41; *UCR-1991,* pp. 5, 10; *UCR-1992,* p. 58; *Sourcebook-1987,* p. 240; BJS, *Criminal Victimization, 1991,* p. 2.
7. See, for example, Walter Gove, Michael Hughes, and Michael Geerken, "Are Uniform Crime Reports a Valid Indicator of the Index Crimes? An Affirmative Answer With Minor Qualifications," *Criminology* 23 (1985), pp. 451–501.
8. *UCR-1991,* p. 11; *UCR-1992,* p. 58; BJS, *Criminal Victimization, 1991,* p. 1. For 1992, the UCR reports a small drop in the number of property crimes, bringing the total number of Index crimes to 14,438,200, a 2.9 percent decrease compared with 1991. This in turn was matched by a population increase of nearly 3,000,000. The overall effect was to reduce the rate of Index crimes from 5,139.7 per 100,000 inhabitants to 4,902.7. Note, however, that the increase in violent crime was close to the increase in population, so that the rate of violent crimes per 100,000 inhabitants decreased only one-tenth of one percent compared with 1991.
9. *Challenge,* p. 35.
10. *UCR-1986,* p. 41; *UCR-1991,* p. 5.
11. *Sourcebook-1991,* p. 2, Table no. 1.1; and p. 22, Table no. 1.16.

12. On this issue, I have made ample use of the discussion and references in Victor Kappeler, Merle Blumberg, and Gary Potter, *The Mythology of Crime and Criminal Justice* (Prospect Heights, Ill.: Waveland, 1993), chap. 10: "The Myth of Lenient Criminal Justice System in the United States," pp. 193–211.

13. *Sourcebook-1992,* p. 197, Table no. 2.45; Ernest van den Haag, "When Felons Go Free: Worse Than a Crime," *National Review* (January 20, 1992), p. 50.

14. Kappeler et al., *The Mythology of Crime and Criminal Justice,* pp. 195–96.

15. "When the range of crimes examined is made more comparable in terms of seriousness and when the rates are standardized for differences in the level of crime cross-nationally, the extreme differences in the use of incarceration between the United States and several other Western democracies are lessened considerably and, in some cases, disappear." James Lynch, "A Comparison of Prison Use in England, Canada, West Germany, and the United States: A Limited Test of the Punitiveness Hypothesis," *Journal of Criminal Law and Criminology* 79, no. 1 (1988), p. 196, cf. p. 181. This conclusion is based on cross-national comparison of the rates at which convicted persons are sentenced to prison, irrespective of the length of the sentence or eventual time actually served. Cross-national comparisons of actual time served show the United States to be roughly comparable to other Western democracies. See James Lynch, "A Cross-National Comparison of the Length of Custodial Sentences for Serious Crimes," *Justice Quarterly* 10, no. 4 (December 1993), pp. 801–23.

16. Clifford Krauss, "Senate Approves Broad Crime Bill; Split Over Guns," *New York Times,* November 20, 1993, p. 1.

17. Sharon LaFraniere, "U.S. Has Most Prisoners Per Capita in the World," *Washington Post,* January 5, 1991, p. A3; and Kappeler et al., *The Mythology of Crime and Criminal Justice,* pp. 195, 199.

18. Elliott Currie, *Confronting Crime: An American Challenge* (New York: Pantheon, 1985), p. 12; cited in Kappeler et al., *The Mythology of Crime and Criminal Justice,* p. 207.

19. Krauss, "Senate Approves Broad Crime Bill; Split Over Guns," p. 1.

20. William Claiborne, "Gun Control Battle Behind It, NRA Pushes Effort on Crime Control," *Washington Post,* December 5, 1993, p. A20.

21. INTERPOL, *International Crime Statistics 1989–1990,* p. 97.

22. Louise I. Shelley, *Crime and Modernization* (Carbondale: Southern Illinois University Press, 1981), p. 76.

23. INTERPOL, *International Crime Statistics 1989–1990,* pp. 2, 22, 58, 97, 148, 172.

24. *UCR-1991,* pp. 62–64.

25. Quoted in *Violence: An Element of American Life,* eds. K. Taylor and F. Soady (Boston: Holbrook Press, 1972), p. 49.

26. *UCR-1991,* pp. 60, 64, 66, 84, 89, 93, 97.

27. *UCR-1991,* pp. 93, 97, 105 (figures have been rounded to the nearest integer).

28. *UCR-1991,* pp. 35–37, Table no. 38; *StatAbst-1992,* pp. 84–105.

29. *Time,* June 30, 1975, p. 11.

30. *StatAbst-1992,* p. 15, Table no. 13; and *UCR-1991,* pp. 223–24.

31. *UCR-1990,* p. 50, Table no. 1; *UCR-1985,* p. 41, Table no. 1; *StatAbst-1992,* p. 14, Table no. 12.

32. I have calculated the population of 16- to 24-year-olds from *Economic Report of the President* (Washington, D.C.: U.S. Government Printing Office, 1988), p. 283, Table B-31; the victimization figures are from *Sourcebook-1987,* p. 240.

33. *UCR-1992,* p. 58; *StatAbst-1992,* p. 15, Table no. 13.

34. "Serious Crime Rises Again in New York," *New York Times,* March 22, 1988, pp. B1, B6.

35. See, for example, Darrell Steffensmeier and Miles D. Harer, "Did Crime Rise or Fall During the Reagan Presidency? The Effects of an 'Aging' U.S. Population on the Nation's Crime Rate," *Journal of Research in Crime and Delinquency* 28, no. 3 (August 1991), pp. 330–59.

36. Steffensmeier and Harer, "Did Crime Rise or Fall During the Reagan Presidency?," p. 331.

37. Morton O. Schapiro and Dennis A. Ahlberg, "Why Crime Is Down," *American Demographics,* October 1986, p. 56.

38. Steffensmeier and Harer, "Did Crime Rise or Fall During the Reagan Presidency?," pp. 347–48.

39. *Washington Post,* August 4, 1975, p. A2.

40. *Washington Post,* August 17, 1975, pp. A1, A4.

41. Yale Kamisar, "Why the Bad Guys Keep Winning" (review of Lawrence Friedman's *Crime and Punishment in American History* [New York: Basic Books, 1993]), *New York Times Book Review,* September 26, 1993, p. 11.

42. Athelia Knight, "Strategies to End the Carnage," *Washington Post,* October 27, 1993, pp. A1 and A16.

43. Writing on the crime bill before its passage, columnist William Raspberry says, "My objections are ... principally that the legislation has nothing to do with crime *prevention*.... The crime bill would make the principle investment at the back end—in the criminal justice system—where it's already too late." "A Crime Bill With No Hope," *Washington Post,* October 27, 1993, p. A25.

44. "UnAmerican Thoughts," *Economist* (October 26, 1991), p. 23.

45. *StatAbst-1992,* p. 450, Table no. 704.

46. Guy Gugliotta, "Number of Poor Americans Rises for 3rd Year," *Washington Post,* October 5, 1993, p. A6.

47. See, for example, John Braithwaite, "Poverty, Power, and White-Collar Crime," in Kip Schlegel and David Weisburd, eds., *White Collar Crime Reconsidered* (Boston: Northeastern University Press, 1992), pp. 78–107.

48. *Washington Post,* September 6, 1982, p. 2; the report was issued by the Full Employment Action Council (a coalition of religious, civil rights, and union groups) and the National Policy Exchange (an economic research and educational organization).

49. *Washington Post,* September 14, 1982, pp. 1, 4.

50. Karen Pennar, "The Rich Are Richer—And America May Be the Poorer," *Business Week* (November 18, 1991), pp. 85, 88.

51. *StatAbst-1992,* p. 399, Table no. 635. See also, "*Racial Gulf:* Blacks' Hopes, Raised by '68 Kerner Report, Are Mainly Unfulfilled," *Wall Street Journal,* February 26, 1988, pp. 1, 9; *StatAbst-1992,* p. 80, Table no. 109; "Today's Native Sons," *Time,* December 1, 1986, pp. 26–29; and *StatAbst-1988,* p. 75, Table no. 113.

52. Todd R. Clear, " 'Tougher' Is Dumber," *New York Times,* December 4, 1993, p. 21.

53. BJS, *Correctional Populations in the United States, 1990,* p. 46. Nearly 22 percent of state facilities are under a state or federal consent decree to limit population (ibid., p. 47).

54. Robert Johnson and Hans Toch, "Introduction," in Johnson and Toch, eds., *The Pains of Imprisonment* (Beverly Hills, Calif.: Sage, 1982), pp. 19–20.

55. Franklin Zimring, *Firearms and Violence in American Life* (Washington, D.C.: U.S. Government Printing Office, 1968), pp. 6–7 (emphasis added).

56. Gary Kleck, *Point Blank: Guns and Violence in America* (New York: Aldine de Gruyter, 1991), p. 17. Kleck's estimate of the number of guns is supported by the Bureau of Alcohol, Tobacco and Firearms, which calculated 200 million in 1990 (cited in Albert Reiss and Jeffrey Roth, eds., *Understanding and Preventing Violence* [Washington D.C.: National Academy Press, 1993], p. 256).

57. Kleck, *Point Blank: Guns and Violence in America,* p. 54. Kleck's claim is based in part on a 1989 Gallup poll that found 47 percent of households had firearms and the *Time/CNN* poll of the same year found 48 percent of households with firearms. Also, see Douglas Weil and David Henenway, "Loaded Guns in the Home: Analysis of a National Random Survey of Gun Owners" *Journal of the American Medical Association* 267, no. 22 (June 10, 1992). They report that 46 percent of households had firearms, including 25 percent that had a handgun, half of which were currently loaded (p. 3033).

58. *Challenge,* p. 239 (emphasis added).

59. *UCR-1991,* pp. 11, 17.

60. Don Colburn and Abigail Trafford, "Guns at Home: Doctors Target Growing Epidemic of Violence," *Washington Post Health,* October 12, 1993, p. 12.

61. Ibid., p. 13.

62. Barbara Vobejda, "Homicide Risk Found to Outweigh Benefit of Gun for Home Protection," *Washington Post,* October 7, 1993, p. A4.

63. "Rate of Gun Deaths Rises Sharply Among 15–24 Age Group," *Washington Post,* March 24, 1993, p. A4.

64. Barbara Vobejda, "Children's Defense Fund Cites Gun Violence," *Washington Post,* January 21, 1994, p. A3.

65. Presidential news conference, June 16, 1981; see also "Reagan Denounces Gun Control Laws," *Washington Post,* May 7, 1983, p. A8.

66. "Whenever there is a crime involving a firearm, there are various groups, some of them quite persuasive in their logic, that think you can ban certain kinds of guns, and I am not in that mode" (George Bush, quoted in George Will, "Playing With Guns," *Newsweek,* March 27, 1989, p. 78).

67. Pierre Thomas, "Brady Gun Law Contains No Penalties, Little Money for States," *Washington Post,* December 3, 1993, p. A3.

68. Zimring, *Firearms and Violence in American Life,* chap. 11.

69. Linda Saltzman et al., "Weapon Involvement and Injury Outcomes in Family and Intimate Assaults," *Journal of the American Medical Association,* 276, no. 22 (June 10, 1992), p. 3043.

70. Arnold S. Trebach, *The Heroin Solution* (New Haven, Conn.: Yale University Press, 1982), pp. 3–24, 246.

71. BJS, *Drugs, Crime, and the Justice System* (December 1992), pp. 26, 28.

72. Majority Staffs of the Senate Judiciary Committee and the International Narcotics Control Caucus, *The President's Drug Strategy: One Year Later* (September 1990), p. 8B; cited in Doug Bandow, "War on Drugs or War on America?," *Stanford Law & Policy Review* (Fall 1991), pp. 245, 253. See also, Michael Isikoff, "International Opium Production Up 8% Last Year," *Washington Post,* March 1, 1992, p. A4, where the number of heroin addicts in the United States is estimated to be between 500,000 and 750,000.

73. Quoted in Doug Bandow, "War on Drugs or War on America?," p. 246.

74. Surgeon General Koop quoted, and reports on the relative addictiveness of cigarettes and cocaine, in Bandow, "War on Drugs or War on America?," p. 249.

75. "The largest study ever made of drug abuse in this country shows that two widely available legal drugs—alcohol and the tranquilizer Valium—are responsible for the greatest amount of drug-related illness, the government reported yesterday." Stuart Auerbach, "2 Drugs Widely Abused," *Washington Post,* July 9, 1976, p. A1.

76. Quoted in Doug Bandow, "War on Drugs or War on America?," p. 250.

77. M. Douglas Anglin and George Speckart, "Narcotics Use and Crime: A Multisample, Multimethod Analysis," *Criminology* 26, no. 2 (1988), p. 226.

78. United States Department of Health, Education and Welfare, Public Health Service, National Institute on Alcohol Abuse and Alcoholism, Special Action Office for Drug Abuse Prevention, *Social Cost of Drug Abuse* (Washington, D.C.: U.S. Government Printing Office, 1974), pp. 20–21.

79. *UCR-1992,* p. 36.

80. BJS, *Drugs and Crime Facts, 1992,* p. 8.

81. Trebach, *The Heroin Solution,* p. 246.

82. Troy Duster, *The Legislation of Morality: Law, Drugs, and Moral Judgment* (New York: Free Press, 1970), pp. 3, 7, inter alia.

83. Cf. Philip C. Baridon, *Addiction, Crime, and Social Policy* (Lexington, Mass.: Lexington Books, 1976), pp. 4–5.

84. Anglin and Speckart, "Narcotics Use and Crime: A Multisample, Multimethod Analysis," p. 197.

85. Bandow, "War on Drugs or War on America?," pp. 245, 248; also Alfred W. McCoy and Alan A. Block, "U.S. Narcotics Policy: An Anatomy of Failure," in McCoy and Block, eds., *War on Drugs: Studies in the Failure of U.S. Narcotics Policy* (Boulder, Colo.: Westview Press, 1992), p. 3.

86. Arnold S. Trebach, Testimony at the Hearings on Proposals to Legalize Drugs held by the House Select Committee on Narcotics Abuse and Control, September 29, 1988, p. 2.

87. "Enemy Within: Drug Money Is Corrupting the Enforcers," *New York Times,* April 11, 1988, p. A12.
88. "U.S. Anti-Drug Effort Criticized," *Washington Post,* November 12, 1988, p. A15.
89. McCoy and Block, "U.S. Narcotics Policy: An Anatomy of Failure," p. 3.
90. Michael Isikoff, "International Opium Production Up 8% Last Year," *Washington Post,* March 1, 1992, p. A4.
91. Bandow, "War on Drugs or War on America?," p. 244; and BJS, *Drugs, Crime, and the Justice System* (December 1992), p. 44.
92. "Cocaine Down: Signs Indicate That America's Cocaine Habit Is Easing," *Wall Street Journal,* July 20, 1987, p. 21.
93. BJS, *Drugs, Crime and the Justice System* (December 1992), p. 42.
94. Reported in McCoy and Block, "U.S. Narcotics Policy: An Anatomy of Failure," p. 3.
95. "Prosecutors Admit: No Victory in Sight," *National Law Journal* (August 8, 1988), p. S-2.
96. BJS, *Drugs, Crime and the Justice System* (December 1992), pp. 126, 131.
97. "Drug Wars Push D.C. to Brink of Homicide Record: Police Efforts Futile as Turf Disputes Raise 1988 Slaying Total to 285," *Washington Post,* October 26, 1988, p. A1. By year's end, the record was soundly broken, with the number of murders reaching 372! And the carnage continues: In 1991, there were 482 homicides in the nation's capital *(UCR-1991,* p. 64).
98. "Enemy Within: Drug Money Is Corrupting the Enforcers," pp. A1, A12.
99. Ibid.
100. Marvin D. Miller, National Organization for the Reform of Marijuana Laws, Testimony at the Hearings on Proposals to Legalize Drugs held by the House Select Committee on Narcotics Abuse and Control, September 29, 1988, pp. 12-13; *UCR-1986,* p. 163.
101. Miller, testimony, p. 19.
102. U.S. Department of Justice, Drug Enforcement Administration, Opinion and Recommended Ruling, Findings of Fact, Conclusions of Law and Decision of Administrative Law Judge Francis L. Young, In The Matter of MARIJUANA RESCHEDULING PETITION, Docket No. 86-22, September 6, 1988, pp. 56–57.
103. Trebach, testimony, pp. 11–12. Doug Bandow of the Cato Institute confirms Trebach's numbers: "Tobacco kills roughly 390,000 people annually and alcohol is responsible for some 150,000 deaths a year. . . . In contrast, all illicit drugs combined account for about 5,000 deaths, most of which, as explained below, are caused by the effects of prohibition. For 100,000 users, tobacco kills 650, alcohol 150, heroin 80, and cocaine 4." (Bandow, "War on Drugs or War on America?," p. 245). In a footnote, the author mentions that these figures have been reduced to reflect only the drug use, not the effects of prohibition.
104. Bandow, "War on Drugs or War on America?," p. 243; McCoy and Block, "U.S. Narcotics Policy: An Anatomy of Failure," p. 6.
105. Jerry V. Wilson, "Our Wasteful War on Drugs," *Washington Post,* January 18, 1994, p. A20.

106. Ibid., p. 31; Surgeon General Joycelyn Elders's statement was reported in *International Herald Tribune,* December 8, 1993, p. 1. She reiterated the suggestion after "reviewing many studies," and even after President Clinton's opposition to the idea was reported. "Elders Reiterates Her Support for Study of Drug Legalization," *Washington Post,* January 15, 1994, p. A8.
107. Wilson, "Our Wasteful War on Drugs," p. A20.
108. *Time,* June 30, 1975, p. 17 (emphasis added).
109. Kai T. Erikson, *Wayward Puritans* (New York: Wiley, 1966), p. 4. Reprinted by permission of John Wiley & Sons, Inc.
110. Ibid., p. 11.
111. Ibid., pp. 13–15 (emphasis added).

2

A Crime by Any Other Name . . .

If one individual inflicts a bodily injury upon another which leads to the death of the person attacked we call it manslaughter; on the other hand, if the attacker knows beforehand that the blow will be fatal we call it murder. Murder has also been committed if society places hundreds of workers in such a position that they inevitably come to premature and unnatural ends. Their death is as violent as if they had been stabbed or shot. . . . Murder has been committed if society knows perfectly well that thousands of workers cannot avoid being sacrificed so long as these conditions are allowed to continue. Murder of this sort is just as culpable as the murder committed by an individual.

Frederick Engels, *The Condition of the Working Class in England*

What's In a Name?

If it takes you an hour to read this chapter, by the time you reach the last page, three of your fellow citizens will have been murdered. *During that same time, at least four Americans will die as a result of unhealthy or unsafe conditions in the workplace!* Although these work-related deaths could have been prevented, they are not called murders. Why not? Doesn't a crime by any other name still cause misery and suffering? What's in a name?

The fact is that the label "crime" is not used in America to name all or the worst of the actions that cause misery and suffering to Americans. It is primarily reserved for the dangerous actions of the poor.

In the February 21, 1993, edition of the *New York Times*, an article appears with the headline: "Company in Mine Deaths Set to Pay Big Fine." It describes an agreement by the owners of a Kentucky mine to pay a fine for safety misconduct that may have led to "the worst American mining accident in nearly a decade." Ten workers died in a methane explosion, and the company pleaded guilty to "a pattern of safety misconduct" that included falsifying reports of methane levels and requiring miners to work under unsupported roofs. The company was fined $3.75 million. The acting foreman at the mine was the only individual charged by the federal government, and for his cooperation with the investigation, prosecutors were recommending that he receive the minimum sentence: probation to six months in prison. The company's president expressed regret for the tragedy that occurred. And the U.S. attorney said he hoped the case "sent a clear message that violations of Federal safety and health regulations that endanger the lives of our citizens will not be tolerated."[1]

Compare this with the story of Colin Ferguson, who prompted an editorial in the *New York Times* of December 10, 1993, with the headline: "Mass Murder on the 5:33."[2] A few days earlier, Colin had boarded a commuter train in Garden City, Long Island, and methodically shot passengers with a 9-millimeter pistol, killing 5 and wounding 18. Colin Ferguson was surely a murderer, maybe a mass murderer. My question is, Why wasn't the death of the miners also murder? Why weren't those responsible for subjecting ten miners to deadly conditions also "mass murderers"?

Why do ten dead miners amount to an "accident," a "tragedy," and five dead commuters a "mass murder"? "Murder" suggests a murderer, whereas "accident" and "tragedy" suggest the work of impersonal forces. But the charge against the company that owned the mine said that they "repeatedly exposed the mine's work crews to danger and that such conditions were frequently concealed from Federal inspectors responsible for enforcing the mine safety act." And the acting foreman admitted to falsifying records of methane levels only two months before the fatal blast. Someone was responsible for the conditions that led to the death of ten miners. Is that person not a murderer, perhaps even a *mass murderer*?

These questions are at this point rhetorical. My aim is not to discuss this case but rather to point to the blinders we wear when we look at such an "accident." There was an investigation. One person, the acting foreman, was held responsible for falsifying records. He is to be sentenced to six months in prison (at most). The company was fined. But no one will be tried for *murder*. No one will be thought of as a murderer. *Why not?* Would the miners not be safer if such people were treated as murderers? Might they not still be alive? Will a president of the United States address the Yale Law

School and recommend mandatory prison sentences for such people? Will he mean these people when he says,

> *These relatively few, persistent criminals who cause so much misery and fear are really the core of the problem. The rest of the American people have a right to protection from their violence[?]*[3]

Didn't those miners have a right to protection from the violence that took their lives? *And if not, why not?*

Once we are ready to ask this question seriously, we are in a position to see that the reality of crime—that is, the acts we label crime, the acts we think of as crime, the actors and actions we treat as criminal—is *created:* It is an image shaped by decisions as to *what* will be called crime and *who* will be treated as a criminal.

The Carnival Mirror

It is sometimes coyly observed that the quickest and cheapest way to eliminate crime would be to throw out all the criminal laws. There is a sliver of truth to this view. Without criminal laws, there would indeed be no "crimes." There would, however, still be dangerous acts. This is why we cannot really solve our crime problem quite so simply. The criminal law *labels* some acts "crimes." In doing this, it identifies those acts as so dangerous that we must use the extreme methods of criminal justice to protect ourselves against them. This does not mean the criminal law *creates* crime—it simply "mirrors" real dangers that threaten us. What is true of the criminal law is true of the whole justice system. If police did not arrest or prosecutors charge or juries convict, there would be no "criminals." This does not mean that police or prosecutors or juries create criminals any more than legislators do. They *react* to real dangers in society. The criminal justice system—from lawmakers to law enforcers—is just a mirror of the real dangers that lurk in our midst. *Or so we are told.*

How accurate is this mirror? We need to answer this in order to know whether or how well the criminal justice system is protecting us against the real threats to our well-being. The more accurate a mirror is, the more the image it shows is created by the reality it reflects. The more misshapen a mirror is, the more the distorted image it shows is created by the mirror, not by the reality reflected. It is in this sense that I will argue that the image of crime is created: The American criminal justice system is a mirror that shows a distorted image of the dangers that threaten us—an image created more by the shape of the mirror than by the reality reflected. What do we see when we look in the criminal justice mirror?

On the morning of September 16, 1975, the *Washington Post* carried an article in its local news section headlined "Arrest Data Reveal Profile of a Suspect." The article reported the results of a study of crime in Prince George's County, a suburb of Washington, D.C. It read in part as follows:

> *The typical suspect in serious crime in Prince George's County is a black male, aged 14 to 19, who lives in the area inside the Capital Beltway where more than half of the county's 64,371 reported crimes were committed in 1974. [The study] presents a picture of persons, basically youths, committing a crime once every eight minutes in Prince George's County.*[4]

This report is hardly a surprise. The portrait it paints of "the typical suspect in serious crime" is probably a pretty good rendering of the image lurking in the back of the minds of most people who fear crime. Furthermore, although the crime rate in Prince George's County is somewhat above the national average and its black population somewhat above that of the average suburban county, the portrait generally fits the national picture presented in the FBI's *Uniform Crime Reports* for the same year, 1974. In Prince George's County, "youths between the ages of 15 and 19 were accused of committing nearly half [45.5 percent] of all 1974 crimes."[5] For the nation in 1974, the FBI reported that persons in this age group accounted for 39.5 percent of arrests for the FBI Index crimes (criminal homicide, forcible rape, robbery, aggravated assault, burglary, larceny, and motor vehicle theft.)[6] These youths were male and (disproportionately) black. In Prince George's County, males "represented three of every four serious crime defendants."[7] In the nation in 1974, out of 1,289,524 persons arrested for FBI Index crimes, 1,043,155, or more than 80 percent, were males.[8] In Prince George's County, where blacks make up approximately 25 percent of the population, "blacks were accused of 58 percent of all serious crimes."[9] In the nation, where blacks made up 11.4 percent of the population in 1974, they accounted for 34.2 percent of arrests for Index crimes.[10]

That was 1974. But little has changed since. In his 1993 book, *How to Stop Crime*, retired police chief Anthony Bouza writes: "Street crime is mostly a black and poor young man's game."[11] And listen to the sad words of the Reverend Jesse Jackson: "There is nothing more painful to me at this stage of my life than to walk down the street and hear footsteps and start thinking about robbery—and then look around and see someone white and feel relieved."[12]

This, then, is the Typical Criminal, the one whose portrait President Reagan described as "that of a stark, staring face, a face that belongs to a frightening reality of our time—the face of a human predator, the face of the habitual criminal. Nothing in nature is more cruel and more dangerous."[13] This is the face that Ronald Reagan saw in the criminal justice mirror, more than a decade ago. Let us look more closely at the face in today's criminal justice mirror, and we shall see much the same Typical Criminal:

He is, first of all, a *he.* Out of 2,012,906 persons arrested for FBI Index crimes in 1991, 1,572,591, or 78 percent, were males.[14] Second, he is a *youth.* In 1991, more than half of arrests for FBI Index crimes were of individuals aged 22 and under.[15] Third, he is predominantly *urban:* "Among city population groupings, those with more than 250,000 inhabitants recorded the highest rate [of arrests], 7,579 [per 100,000 inhabitants]."[16] Fourth, he is disproportionately *black*—blacks are arrested for Index crimes at a rate three times that of their percentage in the national population. In 1991, when blacks were about 12 percent of the nation's population, they made up 34.6 percent of Index crime arrests.[17] Finally, he is *poor:* Among state prisoners in 1991, 33 percent were unemployed prior to being arrested—a rate nearly four times that of males in the general population. Among those state prisoners who had incomes prior to being arrested, 19 percent earned less than $3,000 a year (compared with 6.8 percent of males in the civilian labor force), and half earned less than $10,000 a year (compared with 25 percent of noninstitutionalized males).[18] As the President's Commission reported nearly 30 years ago: "The offender at the end of the road in prison is likely to be a member of the lowest social and economic groups in the country."[19]

This is the Typical Criminal feared by most law-abiding Americans. Poor, young, urban, (disproportionately) black males make up the core of the enemy forces in the war against crime. They are the heart of a vicious, unorganized guerrilla army, threatening the lives, limbs, and possessions of the law-abiding members of society—necessitating recourse to the ultimate weapons of force and detention in our common defense.

But how do we know who the criminals are who so seriously endanger us that we must stop them with force and lock them in prisons?

"From the arrest records, probation reports, and prison statistics," the authors of *The Challenge of Crime in a Free Society* tell us, the "'portrait' of the offender emerges."[20] *These sources are not merely objective readings taken at different stages in the criminal justice process: Each of them represents human decisions.* "Prison statistics" and "probation reports" reflect *decisions* of juries on who gets convicted and decisions of judges on who gets probation or prison and for how long. "Arrest records" reflect decisions about which crimes to investigate and which suspects to take into custody. All these decisions rest on the most fundamental of all *decisions:* the decisions of legislators as to which acts shall be labeled "crimes" in the first place.

The reality of crime as the target of our criminal justice system and as perceived by the general populace is not a simple objective threat to which the system reacts: *It is a reality that takes shape as it is filtered through a series of human decisions running the full gamut of the criminal justice system*—from the lawmakers who determine what behavior shall be in the province of criminal justice to the law enforcers who decide which individuals will be brought within that province.

Note that by emphasizing the role of "human decisions," I do not mean to suggest that the reality of crime is voluntarily and intentionally "created" by individual "decision makers." Their decisions are themselves shaped by the social system, much as a child's decision to become an engineer rather than a samurai warrior is shaped by the social system in which he or she grows up. Thus, to have a full explanation of how the reality of crime is created, we have to understand how our society is structured in a way that leads people to make the decisions they do. In other words, these decisions are part of the social phenomena to be explained—they are not the explanation.

For the present, however, I emphasize the role of the decisions themselves for the following reasons: First, they are conspicuous points in the social process, easy to spot and verify empirically. Second, because they are decisions aimed at protecting us from the dangers in our midst, we can compare the decisions with the real dangers and determine whether they are responding to the real dangers. Third, because the reality of crime—the real actions labeled crimes, the real individuals identified as criminals, the real faces we watch in the news as they travel from arrest to court to prison—results from these decisions, we can determine whether that reality corresponds to the real dangers in our society. Where that reality does correspond to the real dangers, we can say that the reality of crime simply reflects the real dangers in society. Where the reality of crime does not correspond to the real dangers, we can say that it is a reality *created* by those decisions. And then we can investigate the role played by the social system in encouraging, reinforcing, and otherwise shaping those decisions.

It is to capture this way of looking at the relation between the reality of crime and the real dangers "out there" in society that I refer to the criminal justice system as a "mirror." Whom and what we see in this mirror is a function of the decisions about who and what are criminal, and so on. Our poor, young, urban, black male, who is so well represented in arrest records and prison populations, appears not simply because of the undeniable threat he poses to the rest of society. As dangerous as he may be, he would not appear in the criminal justice mirror *if* it had not been decided that the acts he performs should be labeled "crimes," *if* it had not been decided that he should be arrested for those crimes, *if* he had access to a lawyer who could persuade a jury to acquit him and perhaps a judge to expunge his arrest record, and *if* it had not been decided that he is the type of individual and his the type of crime that warrants imprisonment. *The shape of the reality we see in the criminal justice mirror is created by all these decisions*. We want to know

how accurately the reality we see in this mirror reflects the real dangers that threaten us in society.

It is not my view that this reality is created out of nothing. The mugger, the rapist, the murderer, the burglar, the robber all pose a definite threat to our well-being, and they ought to be dealt with in ways that effectively reduce that threat to the minimum level possible (without making the criminal justice system itself a threat to our lives and liberties). Of central importance, however, is that the threat posed by the Typical Criminal is not the greatest threat to which we are exposed. The acts of the Typical Criminal are not the only acts that endanger us, nor are they the acts that endanger us the most. As I shall show in this chapter, we have as great or sometimes even a greater chance of being killed or disabled by an occupational injury or disease, by unnecessary surgery, or by shoddy emergency medical services than by aggravated assault or even homicide! Yet even though these threats to our well-being are graver than that posed by our poor young criminals, they do not show up in the FBI's Index of serious crimes. The individuals responsible for them do not turn up in arrest records or prison statistics. *They never become part of the reality reflected in the criminal justice mirror, although the danger they pose is at least as great and often greater than the danger posed by those who do!*

Similarly, the general public loses more money *by far* (as I show below) from price-fixing and monopolistic practices and from consumer deception and embezzlement than from all the property crimes in the FBI's Index combined. Yet these far more costly acts are either not criminal, or if technically criminal, not prosecuted, or if prosecuted, not punished, or if punished, only mildly. In any event, although the individuals responsible for these acts take more money out of the ordinary citizen's pocket than our Typical Criminal, they rarely show up in arrest statistics and almost never in prison populations. *Their faces rarely appear in the criminal justice mirror, although the danger they pose is at least as great and often greater than that of those who do.*

The inescapable conclusion is that the criminal justice system does not simply *reflect* the reality of crime; it has a hand in *creating* the reality we see.

The criminal justice system is like a mirror in which society can see the face of the evil in its midst. Because the system deals with some evil and not with others, because it treats some evils as the gravest and treats some of the gravest evils as minor, the image it throws back is distorted like the image in a carnival mirror. Thus, the image cast back is false not because it is invented out of thin air but because the proportions of the real are distorted: Large becomes small and small large; grave becomes minor and minor grave. Like a carnival mirror, although nothing is reflected that does not exist in the world, the image is more a creation of the mirror than a picture of the world.

If criminal justice really gives us a carnival-mirror image of "crime," we are doubly deceived. First, we are led to believe that the criminal justice system is protecting us against the gravest threats to our well-being when, in fact, the system is protecting us against only some threats and not necessarily the gravest ones. We are deceived about how much protection we are receiving and thus left vulnerable. The second deception is just the other side of this one. If people believe that the carnival mirror is a true mirror—that is, if they believe the criminal justice system simply *reacts* to the gravest threats to their well-being—they come to believe that whatever is the target of the criminal justice system must be the greatest threat to their well-being. In other words, if people believe that the most drastic of society's weapons are wielded by the criminal justice system *in reaction to* the gravest dangers to society, they will believe the reverse as well: that those actions that call forth the most drastic of society's weapons *must be* those that pose the gravest dangers to society.

A strange alchemy takes place when people uncritically accept the legitimacy of their institutions: What *needs* justification becomes *proof* of justification. People come to believe that prisoners must be criminals *because* they are in prison and that the inmates of insane asylums must be *crazy* because they are in insane asylums.[21] The criminal justice system's use of extreme measures—such as force and imprisonment—is thought to be justified by the extreme gravity of the dangers it combats. By this alchemy, these extreme measures become *proof* of the extreme gravity of those dangers, and the first deception, which merely misleads the public about how much protection the criminal justice system is actually providing, is transformed into the second, which deceives the public into believing that the acts and actors that are the target of the criminal justice system pose the gravest threats to its well-being. Thus, the system may not only fail to protect us from dangers as great or greater than those listed in the FBI Crime Index; it may do still greater damage by creating the false security of the belief that only the acts on the FBI Index really threaten us and require control.

In the following discussion, I describe how and why the criminal justice carnival mirror distorts the image it creates.

Criminal Justice as Creative Art

In Chapter 1, I introduced the Pyrrhic defeat explanation for the "failure" of criminal justice in America: Criminal justice *fails* (or what amounts to the same thing, crime is maintained) to project a particular *image* of crime.

It is the task of this chapter and the next to prove that the reality of crime is *created* and that it is created in a way that promotes a particular *image* of crime: *The image that serious crime—and therefore the greatest danger to society—is the work of the poor.* The notion that the reality of crime is created is derived from Richard Quinney's theory of the *social reality of crime.*[22] But here as elsewhere, an idea that contributes to the Pyrrhic defeat theory gets transformed along the way. Because I understand the idea that the social reality of crime is created in a way different from its meaning for Quinney, it will help in presenting my view to compare it with Quinney's.

Quinney maintains that crime has a "social reality" rather than an objective reality. What he means can be explained with an example: Wherein lies the reality of money? Certainly not in the "objective" characteristics of green printed paper. It exists rather in the "social" meaning attributed to that paper and the pattern of "social" behavior that is a consequence of that meaning. If people did not act as if that green printed paper had value, it would be just green paper, not real money. The reality of a crime *as a crime* does not lie simply in the objective characteristics of an action. It lies in the "social" meaning attached to that action and the pattern of "social" behavior—particularly the behavior of criminal justice officials—that is a product of that meaning. I think Quinney is right in this. When I speak of the reality of crime, I am referring to much more than physical actions like stabbing or shooting. I mean the reality that a society gives those physical actions by labeling them and treating them as criminal.

Quinney further maintains that this reality of crime is *created.* By this he means that crime is a definition of behavior applied by lawmakers and other criminal justice decision makers. "Crime," Quinney writes,

> *is a* definition *of behavior that is conferred on some persons by others. Agents of the law (legislators, police, prosecutors, and judges), representing segments of a politically organized society, are responsible for formulating and administering criminal laws. Persons and behaviors, therefore, become criminal because of the formulation and application of criminal definitions. Thus, crime is* created.[23]

Now this is *not* what I have in mind when I say that the reality of crime is created. Here is the difference. Quinney's position amounts to this: Crimes are established by the criminal law and the criminal law is a human creation; ergo, crime is created. This is true, but it does not take us very far. After all, who can deny that crime is created *in this sense?* Only someone who has been hypnotized into forgetting that law books are written by lawmakers could deny that "crime" is a label that human beings apply to certain actions. What *is* controversial, however, is whether the label is applied appropriately. "Crime," after all, is not merely a sound—it is a word with a generally accepted meaning. Roughly speaking, it means at least "an intentional action that is harmful to society." (Now, of course, "crime" has a technical definition, namely, "an act prohibited by a criminal law." The point of prohibiting an act by the criminal law is to protect society from an injurious act. Thus, though any act prohibited by criminal law is rightly labeled a crime in the technical sense, not every act so prohibited is rightly prohibited, and thus not every act labeled "crime" is appropriately labeled. To determine whether the label crime is applied appropriately, we must use the more general definition.) The label is applied appropriately when it is used to identify all, or at least the worst of, the acts that are harmful to society. The label is applied inappropriately when it is attached to any harmless act or when it is not attached to seriously harmful acts. When I argue that the reality of crime is created, I mean that the label "crime" has not been applied appropriately.

Thus, by calling the social reality of crime created, I mean not just that the label "crime" is applied by human beings but that it is applied inappropriately. One might ask why the inappropriate use of the label "crime" is a reason for saying that crime is created. My answer is this: By calling something *created,* we call attention to the fact that human actors are responsible for it. By calling crime created, I point to human actors rather than objective dangers as determining the shape that the reality of crime takes in our society. If the label "crime" is consistently applied to the most dangerous or harmful acts, then it is misleading to point to the fact that human decision makers are responsible for how the label is applied because their decisions are dictated by compelling objective reasons. Rather than creating a reality, their decisions trace a reality that already exists. On the other hand, if the label is not applied appropriately, it is sensible to assume that it is applied for reasons that lie with the decision makers and not in the realm of objective dangers. This means that when the label "crime" is applied inappropriately, it is essential to call attention to the fact that human actors are responsible for it. Thus, it is precisely when the label "crime" is applied inappropriately that it is important to point out that the reality of crime is *created.*

By calling crime created, I want to emphasize the human responsibility for the shape of crime, not in the trivial sense that humans write the criminal law, *but rather to call attention to the fact that decisions as to what to label and treat as crime are not compelled by objective dangers, and thus that to understand the reality of crime, we must look to the social processes that shape those decisions.*

By calling crime created, I suggest that our picture of crime—the portrait that emerges from arrest statistics, prison populations, politicians' speeches, news media, and fictionalized presentations, the portrait that in turn influences lawmakers and criminal justice policymakers—is not a photograph of the real dangers that threaten us. Its features are not simply traced from the real dangers in the social world. Instead, it is a piece of creative art. It is a picture in which some dangers are portrayed and others omitted. Because it cannot be explained as a straight reflection of real dangers, we must look elsewhere to understand the shape it takes.

This argument, which will occupy us in this chapter and the next, leads to *five hypotheses* about the way in which criminal justice policy is made. To demonstrate that the reality of crime is created, that the criminal justice system is a carnival mirror that gives us a distorted image of the dangers that threaten us, I will try to prove that, at each of the crucial decision-making points in criminal justice, the decisions made do not reflect the real and most serious dangers we face.

1. **Of the Decisions of Legislators:** That the definitions of crime in the criminal law do not reflect the only or the most dangerous of antisocial behaviors.
2. **Of the Decisions of Police and Prosecutors:** That the decisions on whom to arrest or charge do not reflect the only or the most dangerous behaviors legally defined as "criminal."
3. **Of the Decisions of Juries and Judges:** That criminal convictions do not reflect the only or the most dangerous individuals among those arrested and charged.
4. **Of the Decisions of Sentencing Judges:** That sentencing decisions do not reflect the goal of protecting society from the only or the most dangerous of those convicted by meting out punishments proportionate to the harmfulness of the crime committed.
5. **Of All These Decisions Taken Together:** That what criminal justice policy decisions (in hypotheses 1 to 4) do reflect is the implicit identification of crime with the dangerous acts of the poor.

The Pyrrhic defeat theory is composed of these five hypotheses, *plus* the proposition that the criminal justice system is failing in avoidable ways to reduce crime (argued in Chapter 1), *plus* the *historical inertia* explanation of how this failure is generated and left uncorrected because of the ideological benefits it produces (argued in Chapter 4). In presenting this explanation, I try to show how the decisions that create the reality of crime are caused by historical forces and left unchanged because the particular distribution of costs and benefits to which those decisions give rise serves to make the system self-reinforcing.

A Crime by Any Other Name . . .

Think of a crime, any crime. Picture the first "crime" that comes into your mind. What do you see? The odds are you are not imagining a mining company executive sitting at his desk, calculating the costs of proper safety precautions and deciding not to invest in them. Probably what you do see with your mind's eye is one person physically attacking another or robbing something from another via the threat of physical attack. Look more closely. What does the attacker look like? It's a safe bet he (and it is a *he,* of course) is not wearing a suit and tie. In fact, my hunch is that you—like me, like almost anyone else in America—picture a young, tough, lower-class male when the thought of crime first pops into your head. You (we) picture someone like the Typical Criminal described above. The crime itself is one in which the Typical Criminal sets out to attack or rob some specific person.

This last point is important. It indicates that we have a mental image not only of the Typical Criminal but also of the Typical Crime. If the Typical Criminal is a young, lower-class male, the Typical Crime is *one-on-one harm*—where harm means either physical injury or loss of something valuable or both. If you have any doubts that this is the Typical Crime, look at any random sample of police or private eye shows on television. How often do you see the cops on "NYPD Blue" investigate consumer fraud or failure to remove occupational hazards? And when Jessica Fletcher (on "Murder, She Wrote") tracks down well-heeled criminals, it is almost always for garden-variety violent crimes like murder. A study of TV crime shows by The Media Institute in Washington, D.C., indicates that, while the fictional criminals portrayed on television are on the average both older and wealthier than the real criminals who figure in the FBI *Uniform Crime Reports,* "TV crimes are almost 12 times as likely to be violent as crimes committed in the real world."[24] TV crime shows broadcast the double-edged message that the one-on-one crimes of the poor are the typical crimes of all and thus not uniquely caused by the pressures of poverty; *and* that the criminal justice system pursues rich and poor alike—thus, when the criminal justice system happens mainly to pounce on the poor in real life, it is not out of any class bias.[25]

In addition to the steady diet of fictionalized TV violence and crime, there has been an increase in the graphic display of crime on many TV news programs. Crimes reported on TV news are also far more frequently violent than real crimes are.[26] An article in *The Washingtonian* says that the word around two prominent local TV news programs is, "If it bleeds, it leads."[27] What's more, a new breed of nonfictional "tabloid" TV show has appeared in which viewers are shown films of actual violent crimes—blood, screams, and all—or reenactments of actual violent crimes, sometimes using the actual victims playing themselves! Among these are "COPS," "Real Stories of the Highway Patrol," "America's Most Wanted," and "Unsolved Mysteries." Here, too, the focus is on crimes of one-on-one violence, rather than, say, corporate pollution. The *Wall Street Journal,* reporting on the phenomenon of tabloid TV, informs us that "Television has gone tabloid. The seamy underside of life is being bared in a new rash of true-crime series and contrived-confrontation talk shows."[28] Is there any surprise that a survey by *McCall's* indicates that its readers have grown more afraid of crime in the mid-1980s—even though victimization studies show a stable level of crime for most of this period?[29]

It is important to identify this model of the Typical Crime because it functions like a set of blinders. It keeps us from calling a mine disaster a mass murder even if ten men are killed, even if someone is responsible for the unsafe conditions in which they worked and died. I contend that this particular piece of mental furniture so blocks our view that it keeps us from using the criminal justice system to protect ourselves from the greatest threats to our persons and possessions.

What keeps a mine disaster from being a mass murder in our eyes is that it is not a one-on-one harm. What is important in one-on-one harm is not the numbers but the *desire of someone (or ones) to harm someone (or ones) else.* An attack by a gang on one or more persons or an attack by one individual on several fits the model of one-on-one harm; that is, for each person harmed there is at least one individual who wanted to harm that person. Once he selects his victim, the rapist, the mugger, the murderer all want this person they have selected to suffer. A mine executive, on the other hand, does not want his employees to be harmed. He would truly prefer that there be no accident, no injured or dead miners. What he does want is something legitimate. It is what he has been hired to get: maximum profits at minimum costs. If he cuts corners to save a buck, he is just doing his job. If ten men die because he cut corners on safety, we may think him crude or callous but not a murderer. He is, at most, responsible for an *indirect harm,* not a one-on-one harm. For this, he may even be criminally indictable for violating safety regulations—but not for murder. The ten men are dead as an unwanted consequence of his (perhaps overzealous or undercautious) pursuit of a legitimate goal. So, unlike the Typical Criminal, he has not committed the Typical Crime—or so we generally believe. As a result, ten men are dead who might be alive now if cutting corners of the kind that leads to loss of life, whether suffering is specifically aimed at or not, were treated as murder.

This is my point. Because we accept the belief—encouraged by our politicians' statements about crime and by the media's portrayal of crime—that the model for crime is one person specifically trying to harm another, we accept a legal system that leaves us unprotected against much greater dangers to our lives and well-being than those threatened by the Typical Criminal. Before developing this point further, let us anticipate and deal with some likely objections. Defenders of the present legal order are likely to respond to my argument at this point with irritation. Because this will surely turn to outrage in a few pages, let's talk to them now while the possibility of rational communication still exists.

The Defenders of the Present Legal Order (I'll call them "the Defenders" for short) are neither foolish nor evil people. They are not racists, nor are they oblivious to the need for reform in the criminal justice system to make it more evenhanded, and for reform in the larger society to make equal opportunity a reality for all Americans. In general, their view is that—given our limited resources, particularly the resource of human altruism—the political and legal institutions we have are the best that can be. What is necessary is to make them work better and to weed out those who are intent on making them work shoddily. Their response to my argument at this point is that the criminal justice system *should* occupy itself primarily with one-on-one harm. Harms of the sort exemplified in the "mine tragedy" are really *not* murders and are better dealt with through stricter government enforcement of safety regulations. The Defenders admit that this enforcement has been rather lax and recommend that it be improved. Basically, though, they think this division of labor is right because it fits our ordinary moral sensibilities.

The Defenders maintain that, according to our common moral notions, someone who tries to do another harm and does is really more evil than someone who jeopardizes others while pursuing legitimate goals but doesn't aim to harm anyone. The one who jeopardizes others in this way at least doesn't try to hurt them. He or she doesn't have the goal of hurting someone in the way that a mugger or a rapist does. Moreover, being directly and purposely harmed by another person, the Defenders believe, is terrifying in a way that being harmed indirectly and impersonally, say, by a safety hazard, is not—even if the resultant injury is the same in both cases. And we should be tolerant of the one responsible for lax safety measures because he or she is pursuing a legitimate goal, that is, his or her dangerous action occurs as part of a productive activity, something that ultimately adds to social wealth and thus benefits everyone—whereas doers of direct harm benefit no one but themselves. Thus, the latter are rightfully in the province of the criminal justice system with its drastic weapons, and the former appropriately dealt with by the milder forms of regulation.

Further, the Defenders insist, the crimes identified as such by the criminal justice system are imposed on their victims totally against their will, whereas the victims of occupational hazards chose to accept their risky jobs and thus have in some degree consented to subject themselves to the dangers. Where dangers are consented to, the appropriate response is not blame but requiring improved safety, and this is most efficiently done by regulation rather than with the guilt-seeking methods of criminal justice.

In sum, the Defenders make four objections: 1. That someone who purposely tries to harm another is really more evil than someone who harms another without aiming to, even if the degree of harm is the same. 2. That being harmed directly by another person is more terrifying than being harmed indirectly and impersonally, as by a safety hazard, even if the degree of harm is the same. 3. That someone who harms another in the course of an illegitimate and purely self-interested action is more evil than someone who harms another as a consequence of a legitimate and socially productive endeavor. 4. That the harms of typical crimes are imposed on their victims against their wills, while harms like those due to occupational hazards are consented to by workers when they agree to a job. This too is thought to make the harms of typical crimes evil in a way that occupational harms are not.

All four of these objections are said to reflect our common moral beliefs, which are a fair standard for a legal system to match. Together they are said to show that the typical criminal does something worse than the one responsible for an occupational hazard, and thus deserves the special treatment provided by the criminal justice system. Some or all of these objections may have already occurred to the reader. Thus, it is important to respond to the Defenders. For the sake of clarity I shall number the paragraphs in which I start to take up each objection in turn.

1. The Defenders' first objection confuses intention with specific aim or purpose, and it is intention that brings us properly within the reach of the criminal law. It is true that a mugger aims to harm his victim in the way that a corporate executive who maintains an unsafe workplace does not. But the corporate executive acts intentionally nonetheless, and that's what makes his actions appropriately subject to criminal law. What we intend is not just what we try to make happen but what we know is likely to happen as the normal causal product of our chosen actions. As criminal law theorist Hyman Gross points out: "What really matters here is whether conduct of a particular degree of dangerousness was done intentionally."[30] Whether we want or aim for that conduct to harm someone is a different matter, which is relevant to the actor's *degree* of culpability (not to whether he or she is culpable at all). Gross describes the degrees of culpability for intentional action by means of an example in which a sailor dies when his ship is fumigated while he is asleep in the hold. Fumigation is a dangerous activity; it involves spraying the ship with poison that is normally fatal to humans. If the fumigation was done in order to kill the sailor, we can say that his death is caused *purposely*. But suppose that the fumigation was done knowing that a sailor was in the hold but not in order to kill him. Then, according to Gross, we say that his death was brought about *knowingly*. If the fumigation was done without

knowledge that someone was in the hold but without making sure that no one was, then the sailor's death is brought about *recklessly*. Finally, if the fumigation was done without knowledge that the sailor was there and some, but inadequate, precautions were taken to make sure no one was there, then the sailor's death is brought about *negligently*.

How does this apply to the executive who imposes dangerous conditions on his workers, conditions that, as in the mine explosion, do finally lead to death? The first thing to note is that, the difference between purposely, knowingly, recklessly, or negligently causing death is a difference within the range of intentional (and thus to some extent culpable) action. What is done recklessly or negligently is still done intentionally. Second, culpability decreases as we go from purposely to knowingly to recklessly to negligently killing because, according to Gross, the outcome is increasingly due to chance and not to the actor; that is, the one who kills on purpose leaves less room to chance that the killing will occur than the one who kills knowingly (the one who kills on purpose will take precautions against the failure of his killing, while the one who kills knowingly won't), and likewise the one who kills recklessly leaves wholly to chance whether there is a victim at all. And the one who kills negligently reduces this chance, but insufficiently.

Now, we may say that the kernel of truth in the Defenders' objection is that the common street mugger harms on purpose, while the executive harms only knowingly or recklessly or negligently. This does not justify refusing to treat the executive killer as a criminal, however, because we have criminal laws against reckless or even negligent harming—thus the kid-glove treatment meted out to those responsible for occupational hazards and the like is no simple reflection of our ordinary moral sensibilities, as the Defenders claim. Moreover, don't be confused into thinking that, because all workplaces have some safety measures, all workplace deaths are at most due to negligence. To the extent that precautions are not taken against particular dangers (like leaking methane), deaths due to those dangers are—by Gross's standard—caused recklessly or even knowingly (because the executive knows that potential victims are in harm's way from the danger he fails to reduce). And Nancy Frank concludes from a review of state homicide statutes that "a large number of states recognize unintended deaths caused by extreme recklessness as murder."[31]

But there is more to be said. Remember that Gross attributes the difference in degrees of culpability to the greater role left to chance as we descend from purposely to recklessly to negligently harming. In this light it is important to note that the executive (say, the mine owner) imposes danger on a larger number of individuals than the typical criminal typically does. So while the typical criminal purposely harms a particular individual, the executive knowingly subjects a large number of workers to a risk of harm. But as the risk gets greater and the number of workers gets greater, it becomes increasingly likely that one or more workers will get harmed. This means that the gap between the executive and the typical criminal shrinks. By not harming workers purposely, the executive leaves more to chance; but by subjecting large numbers to risk, he leaves it less and less to chance that someone will be harmed, and thus he roles back his advantage over the typical criminal. If you keep your workers in mines or factories with high levels of toxic gases or chemicals, you start to approach 100 percent likelihood that at least one of them will be harmed as a result. And that means that the culpability of the executive approaches that of the typical criminal.

A different way to make the Defenders' argument is to say that the executive has failed to protect his workers, while the typical criminal has positively acted to harm his victim. In general, we think it is worse to harm someone than to fail to prevent their being harmed (perhaps you should feed starving people on the other side of town or of the world, but few people will think you are a murderer if you don't and the starving die). But at least in some cases we are responsible for the harm that results from our failure to act (for example, parents are responsible for failing to provide for their children). Some philosophers go further and hold that we are responsible for all the foreseeable effects of what we do, including the foreseeable effects of failing to act certain ways.[32] While this view supports the position for which I am arguing here, I think it goes too far. It entails that we are murderers every time we are doing anything other than saving lives, which surely goes way beyond our ordinary moral beliefs. My view is that in most cases, we are responsible only for the foreseeable effects likely to be caused by our action—and not responsible for those caused by our inaction. We are, however, responsible for the effects of our inaction in at least one special type of case: where we have a special obligation to aid people. This covers the parent who causes his child's death by failing to feed him, the doctor who causes her patient's death by failing to care for her, and the coal mine owner who causes his employees' death by failing to take legally mandated safety precautions. It may also cover the society that fails to rectify harm-producing injustices in its midst. This is another way in which the moral difference between the safety-cutting executive and the typical criminal shrinks away.

Further on this first objection, I think the Defenders overestimate the importance of specifically trying to do evil in our moral estimate of people. The mugger who aims to hurt someone is no doubt an ugly character. But so too is the well-heeled executive who calmly and callously chooses to put others at risk. Compare the mine executive who cuts corners with the typical murderer. Most murders, we know, are committed in the heat of some passion like rage or jealousy. Two lovers or neighbors or relatives find themselves in a heated argument. One (often it is a matter of chance *which* one) picks up a weapon and strikes the other a fatal blow. Such a person is clearly a murderer and rightly subject to punishment by the criminal justice system. Is this person more evil than the executive who, knowing the risks, calmly chooses not to pay for safety equipment?

The one who kills in a heated argument kills from passion. What she does she probably would not do in a cooler moment. She is likely to feel "she was not herself." The one she killed was someone she knew, a specific person who at the time seemed to her to be the embodiment of all that frustrates her, someone whose very existence makes life unbearable. I do not mean to suggest that this is true of all killers, although there is reason to believe it is true of many. Nor do I mean to suggest that such a state of mind justifies murder. What it does do, however, is suggest that the killer's action, arising out of anger at a particular individual, does not show general disdain for the lives of her fellows. Here is where she is different from our mine executive. Our mine executive wanted to harm no one in particular, but he *knew his acts were likely to harm someone*—and once someone is harmed, the victim is someone in particular. Nor can our executive claim that "he was not himself." His act is done not out of passion but out of cool reckoning. Precisely here his evil shows. In his willingness to jeopardize the lives of unspecified others who pose him no real or imaginary threat in order to make a few dollars, he shows his general disdain for all his fellow human beings. Can it really be said that he is less evil than one who kills from passion? The Model Penal Code includes within the definition of murder any death caused by "extreme indifference to human life."[33] Is our executive not a murderer by this definition?

It's worth noting that in answering the Defenders here, I have portrayed harms from occupational hazards in their best light. They are not, however, all just matters of well-intentioned but excessive risk taking. Consider, for example, the Manville (formerly Johns Manville) asbestos case. It is predicted that 240,000 Americans working now or who previously worked with asbestos will die from asbestos-related cancer in the next 30 years. But documents made public during congressional hearings in 1979 show "that Manville and other companies within the asbestos industry covered up and failed to warn millions of Americans of the dangers associated with the fireproof, indestructible insulating fiber."[34] An article in the *American Journal of Public Health* attributes thousands of deaths to the cover-up.[35] Later in this chapter I document similar intentional cover-ups, such as the falsification of reports on coal dust levels in mines, which leads to crippling and often fatal black lung disease. Surely someone who knowingly subjects others to risks and tries to hide those risks from them is culpable in a high degree.

2. I think the Defenders are right in believing that direct personal assault is terrifying in a way that indirect impersonal harm is not. This difference is no stranger to the criminal justice system. Prosecutors, judges, and juries constantly have to consider how terrifying an attack is in determining what to charge and what to convict offenders for. This is why we allow gradations in charges of homicide or assault and allow particularly grave sentences for particularly grave attacks. In short, the difference the Defenders are pointing to here might justify treating a one-on-one murder as graver than murder due to lax safety measures, but it doesn't justify treating one as a grave crime and the other as a mere regulatory (or very minor criminal) matter. After all, although it is worse to be injured with terror than without, it is still the injury that constitutes the worst part of violent crime. Given the choice, seriously injured victims of crime would surely rather have been terrorized and not injured than injured and not terrorized. If that is so, then the worst part of violent crime is still shared by the indirect harms that the Defenders would relegate to regulation.

Furthermore, if direct personal assault is more frightening than impersonal harm, impersonal harm often takes its toll on trust. Impersonal harms from occupational hazards, dangerous consumer products, pollution, and lax government enforcement of rules against these things weaken people's trust in their employers, in their producers and merchants, and in their government. And this is likely to spread to undermine trust generally in one's fellow citizens. Both a sense of personal security and a sense of trust in one's fellows are essential aspects of civility. Where direct harm undermines the first, indirect harm undermines the second.

3. There is also something to the Defenders' claim that indirect harms, such as ones that result from lax safety measures, are part of legitimate productive activities, whereas one-on-one crimes are not. No doubt we must tolerate the risks that are necessary ingredients of productive activity (unless those risks are so great as to outweigh the gains of the productive activity). But this doesn't imply we shouldn't identify the risks, or levels of danger, that are unnecessary and excessive, and use the law to protect innocent people from them. And if those risks are great enough, the fact that they may further a productive or otherwise legitimate activity is no reason against making them crimes—if that's what's necessary to protect workers. A person can commit a crime to further an otherwise legitimate endeavor and it is still a crime. If, say, I threaten to assault my workers if they don't work faster, this doesn't make my act any less criminal. And, in general, if I do something that by itself ought to be a crime, the fact that I do it as a means to a legitimate aim doesn't change the fact that it ought to be a crime. If acts that intentionally endanger others ought to be crimes, then

the fact that the acts are means to legitimate aims doesn't change the fact that they ought to be crimes.

4. Cases like the Manville asbestos case show that the Defenders overestimate the reality of the "free consent" with which workers take on the risks of their jobs. You can consent to a risk only if you know about it, and often the risks are concealed. Moreover, the Defenders overestimate generally the degree to which workers freely consent to the conditions of their jobs. Although no one is forced at gunpoint to accept a particular job, virtually everyone is forced by the requirements of necessity to take some job. At best, workers can choose among the dangers present at various work sites, but they cannot choose to face no danger at all. Moreover, workers can choose jobs only where there are openings, which means they cannot simply pick their place of employment at will. For nonwhites and women, the choices are even more narrowed by discriminatory hiring, long-standing occupational segregation (funneling women into secretarial, nursing, or teaching jobs and blacks into janitorial and other menial occupations), not to mention subtle and not so subtle practices that keep nonwhites and women from advancing within their occupations. Consequently, for all intents and purposes, most workers *must* face the dangers of the jobs that are available to them. What's more, remember that while here we have been focusing on harms due to occupational hazards, much of the indirect harm that I shall document in what follows is done not to workers but to consumers (of food with dangerous chemicals) and citizens (breathing dangerous concentrations of pollutants).

Finally, recall that the basis of all the Defenders' objections is that the idea that one-on-one harms are more evil than indirect harms is part of our common moral beliefs, and that this makes it appropriate to treat the former with the criminal justice system and the latter with milder regulatory measures. Here I think the Defenders err by overlooking the role of legal institutions in shaping our ordinary moral beliefs. Many who defend the criminal justice system do so precisely because of its function in educating the public about the difference between right and wrong. The great historian of English law, Sir James Fitzjames Stephens, held that a

> *great part of the general detestation of crime which happily prevails amongst the decent part of the community in all civilized countries arises from the fact that the commission of offences is associated in all such communities with the solemn and deliberate infliction of punishment wherever crime is proved.*[36]

One cannot simply appeal to ordinary moral beliefs to defend the criminal law because the criminal law has already had a hand in shaping ordinary moral beliefs. At least one observer has argued that making narcotics use a crime in the beginning of this century *caused* a change in the public's ordinary moral notions about drug addiction, which prior to that time had been viewed as a medical problem.[37] It is probably safe to say that in our own time, civil rights legislation has sharpened the public's moral condemnation of racial discrimination. Hence, we might speculate that if the criminal justice system began to prosecute—and if the media began to portray—those who inflict *indirect harm* as serious criminals, our ordinary moral notions would change on this point as well.

I think this disposes of the Defenders for the time being. We are left with the conclusion that there is no moral basis for treating *one-on-one harm* as criminal and *indirect harm* as merely a regulatory affair. What matters, then, is whether the purpose of the criminal justice system will be served by including, in the category of serious crime, actions that are predictably likely to produce serious harm, yet that are done in pursuit of otherwise legitimate goals and without the aim of harming anyone.

What is the purpose of the criminal justice system? No esoteric answer is required. Norval Morris and Gordon Hawkins write that "the prime function of the criminal law is to protect our persons and our property."[38] *The Challenge of Crime in a Free Society,* the report of the President's Commission on Law Enforcement and Administration of Justice, tells us that "any criminal justice system is an apparatus society uses to enforce the standards of conduct necessary to protect individuals and the community."[39] Whatever else we think a criminal justice system should accomplish, I doubt if anyone would deny that its central purpose is to protect us against the most serious threats to our well-being. This purpose is seriously undermined by taking one-on-one harm as the model of crime. Excluding harm caused without the aim of harming someone in particular prevents the criminal justice system from protecting our persons and our property from dangers at least as great as those posed by one-on-one harm. This is so because, as I will show, there are a large number of actions that are not labeled *criminal* but that lead to loss of life, limb, and possessions on a scale comparable to those actions that are represented in the FBI Crime Index—and a crime by any other name still causes misery and suffering.

* * *

In the remainder of this chapter, I identify some acts that are *crimes by any other name*—acts that cause harm and suffering comparable to that caused by acts called crimes. My purpose is to confirm the first hypothesis: that the definitions of crime in the criminal law do not reflect the only or the most dangerous behaviors in our society. To do this, we will need some measure of the harm and suffering caused by crimes with which we can compare the harm and suffering caused by noncrimes. Our measure need not be too refined because my point can be made if I can show that there are some acts that we do not treat as crime but that cause harm *roughly comparable* to that caused by acts that we do treat as crimes. For that, it is not necessary to compare the harm caused by noncriminal acts with the harm caused by *all* crimes. I need only show that the harm produced by some type of noncriminal act is comparable to the harm produced by *any* serious crime. Because the harms caused by noncriminal acts fall into the categories of death, bodily injury (including the disabling effects of disease), and property loss, I will compare the harms done by noncriminal acts with the injuries caused by the crimes of murder, aggravated assault, and theft.

According to the FBI's *Uniform Crime Reports,* in 1991, there were 24,703 murders and nonnegligent manslaughters, and 1,092,739 aggravated assaults. In 1992, there were 23,760 murders and nonnegligent manslaughters, and 1,126,970 aggravated assaults. "Murder and nonnegligent manslaughter" includes all "willful (nonnegligent) killing of one human being by another." "Aggravated assault" is defined as an "attack by one person on another for the purpose of inflicting severe or aggravated bodily injury."[40] Thus, as a measure of the physical harm done by crime in the beginning of the 1990s, we can say that reported crimes lead to roughly 24,000 deaths and 1,000,000 instances of serious bodily injury short of death a year. As a measure of monetary loss due to property crime, we can use $15.1 billion—the total estimated dollar losses due to property crime in 1992 according to the UCR.[41] Whatever the shortcomings of these reported crime statistics, they are the statistics upon which public policy has traditionally been based. Thus, I will consider any actions that lead to loss of life, physical harm, and property loss comparable to the figures in the UCR as actions that pose grave dangers to the community comparable to the threats posed by crimes. They are surely precisely the kind of harmful actions from which a criminal justice system whose purpose is to protect our persons and property ought to protect us. *They are crimes by other names.*

Work May Be Dangerous to Your Health

Since the publication of *The President's Report on Occupational Safety and Health*[42] in 1972, numerous studies have documented the astounding incidence of disease, injury, and death due to hazards in the workplace *and* the fact that much or most of this carnage is the consequence of the refusal of management to pay for safety measures and of government to enforce safety standards—and sometimes of willful defiance of existing law.[43]

In that 1972 report, the government estimated the number of job-related illnesses at 390,000 per year and the number of annual deaths from industrial disease at 100,000. For 1990, the Bureau of Labor Statistics (BLS) of the U.S. Department of Labor estimates 330,800 job-related illnesses and 2,900 work-related deaths.[44] Note that the latter figure applies only to private-sector work environments with 11 or more employees. And it is not limited to death from occupational disease but includes all work-related deaths, including those resulting from accidents on the job.

Before we celebrate what appears to be a dramatic drop in work-related mortality, we should point out that the BLS itself "believes that the annual survey significantly understates the number of work-related fatalities."[45] And there is wide agreement that occupational diseases are seriously underreported. *The Report of the President to the Congress on Occupational Safety and Health* for 1980 stated that

> *recording and reporting of illnesses continue to present measurement problems, since employers (and doctors) are often unable to recognize some illnesses as work-related. The annual survey includes data only on the visible illnesses of workers. To the extent that occupational illnesses are unrecognized and, therefore, not recorded or reported, the illness survey estimates may understate their occurrence.*[46]

Part of the difficulty is that there may be a substantial delay between contracting a fatal disease on the job and the appearance of symptoms, and from these to death. Moreover, the Occupational Safety and Health Administration (OSHA) relies on employer reporting for its figures, and there are many incentives for underreporting. Writing in the journal *Occupational Hazards,* Robert Reid states that

> *OSHA concedes that many factors—including insurance rates and supervisor evaluations based on safety performance—are incentives to underreport. And the agency acknowledges that recordkeeping violations have increased more than 27 percent since 1984, with most of the violations recorded for not maintaining the injuries and illnesses log examined by compliance officers and used for BLS' annual survey.*[47]

A study by the National Institute for Occupational Safety and Health (NIOSH) concludes that "there may be several thousand more workplace deaths each year than employers report."[48]

For these reasons, plus the fact that BLS's figures on work-related deaths are only for private workplaces with 11 or more employees, we must supplement the BLS figures with other estimates. In 1982, then U.S. Secretary of Health and Human Services Richard Schweiker stated that "current estimates for overall workplace-associated cancer mortality vary within a range of five to fifteen percent."[49] With annual cancer deaths currently running at about 500,000, that translates into about 25,000 to 75,000 job-related cancer deaths per year. More recently, Edward Sondik, of the National Cancer Institute, states that the best estimate of cancer deaths attributable to occupational exposure is 4 percent of the total, with the range of acceptable estimates running between 2 and 8 percent. That translates into a best estimate of 20,000 job-related cancer deaths a year, within a range of acceptable estimates between 10,000 and 40,000.[50]

Death from cancer is only part of the picture of death-dealing occupational disease. In testimony before the Senate Committee on Labor and Human Resources, Dr. Philip Landrigan, director of the Division of Environmental and Occupational Medicine at the Mount Sinai School of Medicine in New York City, stated that

> *Recent data indicate that occupationally related exposures are responsible each year in New York State for 5,000 to 7,000 deaths and for 35,000 new cases of illness (not including work-related injuries). These deaths due to occupational disease include 3,700 deaths from cancer. . . .*
>
> *Crude national estimates of the burden of occupational disease in the United States may be developed by multiplying the New York State data by a factor of 10. New York State contains slightly less than 10 percent of the nation's workforce, and it includes a broad mix of employment in the manufacturing, service and agricultural sectors. Thus, it may be calculated that occupational disease is responsible each year in the United States for 50,000 to 70,000 deaths, and for approximately 350,000 new cases of illness.*[51]

It is some confirmation of Dr. Landrigan's estimates that they imply work-related cancer deaths of approximately 37,000 a year—a figure that is toward the low end of the range in Secretary Schweiker's statement on this issue, and toward the top end of the range of acceptable estimates according to Sondik. Landrigan's estimates of deaths from occupational disease are also corroborated by a study reported by the National Safe Workplace Institute, which estimates that the number of occupational disease deaths is between 47,377 and 95,479. Mark Cullen, director of the occupational medicine program at the Yale University School of Medicine, praised this study as "a very balanced, very comprehensive overview of occupational health." The study's figures are low compared with a 1985 report of the Office of Technology Assessment (OTA) that estimated 100,000 Americans die annually from work-related illness.[52] Even if we discount OSHA's 1972 estimate of 100,000 deaths a year due to occupational disease or OTA's 1985 estimate of the same number, we would surely be erring in the other direction to accept the BLS figure of 2,900. We can hardly be overestimating the actual toll if we take the conservative route and set it at 25,000 deaths a year resulting from occupational disease.

The BLS estimate of 330,000 job-related illnesses for 1990 roughly matches Dr. Landrigan's estimates. For 1991, BLS estimates 368,000 job-related illnesses. These illnesses are of varying severity (the majority are so-called "repeated trauma" diseases, such as carpal tunnel syndrome). Because I want to compare these occupational harms with those resulting from aggravated assault, I shall stay on the conservative side here too, as with deaths from occupational diseases, and say that there are annually in the United States approximately 150,000 job-related serious illnesses. Taken together with 25,000 deaths from occupational diseases, how does this compare with the threat posed by crime?

Before jumping to any conclusions, note that the risk of occupational disease and death falls only on members of the labor force, whereas the risk of crime falls on the whole population, from infants to the elderly. Because the labor force is about half the total population (124,810,000 in 1990, out of a total population of 249,900,000), to get a true picture of the *relative* threat posed by occupational diseases compared with that posed by crimes, we should *halve* the crime statistics when comparing them with the figures for industrial disease and death. Using the crime figures for the first years of the 1990s (cited earlier in this chapter), we note that the *comparable* figures would be

	Occupational Disease	***Crime (halved)***
Death	25,000	12,000
Other physical harm	150,000	500,000

If it is argued that this paints an inaccurate picture because so many crimes go unreported, my answer is this: First of all, homicides are by far the most completely reported of crimes. For obvious reasons, the general underreporting of crimes is not equal among crimes. It is easier to avoid reporting a rape or a mugging than a corpse. Second, although not the best, aggravated assaults are among the better-reported crimes. From victimization studies, it is estimated that 59 percent of aggravated assaults were reported to the police in 1980, compared with 29 percent of thefts.[53] On the other hand, we should expect more—not less—underreporting of industrial than criminal victims because diseases and deaths are likely to cost firms money in the form of workdays lost and insurance premiums raised, occupational diseases are frequently first seen by company physicians who have every reason to diagnose complaints as either malingering or not job-related, and many occupationally caused diseases do not show symptoms or lead to death until after the employee has left the job.

> *A survey conducted last year by the University of Washington reported that one in four Americans currently suffers an occupational disease. The report also disclosed that only one of the 10 workers with an occupational disease had been included in either OSHA statistics or in the state's workmen's compensation records.*[54]

In sum, both occupational and criminal harms are underreported, though there is reason to believe that the underreporting is worse with occupational than criminal harms. Finally, note that I have been extremely conservative in estimating occupational deaths and other harms. However one may quibble with figures presented here, I think it is fair to say that, if anything, they understate the extent of occupational harm compared with criminal harm.

Note further that the estimates in the last chart are *only* for occupational *diseases* and deaths from those diseases. They do not include death and disability from work-related injuries. Here, too, the statistics are gruesome. The National Safety Council reported that in 1991, work-related accidents caused 9,600 deaths and 1.7 million disabling work injuries, at a total cost to the economy of $63.3 billion.[55] This brings the number of occupation-related deaths to 34,600 a year and other physical harms to 1,850,000. If, on the basis of these additional figures, we recalculated our chart comparing occupational harms from both disease and accident with criminal harms, it would look like this:

	Occupational Hazard	***Crime (halved)***
Death	34,600	12,000
Other physical harm	1,850,000	500,000

Can there be any doubt that workers are more likely to stay alive and healthy in the face of the danger from the underworld than in the workworld? If any doubt lingers, consider this: Lest we falter in the struggle against crime, the FBI includes in its annual *Uniform Crime Reports* a table of "crime clocks," which graphically illustrates the extent of the criminal menace. For 1992, the crime clock shows a murder occurring every 22 minutes. If a similar clock were constructed for occupational deaths—using the conservative estimate of 34,600 cited above and remembering that this clock ticks only for that half of the population that is in the labor force—this clock would show an occupational death about every 15 minutes! In other words, in the time it takes for three murders on the crime clock, four workers have died *just from trying to make a living.*

To say that some of these workers died from accidents due to their own carelessness is about as helpful as saying that some of those who died at the hands of murderers asked for it. It overlooks the fact that where workers are careless, it is not because they love to live dangerously. They have production quotas to meet, quotas that they themselves do not set. If quotas were set with an eye to keeping work at a safe pace rather than to keeping the production-to-wages ratio as high as possible, it might be more reasonable to expect workers to take the time to be careful. Beyond this, we should bear in mind that the vast majority of occupational deaths result from disease, not accident, and disease is generally a function of conditions outside a worker's control. Examples of such conditions are the level of coal dust in the air ("260,000 miners receive benefits for [black lung] disease, and perhaps as many as 4,000 retired miners die from the illness or its complications each year"; about 10,000 currently working miners "have X-ray evidence of the beginnings of the crippling and often fatal disease")[56] or textile dust (some 100,000 American cotton textile workers presently suffer breathing impairments caused by acute byssinosis, or brown lung, and another 35,000 former mill workers are totally disabled with chronic brown lung)[57] or asbestos fibers (it has been estimated that, under the lenient asbestos standard promulgated by OSHA in 1972, anywhere from 18,400 and 598,000 deaths from lung cancer would result from exposure to asbestos),[58] or coal tars ("workers who had been employed five or more years in the coke ovens died of lung cancer at a rate three and a half times that for all steelworkers"; coke oven workers develop cancer of the scrotum at a rate five times that of the general population).[59] Also, some 800,000 people suffer from occupationally related skin disease each year (according to a 1968 estimate by the U.S. surgeon general),[60] and "the number of American workers experiencing noise conditions that may damage their hearing is estimated [in a 1969 Public Health Service publication of the Department of Health, Education and Welfare] to be in excess of 6 million, and may even reach 16 million."[61]

To blame the workers for occupational disease and deaths is to ignore the history of governmental attempts to compel industrial firms to meet safety standards that would keep dangers (such as chemicals or fibers or dust particles in the air) that are outside the worker's control down to a safe level. This has been a continual struggle, with firms using everything from their own "independent" research institutes to more direct and often questionable forms of political pressure to influence government in the direction of loose standards and lax enforcement. So far, industry has been winning because OSHA has been given neither the personnel nor the mandate to fulfill its purpose. It is so understaffed that, in 1973, when 1,500 federal sky

marshals guarded the nation's airplanes from hijackers, only 500 OSHA inspectors toured the nation's workplaces. By 1980, OSHA employed 1,581 compliance safety and health officers, but this still enabled inspection of only roughly 2 percent of the 2.5 million establishments covered by OSHA. The *New York Times* reports that in 1987 the number of OSHA inspectors was down to 1,044. As might be expected, the agency performs fewer inspections than it did a dozen years ago.[62] Don Lofgren, a former OSHA inspector, writes that

> *because of understaffing, OSHA attorneys are sometimes forced to enter into penalty-slashing settlements just to keep a burgeoning backlog of cases at bay. Perhaps more influential, OSHA managers and attorneys know that appeal judges often discount penalties regardless of the formal procedures OSHA used in calculating the fine.*[63]

According to a report issued by the AFL-CIO in 1992, "The median penalty paid by an employer during the years 1972–1990 following an incident resulting in death or serious injury of a worker was just $480."[64] The same report claims that the federal government spends $1.1 billion a year to protect fish and wildlife and only $300 million a year to protect workers from health and safety hazards on the job.

An editorial in the January 1983 issue of the *American Journal of Public Health,* titled "Can Reagan Be Indicted for Betraying Public Health?," answers the question in its title affirmatively by listing the Reagan administration's attempts to cut back government support for public health programs. On the issue of occupational safety and health, the editorial states:

> *The Occupational Safety and Health Administration (OSHA) has delayed the cotton and lead [safe exposure level] standards. It proposes to weaken the generic carcinogen policy, the labeling standard, the access to medical and exposure records standard. Mine fatalities are rising again, but the Mine Safety and Health Administration and OSHA enforcement have been cut back. Research on occupational safety and health has been slashed more than any other research program in the Department of Health and Human Services. The National Institute for Occupational Safety and Health funding in real dollars is lower in 1983 than at any time in the 12-year history of the Institute. Reporting and data requirements have been devastated.*[65]

The editorial ends by asking rhetorically, "How can anyone believe that the Reagan Administration wishes to prevent disease or promote health or preserve public health in America?"

And so it goes on.

Is a person who kills another in a bar brawl a greater threat to society than a business executive who refuses to cut into his profits to make his plant a safe place to work? By any measure of death and suffering the latter is by far a greater danger than the former. Because he wishes his workers no harm, because he is only indirectly responsible for death and disability while pursuing legitimate economic goals, his acts are not called "crimes." Once we free our imagination from the blinders of the one-on-one model of crime, can there be any doubt that the criminal justice system does *not* protect us from the gravest threats to life and limb? It seeks to protect us when danger comes from a young, lower-class male in the inner city. When a threat comes from an upper-class business executive in an office, the criminal justice system looks the other way. This is in the face of growing evidence that for every three American citizens murdered by thugs, at least four American workers are killed by the recklessness of their bosses and the indifference of their government.

Health Care May Be Dangerous to Your Health

More than 25 years ago, when the annual number of willful homicides in the nation was about 10,000, the President's Commission on Law Enforcement and Administration of Justice reported that

> *A recent study of emergency medical care found the quality, numbers, and distribution of ambulances and other emergency services severely deficient, and estimated that as many as* 20,000 Americans die unnecessarily each year *as a result of improper emergency care. The means necessary for correcting this situation are very clear and would probably yield greater immediate return in reducing death than would expenditures for reducing the incidence of crimes of violence.*[66]

On July 15, 1975, Dr. Sidney Wolfe of Ralph Nader's Public Interest Health Research Group testified before the House Commerce Oversight and Investigations Subcommittee that there "were 3.2 million cases of unnecessary surgery performed each year in the United States." These unneeded operations, Wolfe added, "cost close to $5 billion a year and kill as many as 16,000 Americans."[67] Wolfe's estimates of unnecessary surgery were based on studies comparing the operations performed and surgery recommended by doctors who are paid for the operations they do with those performed and recommended by salaried doctors who receive no extra income from surgery.

The figure accepted by Dr. George A. Silver, professor of public health at the Yale University School of Medicine, is 15,000 deaths a year "attributable to unnecessary surgery."[68] Silver places the annual cost of excess surgery at $4.8 billion.[69] In an article on an experimental program by Blue Cross and Blue Shield aimed at curbing unnecessary surgery, *Newsweek* reports that

> *a Congressional committee earlier this year [1976] estimated that more than 2 million of the elective operations performed in 1974 were not only unnecessary—but also killed about 12,000 patients and cost nearly $4 billion.*[70]

Because the number of surgical operations performed in the United States rose from 16.7 million in 1975 to 22.4 million in 1991,[71] there is reason to believe that at least somewhere between (the congressional committee's estimate of) 12,000 and (and Dr. Wolfe's estimate of) 16,000 people a year still die from unnecessary surgery. In 1991, the FBI reported that 3,405 murders were committed by a "cutting or stabbing instrument."[72] Obviously, the FBI does not include the scalpel as a cutting or stabbing instrument. If they did, they would have had to report that between 15,405 and 19,405 persons were killed by "cutting or stabbing" in 1991—depending on whether you take Congress's figure or Wolfe's. No matter how you slice it, the scalpel may be more dangerous than the switchblade.

And this is only a fraction of the problem: Data from the Harvard Medical Practice Study (based on over 30,000 records from New York State Hospitals in 1984 and extrapolated to the American population as a whole) indicate that more than 1.3 million Americans are injured by medical treatment, and "that each year 150,000 people die from, rather than in spite of, their medical treatment."[73] One of the authors of the study, Dr. Lucian Leape, a surgeon and lecturer at the Harvard School of Public Health, suggests that one-quarter of these deaths are due to negligence, and two-thirds are preventable.

While they are at it, the FBI should probably add the hypodermic needle and the prescription to their list of potential murder weapons. Silver points out that these are also death-dealing instruments.

> *Of the 6 billion doses of antibiotic medicines administered each year by injection or prescription, it is estimated that 22 percent are unnecessary. Of the doses given, 10,000 result in fatal or near-fatal reactions. Somewhere between 2,000 and 10,000 deaths probably would not have occurred if the drugs, meant for the patient's benefit, had not been given.*[74]

These estimates are supported by the Harvard Medical Practice Study. Its authors write that, of the 1.3 million medical injuries, 19 percent (247,000) were related to medications, and 14 percent of these (34,580) resulted in permanent injury or death.[75]

The danger continues. The Public Citizen Health Research Group reports in its *Health Letter* of October 1988 that

> *two major U.S. drug companies—Lilly and SmithKline—have pleaded guilty to criminal charges for having withheld information from the Food and Drug Administration (FDA) about deaths and life-threatening adverse drug reactions.*

The response of the Justice Department has been predictably merciful:

> *SmithKline, the actions of whose executives resulted in at least . . . 36 deaths, pleaded guilty to 14 criminal misdemeanor counts and was fined $34,000. Lilly*

and its executives, whose criminal negligence was responsible for deaths to at least 49 Americans . . . , were slapped on the wrist with a total of $45,000 in fines.[76]

In fact, if someone had the temerity to publish a *Uniform Crime Reports* that really portrayed the way Americans are murdered, the FBI's statistics on the *type of weapon used* in murder would have to be changed for 1991, from those shown in Table 3a to something like those shown in Table 3b.

The figures shown in Table 3b would give American citizens a much more honest picture of what threatens them—though remember how conservative the estimates of noncriminal harm are. Nonetheless, we are not likely to see such a chart broadcast by the criminal justice system, perhaps because it would also give American citizens a more honest picture of *who* threatens them.

We should not leave this topic without noting that, aside from the other losses it imposes, unnecessary surgery was estimated to have cost between $4 billion and $5 billion in 1974. The price of medical care has roughly quadrupled between 1974 and 1991. Thus, assuming that the same number of unneeded operations were performed in 1991, the cost of unnecessary surgery would be between $16 and $20 billion. To this we should add the unnecessary 22 percent of the 6 billion administered doses of medication. Even at the extremely conservative estimate of $3 a dose, this adds about $4 billion. In short, assuming that earlier trends have continued, there is reason to believe that unnecessary surgery and medication cost the public between $20 and $24 billion annually—far outstripping the $15.1 billion taken by thieves that concern the FBI.[77] This gives us yet another way in which we are robbed of more money by practices that are not treated as criminal than by practices that are.

Waging Chemical Warfare Against America

One in 4 Americans can expect to contract cancer during their lifetimes. The American Cancer Society estimated that 420,000 Americans would die of cancer in 1981. The National Cancer Institute's estimate for 1993 is 526,000 deaths from cancer. "A 1978 report issued by the President's Council on Environmental Quality (CEQ) unequivocally states that 'most researchers agree that 70 to 90 percent of cancers are caused by environmental influences and are hence theoretically preventable.' "[78] This means that a concerted national effort could result in saving 350,000 or more lives a year and reducing each individual's chances of getting cancer in his or her lifetime from 1 in 4 to 1 in 12 or fewer. If you think this would require a massive effort in terms of money and personnel, you are right. How much of an effort, though, would the nation make to stop a foreign invader who was

TABLE 3a

How Americans Are Murdered

Total	*Firearms*	*Knife or Other Cutting Instrument*	*Other Weapon: Club, Arson, Poison, Strangulation, etc.*	*Personal Weapon: Hands, Fists, etc.*
21,505[a]	14,265	3,405	2,642	1,193

[a] Note that this figure diverges somewhat from the figure of murders and nonnegligent manslaughters used elsewhere in the FBI *Uniform Crime Reports,* 1991, since the FBI has data on the weapons used in only 21,505 of the reported murders.

SOURCE: FBI *Uniform Crime Reports,* 1991: "Murder Victims: Weapons Used, 1987–1991."

TABLE 3b

How Americans Are (Really) Murdered

Total	*Occupational Hazard & Disease*	*Inadequate Emergency Medical Care*	*Knife or Other Cutting Instrument Including Scalpel*	*Firearms*	*Other Weapon: Club, Poison, Hypodermic Prescription Drug*	*Personal Weapon: Hands, Fists, etc.*
90,105	34,600	20,000	15,405[a]	14,265	4,642[a]	1,193

[a] These figures represent the relevant figures in Table 3a plus the most conservative figures for the relevant categories discussed in the text.

killing a thousand people a day and bent on capturing one-quarter of the present population?

In face of this "invasion" that is already under way, the U.S. government has allocated $1.9 billion to the National Cancer Institute (NCI) for fiscal year 1992, and NCI has allocated $219 million to the study of the physical and chemical (i.e., environmental) causes of cancer.[79] Compare this with the (at least) $45 billion spent to fight the Persian Gulf War.[80] The simple truth is that the government that strove so mightily to protect the borders of a small, undemocratic nation 7,000 miles away is doing next to nothing to protect us against the chemical war in our midst. This war is being waged against us on three fronts:

- Pollution
- Cigarette smoking
- Food additives

Not only are we losing on all three fronts, but it looks as if we do not even have the will to fight.

In April 1976, Dr. Umberto Saffioti, director of the National Cancer Institute's program of research into the chemical causes of cancer, resigned to protest three years' lack of support by NCI leaders.[81] In a letter stating his reasons for stepping down, he pointed out that there are "people who are now exposed to toxic agents and who are not protected because the necessary support was not provided in time."[82] Earlier the same year, three lawyers for the Environmental Protection Agency resigned "'because of the continued failure of the EPA to take effective action,' to regulate possible cancer-causing and other toxic chemicals in the air, food supply, drinking water and waterways." In a joint statement, the attorneys said:

> *It is clear from recent actions that the agency intends to refrain from vigorous enforcement of available toxic-substances controls and to retrench from the few legal precedents which it has set for evaluating the cancer hazards posed by the chemicals.*[83]

More recent observers believe that

> *EPA is locked into a "pathological cycle of regulatory failure." Others assert that, although making limited progress, the EPA is so crippled by institutional and policy deficiencies that major reform is imperative. Almost nobody believes EPA has been a substantial success.*[84]

The evidence linking *air pollution* and cancer, as well as other serious and often fatal diseases, has been rapidly accumulating in recent years. In 1993, the *Journal of the American Medical Association* reported on research that found "'robust' associations between premature mortality and air pollution levels."[85] They estimate that pollutants cause about 2 percent of all cancer deaths (at least 10,000 a year).[86]

During 1975, the epidemiological branch of the National Cancer Institute did a massive county-by-county analysis of cancer in the United States, mapping the "cancer hotspots" in the nation. The result was summed up by Dr. Glenn Paulson, assistant commissioner of science in the New Jersey Department of Environmental Protection: "If you know where the chemical industry is, you know where the cancer hotspots are."[87] What distinguishes these findings from the material on occupational hazards discussed above is that NCI investigators found higher death rates for *all* those living in the cancer hotspots—not just the workers in the offending plants.

For instance, NCI researchers found that Deer Lodge County in Montana ranked ninth out of 3,021 U.S. counties in lung cancer death rates. Deer Lodge County is the home of the Anaconda Company's giant copper-smelting works. The county's death rate was twice the rate expected for a rural county. A study by the Montana Department of Health and Environmental Sciences showed that the county's death rates for emphysema, asthma, and bronchitis are also well above the national average. Another study by two NCI researchers found that in *all* U.S. counties with smelters, the incidence of lung cancer is above the national average. "The researchers found high lung cancer death rates not only in men—who are often exposed to arsenic on their jobs inside smelters—but also among women, who generally never went inside smelters and were not previously believed to have been exposed to arsenic." Explanation: "neighborhood air pollution from industrial sources of inorganic arsenic."[88]

New Jersey, however, took the prize for having the highest cancer death rate in the nation. NCI investigators found that "19 of New Jersey's 21 counties rank in the top 10 percent of all counties in the nation for cancer death rates." Salem County, home of E. I. Du Pont de Nemours and Company's Chambers Works, which has been manufacturing chemicals since 1919, "has the highest bladder cancer death rate in the nation—8.7 deaths per 100,000 persons."[89]

In 1970, Lester B. Lave and Eugene P. Seskin reviewed more than 50 scientific studies of the relationship between air pollution and morbidity and mortality rates for lung cancer, nonrespiratory-tract cancers, cardiovascular disease, bronchitis, and other respiratory diseases. They found in every instance a *positive quantifiable relationship.* Using sophisticated statistical techniques, they concluded that a 10 percent reduction in air pollution could be expected to "decrease the total death rate by 0.5 percent."[90] At current death rates, that would save more than 10,000 lives.

A more recent study, by Douglas Dockery of the Harvard School of Public Health and Joel Schwartz of the Environmental Protection Agency, concluded that air pollution at 1988 levels was responsible for 60,000 deaths a year.[91] The Natural Resources Defense Council sued the EPA for its foot-dragging in implementation of the Clean Air Act, charging that "One hundred million people live in areas of unhealthy air."[92]

This chemical war is not limited to the air. The National Cancer Institute has identified as carcinogens or suspected carcinogens 23 of the chemicals commonly found in our drinking water.[93] Moreover, according to one observer, we are now facing a "new plague—toxic exposure." Of the extent of contamination, he says,

> *this country generates between 255 million and 275 million metric tons of hazardous waste annually, of which as much as 90 percent is improperly disposed of. . . . The Office of Technology Assessment estimates that there are some 600,000 contaminated sites in the country, of which 888 sites have been designated or proposed by the Environmental Protection Agency for priority cleanup under the Superfund program.*[94]

New Jersey, by the way, has 109 toxic waste sites bad enough to be on the Superfund cleanup list, which makes New Jersey the number one cleanup priority.[95] This may be another reason why New Jersey leads the nation in the cancer death rate. Studies have borne out the correlation between nearness to toxic wastes and above-average cancer mortality rates, as well as the generally negative correlation between residential affluence and nearness to toxic wastes.[96]

As with OSHA, the Reagan administration instituted a general slowing down of enforcement of EPA regulations. Reagan tried to cut EPA's enforcement budget by 45 percent in his first two years. By 1983, the EPA's regional offices were staffed at levels substantially lower than needed to enforce the law effectively, according to the agency's own studies. The president also signaled his tolerant attitude toward environmental hazards in his appointments to top-level posts at EPA of such people as Anne Burford, "who fiercely opposed any legislation regulating hazardous-waste disposal."[97] President Bush followed suit. The EPA's Research and Development staff, whose work provides the scientific basis for such regulations, was reduced by nearly 25 percent between 1981 and 1992.[98]

So the chemical war goes on. No one can deny that we know the enemy. No one can deny that we know the toll it is taking. Indeed, we can compute the number of deaths that result from every day that we refuse to mount an offensive. Yet we still refuse. Thus, for the time being the only advice we can offer someone who values his or her life is: If you must breathe our air, don't inhale.

The evidence linking *cigarette smoking* and cancer is overwhelming and need not be repeated here. The Centers for Disease Control estimates that cigarettes cause 87 percent of lung cancers—approximately 146,000 in 1992.[99] Tobacco continues to kill an estimated 400,000 Americans a year.[100] Cigarettes are widely estimated to cause 30 percent of all cancer deaths.[101]

Cigarettes are also blamed for other lung diseases such as emphysema, and they play a substantial role in heart disease.

This is enough to expose the hypocrisy of running a full-scale war against heroin (which produces no degenerative disease) while allowing cigarette sales and advertising to flourish. It also should be enough to underscore the point that once again there are threats to our lives much greater than criminal homicide. The legal order does not protect us against them. Indeed, not only does our government fail to protect us against this threat, it promotes it! The government provided a price-support program for the tobacco industry (making up the difference when market price fell below a target price) from 1933 to 1982, and in 1986 it wrote off $1.1 billion in loans it had made to tobacco farmers.[102] Moreover, the Reagan administration first supported and then, under intense lobbying pressure from the tobacco industry, withdrew its support for more and stronger warnings on cigarettes.[103] The president is not the only offender here. The U.S. Congress has turned down more than 1,000 proposed tobacco control bills since 1964, the year of the first Surgeon General Report on the dangers of tobacco. This may be related to the fact that Congress has accepted some $9.3 million in campaign contributions from the tobacco companies in the past three elections.[104]

If you think that tobacco harms only people who knowingly decide to take the risk, consider the following: Documents recently made public suggest that, by the mid-1950's, Liggett & Myers, the makers of Chesterfield and L&M cigarettes, had evidence that smoking is addictive and cancer-causing, and that they were virtually certain of it by 1963—but they never told the public and "actively misled" the U.S. surgeon general.[105] Moreover, the cigarette industry intentionally targets young people—who are not always capable of assessing the consequences of their choices—with its ads, and it is successful. Some 2.6 million youngsters between the ages of 12 and 18 are smokers.[106]

In addition, the Environmental Protection Agency has released data on the dangers of "secondhand" tobacco smoke (which nonsmokers breathe when smoking is going on around them). They report that each year secondhand smoke causes 3,000 lung-cancer deaths, contributes to 150,000 to 300,000 respiratory infections in babies, exacerbates the asthmatic symptoms of 400,000 to 1,000,000 children with the disease, and triggers 8,000 to 26,000 new cases of asthma in children who don't yet have the disease.[107] A 1993 issue of the *Journal of the American Medical Association* reports that tobacco contributes to 10 percent of infant deaths.[108]

The average American consumes *one pound* of chemical *food additives* per year.[109] Speaking on the floor of the U.S. Senate in 1972, Sen. Gaylord Nelson said:

People are finally waking up to the fact that the average American daily diet is substantially adulterated with unnecessary and poisonous chemicals and frequently filled with neutral, nonnutritious substances. We are being chemically medicated against our will and cheated of food value by low nutrition foods.[110]

A hard look at the chemicals we eat and at the federal agency empowered to protect us against eating dangerous chemicals reveals the recklessness with which we are being "medicated against our will."

Beatrice Hunter has taken such a hard look and reports her findings in a book aptly titled *The Mirage of Safety*, a catalogue of the possible dangers that lurk in the foods we eat. More than this, however, it is a description of how the Food and Drug Administration, through a combination of lax enforcement and uncritical acceptance of the results of the food industry's own "scientific" research, has allowed a situation to exist in which the American food-eating public is the real guinea pig for nearly *3,000* food additives. As a result, we are subjected to chemicals strongly suspected of producing cancer,[111] gallbladder ailments,[112] hyperkinesis in children,[113] and allergies[114]; to others that inhibit "mammalian cell growth" and "may adversely affect the rate of DNA, RNA, and protein synthesis;[115]" and to still others that are capable of crossing the placental barrier between mother and fetus and are suspected causes of birth defects and congenital diseases.[116]

The food additives are, of course, only part of the dangerous chemicals that we eat. During the 1980s, American farmers normally used about 800 million pounds of the active ingredients in pesticides per year.[117] In 1993, the *New York Times* reported that farmers now use 1 billion pounds of chemicals on crops each year.[118] Dr. Landrigan of the Mount Sinai School of Medicine, writing in a 1992 issue of the *American Journal of Public Health*, points to

recent data from the US Environmental Protection Agency (EPA) showing that infants and young children are permitted to have dietary exposures to potentially carcinogenic and neurotoxic pesticides that exceed published standards by a factor of more than 1000.[119]

Landrigan also estimates that between 3 and 4 million American preschool children have dangerously elevated blood lead levels, which could result in long-term neuropsychological impairment.

To call government and industry practices reckless is mild in view of the fact that, in spite of the growth in knowledge about the prevention and cure of cancer, "between 1950 and 1988, for U.S. Whites, age-adjusted incidence of cancer rose by 43.5 percent."[120] And according "to the March of Dimes Birth Defects Foundation, each year some 233,000 infants are born with birth defects."[121]

Based on the knowledge we have, there can be no doubt that air pollution, tobacco, and food additives amount to a chemical war that makes the crime wave look like a football scrimmage. Even with the most conservative estimates, it is clear that *the death toll in this war is far higher than the number of people killed by criminal homicide!*

Poverty Kills

We are long past the day when we could believe that poverty was caused by forces outside human control. Poverty is "caused" by lack of money, which means that once a society reaches a level of prosperity at which many enjoy a relatively high standard of living, then poverty can be eliminated or at least significantly reduced by transferring some of what the "haves" have to the "have-nots." In other words, regardless of what caused poverty in the past, what causes it to continue in the present is the refusal of those who have more to share with those who have less. Now you may think these remarks trite or naive. They are not offered as an argument for redistribution of income, although I think such a redistribution is long overdue. These remarks are presented to make a much simpler point, which is that poverty exists in a wealthy society like ours *because we allow it to exist.* Therefore, we[122] share responsibility for poverty and for its consequences.

The poverty for which we are responsible "remains," in the words of *Business Week,* "stubbornly high." Moreover, it has particularly nasty features. For example, it affects children and blacks at a rate higher than the national average. Whereas about one out of every seven Americans overall is poor, one out of every five children grows up in poverty, and nearly one out of every two black children is poor. One out of every ten white Americans is below the poverty line, but three out of every ten black Americans are.[123] A study published by the Urban Institute ranked the United States highest in child poverty among eight industrialized nations studied. The other nations were Switzerland, Sweden, Norway, West Germany, Canada, the United Kingdom, and Australia. Moreover, it is estimated that there are now at least 350,000 Americans whose poverty has rendered them homeless. The fastest-growing group among the homeless "consists of families headed by single mothers who can no longer afford to feed their children *and* pay the rent."[124]

We are prone to think that the consequences of poverty are fairly straightforward: less money means fewer things. So poor people have fewer clothes or cars or appliances, go to the theater less often, and live in smaller homes with less or cheaper furniture. This is true and sad, but perhaps not intolerable. However, in addition, one of the things poor people have less of is *good*

health. Less money means less nutritious food, less heat in winter, less fresh air in summer, less distance from other sick people or from unhealthy work

or dumping sites, less knowledge about illness or medicine, fewer doctor visits, fewer dental visits, less preventive health care, and (in the United States at least) less first-quality medical attention when all these other deprivations take their toll and a poor person finds himself or herself seriously ill. The result is that the poor suffer more from poor health and die earlier than do those who are well off. Poverty robs them of their days while they are alive and kills them before their time. A prosperous society that allows poverty in its midst is a party to murder.

A review of more than 30 historical and contemporary studies of the relationship of economic class and life expectancy affirms the obvious conclusion that "class influences one's chances of staying alive. Almost without exception, the evidence shows that classes differ on mortality rates."[125] An article in the November 10, 1993 issue of the *Journal of the American Medical Association* confirms the continued existence of this cost of poverty:

> *People who are poor have higher mortality rates for heart disease, diabetes mellitus, high blood pressure, lung cancer, neural tube defects, injuries, and low birth weight, as well as lower survival rates from breast cancer and heart attacks.*[126]

Interestingly, the poor have higher mortality rates even in countries like Canada and Great Britain, which guarantee access to medical care. The difference can be attributed in large measure to the other disabilities of poverty, such as lower education levels and less healthy work and residential environments. A study of lower respiratory illness in infants found its incidence directly correlated to socioeconomic status, with lower-socioeconomic–status infants showing greater incidence than middle-status infants and more than twice that of higher status infants. A large portion of the difference was attributed to the unhealthy environmental conditions in which poor infants grow up.[127]

Another indication of the correlation between low income and poor health is found in statistics on the number of days of reduced activity due to illness or injury suffered by members of different income groups. In 1989, persons from families earning less than $10,000 a year suffered an average of 26.5 such days, persons from families earning from $10,000 to $19,999 suffered 18.7 days, persons from families earning between $20,000 and $34,999 suffered 13.3 days, and persons from families earning $35,000 and over suffered 9.9 days of reduced activity.[128]

Here, too, things have gotten worse rather than better in recent years. The Census Bureau reports that the number of poor Americans grew for the third year in a row in 1992. It is now at 36.9 million.[129] According to a report in the *Wall Street Journal,* the number of Americans without health insurance grew during the Reagan-Bush years to an estimated 37 million, where it currently stands. The percentage of the poor covered by Medicaid has gone from 65 percent to less than 40 percent. Hardest hit have been poor women and their children, many of whom have been removed from Medicaid coverage because of income eligibility rules that have not kept up with inflation. "In 1986, the average state income cutoff for Medicaid was 48 percent of the federal poverty level, compared to 71 percent in 1975."[130]

A comparison of the health and mortality of blacks and whites in America yields further insight into the relationship of health and mortality to economic class. In 1990, about one out of every three blacks lived below the poverty line, as compared with one out of every ten whites. In 1989, black infant mortality (during the first year of life) was 17.7 per 1,000 live births compared with 8.2 for whites.[131] In short, black mothers lose their babies within the first year of life more than twice as often as white mothers. In the face of this disparity (which has been around for years and recently has even grown), the Reagan administration reduced funding for maternal and child health programs by more than 25 percent and attempted to reduce support for immunization programs for American children.[132] In 1987, only 48 percent of American one-year-olds had received the standard immunizations—every Western European nation was at least ten percentage points higher, with France and the United Kingdom in the eighties.[133]

Numerous studies have suggested that allocation of health services is subject as well to racial bias. A 1992 study of patients under Medicare said that older whites are 3.5 times more likely than older blacks to get bypass surgery for blocked arteries. Black kidney patients are 45 percent less likely than whites to get transplants according to a 1991 New York State Health Department study. There is evidence also of discrimination against Hispanic patients and women.[134] A study of surgery rates in Maryland hospitals by race and income of patient asserts, "The more discretionary the procedure, the lower is the relative incidence among Blacks."[135]

Cancer survival statistics show a similar picture. Between 1981 and 1987, 38.4 percent of blacks diagnosed with cancer were still alive five years after the diagnosis, compared with 52.5 percent of whites. This disparity has been noted since at least the early 1970s.[136] One important cause of this difference is that "white patients tended to have higher percentages of cancers diagnosed while localized,"[137] that is, earlier in their development. This means, at a minimum, that at least some of the difference turns out to be due to such things as better access to medical care, higher levels of education about the early warning signs of cancer, and so on, all of which strongly correlate with higher income levels. Data reported in the journal *Science* suggest that "blacks get more cancer not because they're black, but because they're poor."[138] A study of the stage at which women had breast cancer diagnosed found that white and black women living in areas characterized by lower average income and educational attainment were diagnosed later than those in areas marked by higher income and educational attainment. Within the same areas, black women were diagnosed later than whites, except in the areas of highest income and education, where the black disadvantage disappeared.[139] "And while black women show a lower incidence of breast cancer than white women, they nevertheless die from it more often."[140]

Life expectancy figures paint the most tragic picture of all. In 1990, life expectancy among blacks was 70.3 years, whereas among whites it was 76 years. This difference cannot be wholly attributed to genetic factors because the life expectancy difference between the races has steadily shrunk in response to advances in medicine during this century.[141] This is borne out by a "study of the relative contribution of various risk factors and income levels to mortality among blacks," reported recently in the *Journal of the American Medical Association.* The study "estimated that 38 percent of excess [of black over white] mortality could be accounted for by family income and 31 percent by risk factors (smoking status, blood pressure, cholesterol level, body mass index, alcohol use, and diabetes), with 31 percent remaining unexplained."[142] A stronger conclusion is reached by a study reported in a 1992 issue of the *American Journal of Public Health,* whose authors concluded that "In no instance were Black-White differences in all-cause or coronary mortality significantly different when socioeconomic status was controlled."[143]

In short, *poverty hurts, injures, and kills—just like crime.* A society that could remedy its poverty but does not is an accomplice in crime.

Summary

Once again, our investigations lead to the same result. The criminal justice system does not protect us against the gravest threats to life, limb, or possessions. Its definitions of crime are not simply a reflection of the objective dangers that threaten us. The workplace, the medical profession, the air we breathe, and the poverty we refuse to rectify lead to far more human suffering, far more death and disability, and take far more dollars from our pockets than the murders, aggravated assaults, and thefts reported annually by the FBI. What is more, this human suffering is preventable. A government  really intent on protecting our well-being could enforce work safety regulations, police the medical profession, require that clean air standards be met, and funnel sufficient money to the poor to alleviate the major disabilities of poverty—but it does not. Instead we hear a lot of cant about law and order and a lot of rant about crime in the streets. It is as if our leaders were not only refusing to protect us from the major threats to our well-being but trying to cover up this refusal by diverting our attention to crime—as if this were the only real threat.

As we have seen, the criminal justice system is a carnival mirror that presents a distorted image of what threatens us. The distortions do not end with the definitions of crime. As we will see in what follows, new distortions enter at every level of the system, so that in the end, when we look in our prisons to see who really threatens us, all we see are poor people. By that time, virtually all the well-to-do people who endanger us have been discreetly weeded out of the system. As we watch this process unfold in the following chapter, we should bear in mind the conclusion of the present chapter: All the mechanisms by which the criminal justice system comes down more frequently and more harshly on the poor criminal than on the well-off criminal take place *after* most of the dangerous acts of the well-to-do have been excluded from the definition of crime itself. The bias against the poor within the criminal justice system is all the more striking when we recognize that the door to that system is shaped in a way that excludes in advance the most dangerous acts of the well-to-do. Demonstrating this has been the purpose of the present chapter.

Study Questions

1. What should be our definition of the term *crime*? Why does it matter what we call things? Should there be an overlap between the acts we label crimes and the acts we think are morally wrong?
2. Quickly—without thinking about it—picture to yourself a criminal. Describe what you see. Where did this picture come from? Are there people in our society who pose a greater danger to you than the individual you pictured? Why, or why not?
3. What is meant by likening the criminal justice system to a "carnival mirror"?
4. Do you think a business executive who refuses to invest in safety precautions with the result that several workers die is morally better than, equal to, or worse than a mugger who kills his victim after robbing him? What if the executive knowingly violated a safety regulation? What if the mugger was high on drugs? Explain your response.
5. What is meant by speaking of criminal justice as "creative art"? How does the view presented here differ from that of Quinney?
6. Give examples of social practices that are more dangerous to your well-being than common crime. How should these practices be dealt with?

Additional Readings

FRANK, NANCY, AND MICHAEL LYNCH. *Corporate Crime, Corporate Violence.* Albany: Harrow and Heston, 1992.

HILLS, STUART, ed. *Corporate Violence: Injury and Death for Profit.* Totowa, N.J.: Rowman and Littlefield, 1987.

LOFGREN, DON. *Dangerous Premises: An Insider's View of OSHA Enforcement.* Ithaca: ILR Press/Cornell University, 1989.

MOKHIBER, RUSSELL. *Corporate Crime and Violence: Big Business Power and the Abuse of Public Trust.* San Francisco: Sierra Club Books, 1988.

QUINNEY, RICHARD. *The Social Reality of Crime.* Boston: Little, Brown, 1970.

REGENSTEIN, LEWIS. *How to Survive in America the Poisoned.* Washington, D.C.: Acropolis Books, 1986.

ROBINSON, JAMES. *Toil and Toxics: Workplace Struggles and Political Strategies for Occupational Health.* Berkeley, Calif.: University of California Press, 1991.

TIDWELL, MIKE. *In the Shadow of the White House: Drugs, Death and Redemption on the Streets of the Nation's Capital.* Rocklin, Calif.: Prima Pub, 1992.

WHITE, LAWRENCE. *Merchants of Death: The American Tobacco Industry.* New York: Beech Tree Books, 1988.

Notes to Chapter 2

1. "Company in Mine Deaths Set to Pay Big Fine," *New York Times,* February 21, 1993, p. A19.
2. "Mass Murder on the 5:33," *New York Times,* December 10, 1993, p. A34.
3. Gerald R. Ford, "To Insure Domestic Tranquility: Mandatory Sentence for Convicted Felons," speech delivered at the Yale Law School Sesquicentennial Convocation, New Haven, Connecticut, April 25, 1975, in *Vital Speeches of the Day* 41, no. 15 (May 15, 1975), p. 451.
4. "Arrest Data Reveal Profile of Suspect," *Washington Post,* September 16, 1975, p. C1.
5. Ibid.; see also Maryland-National Capital Parks and Planning Commission, *Crime Analysis 1975: Prince George's County* (August 1975), p. 86.
6. *UCR-1974,* p. 186.
7. Maryland-National Capital Parks and Planning Commission, *Crime Analysis 1975,* p. 3.
8. See *UCR-1974,* p. 190.
9. "Arrest Data Reveal Profile of Suspect," p. C1; and Maryland-National Capital Parks and Planning Commission, *Crime Analysis 1975,* p. 86.
10. *UCR-1974,* p. 191.
11. Anthony Bouza, *How to Stop Crime* (New York: Plenum, 1993), p. 57.
12. Quoted in George Will, "A Measure of Morality," *Washington Post,* December 16, 1993, p. A25.

13. Speech to International Association of Chiefs of Police, September 28, 1981.
14. *UCR-1991,* p. 218.
15. *UCR-1991,* p. 223.
16. *UCR-1991,* p. 212.
17. *StatAbst-1992,* p. 16, Table no. 15. Blacks accounted for 44.8 percent of arrests for violent crime in 1991. For "city arrests," the percentage of blacks for Index crimes is 36.9; for violent crimes it is 48.9 (*UCR-1991,* pp. 231, 240).
18. See Chapter 3 for documentation.
19. *Challenge,* p. 44; see also p. 160.
20. Ibid.
21. This transformation has been noted by Erving Goffman in his sensitive description of total institutions, *Asylums* (Garden City, N.Y.: Doubleday, 1961).

> *The interpretative scheme of the total institution automatically begins to operate as soon as the inmate enters, the staff having the notion that entrance is prima facie evidence that one must be the kind of person the institution was set up to handle. A man in a political prison must be traitorous; a man in a prison must be a law-breaker; a man in a mental hospital must be sick. If not traitorous, criminal, or sick, why else would he be here? [p. 84]*

So, too, a person who calls forth the society's most drastic weapons of defense must pose the gravest danger to its well-being. Why else the reaction? The point is put well and tersely by D. Chapman: "There is a circular pattern in thinking: we are hostile to wicked people, wicked people are punished, punished people are wicked, we are hostile to punished people because they are wicked." "The Stereotype of the Criminal and the Social Consequences," *International Journal of Criminology and Penology* 1 (1973), p. 16.
22. Richard Quinney, *The Society Reality of Crime* (Boston: Little, Brown, 1970). In his later work, for example, *Critique of Legal Order: Crime Control in Capitalist Society* (Boston: Little, Brown, 1973), and *Class, State & Crime* (New York: McKay, 1977), Quinney moves clearly into a Marxist problematic and his conclusions dovetail with many in this book. In my own view, however, Quinney has not yet accomplished a satisfactory synthesis between the "social reality" theory and his later Marxism. Elsewhere, I have examined Quinney's theory from the standpoint of moral philosophy. See Jeffrey H. Reiman, "Doing Justice to Criminology: Reflections on the Implications for Criminology of Recent Developments in the Philosophy of Justice," in *Issues in Criminal Justice: Planning and Evaluation,* eds., Marc Riedel and Duncan Chappell (New York: Praeger, 1976), pp. 134–142.
23. Quinney, *Social Reality of Crime,* p. 15.
24. *Washington Post,* January 11, 1983, p. C10.
25. This answers Graeme Newman, who observes that most criminals on TV are white, and wonders what the "ruling class" or conservatives "have to gain by denying the criminality of Blacks." Graeme R. Newman, "Popular Culture and Criminal Justice: A Preliminary Analysis," *Journal of Criminal Justice* 18 (1990), pp. 261–74.

26. Newman, "Popular Culture and Criminal Justice: A Preliminary Analysis," pp. 263–64.

27. Barbara Matusow, "If It Bleeds, It Leads," *Washingtonian,* January 1988, p. 102.

28. "Titillating Channels: TV Is Going Tabloid As Shows Seek Sleaze and Find Profits, Too," *Wall Street Journal,* May 18, 1988, p. 1.

29. "Crime in America: The Shocking Truth," *McCall's,* March 1987, p. 144.

30. Hyman Gross, *A Theory of Criminal Justice* (New York: Oxford University Press, 1979), p. 78. See generally Chapter 3, "Culpability, Intention, Motive," which I have drawn upon in making the argument of this and the following two paragraphs.

31. Nancy Frank, "Unintended Murder and Corporate Risk-Taking: Defining the Concept of Justifiability," *Journal of Criminal Justice* 16 (1988), p. 18.

32. For example, see John Harris, "The Marxist Conception of Violence," *Philosophy & Public Affairs* 3, no. 2 (Winter 1974), pp. 192–220; Jonathan Glover, *Causing Death and Saving Lives* (Hammondsworth, England: Penguin, 1977), pp. 92–112; and James Rachels, *The End of Life* (Oxford: Oxford University Press, 1986), pp. 106–50.

33. *Model Penal Code,* Final Draft (Philadelphia: American Law Institute, 1962).

34. Russell Mokhiber, *Corporate Crime and Violence: Big Business Power and the Abuse of Public Trust* (San Francisco: Sierra Club, 1988), pp. 278, 285.

35. David E. Lilienfeld, "The Silence: The Asbestos Industry and Early Occupational Cancer Research—A Case Study," *American Journal of Public Health* 81, no. 6 (June 1991), p. 791. This article shows how early the asbestos industry knew of the link between asbestos and cancer and how hard they tried to suppress this information. See also Paul Brodeur, *Outrageous Misconduct: The Asbestos Industry on Trial* (New York: Pantheon, 1985).

36. Sir James Fitzjames Stephen, from his *History of the Criminal Law of England* 2 (1883), excerpted in *Crime, Law and Society,* eds., Abraham S. Goldstein and Joseph Goldstein (New York: Free Press, 1971), p. 21.

37. Troy Duster, *The Legislation of Morality: Law, Drugs and Moral Judgment* (New York: Free Press, 1970), pp. 3–76.

38. Norval Morris and Gordon Hawkins, *The Honest Politician's Guide to Crime Control* (Chicago: University of Chicago Press, 1970), p. 2.

39. *Challenge,* p. 7.

40. *UCR-1991,* pp. 13, 31; *UCR-1992,* pp. 58, 381.

41. *UCR-1992,* p. 36.

42. *The President's Report on Occupational Safety and Health* (Washington, D.C.: U.S. Government Printing Office, 1972).

43. "James Messerschmidt, in a comprehensive review of research studies on job related accidents, determined that somewhere between 35 and 57 percent of those accidents occurred because of direct safety violations by the employer. Laura Shill Schraeger and James Short, Jr. found 30 percent of industrial accidents resulted from safety violations and another 20 percent resulted from unsafe working conditions." Kappeler et al., *Mythology of Crime and Criminal*

Justice, p. 104. See James Messerschmidt, *Capitalism, Patriarchy, and Crime: Toward a Socialist Feminist Criminology* (New Jersey: Rowman and Littlefield, 1986); and Laura Shill Schraeger and James Short, "Toward a Sociology of Organizational Crime," *Social Problems* 25 (April 1978), p. 407–19. See also Joseph A. Page and Mary-Win O'Brien, *Bitter Wages: Ralph Nader's Study Group Report on Disease and Injury on the Job* (New York: Grossman, 1973); Rachel Scott, *Muscle and Blood* (New York: Dutton, 1974); Jeanne M. Stellman and Susan M. Daum, *Work Is Dangerous to Your Health* (New York: Vintage, 1973); Fran Lynn "The Dust in Willie's Lungs," *Nation* 222, no. 7 (February 21, 1976), pp. 209–12; and Joel Swartz, "Silent Killers at Work," *Crime and Social Justice* 3 (Summer 1975), pp. 15–20.

44. *President's Report on Occupational Safety and Health,* p. 111; National Safety Council, *Accident Facts 1992,* pp. 39, 50.

45. National Safety Council, *Accident Facts 1992,* pp. 39.

46. *Report of the President to the Congress on Occupational Safety and Health, 1980* (August 4, 1981), p. 86, reporting on deaths and illnesses for 1979. Robert Johnson, who has conducted extensive interviews with present and former textile workers suffering from brown lung, indicates that another reason for the underreporting of occupational disease is that workers are often hesitant to admit symptoms for fear of being seen as "defective" or "worn out" and therefore losing their jobs (personal communication).

47. Robert Reid, "How Accurate Are Safety and Health Statistics?" *Occupational Hazards,* March 1987, p. 49.

48. "Is OSHA Falling Down on the Job? *New York Times,* August 2, 1987, pp. A1, A6.

49. Letter from Schweiker to B. J. Pigg, Executive Director of the Asbestos Information Association, dated April 29, 1982.

50. Edward Sondik, "Progress in Cancer Prevention and Control," in Russell Maulitz, ed., *Unnatural Causes: Three Leading Killer Diseases in America* (New Brunswick: Rutgers Universitiy Press, 1989), p. 117.

51. Philip Landrigan, Testimony before the Senate Committee on Labor and Human Resources, April 18, 1988, p. 2. For cancer deaths, see StatAbst-1988, p. 77, Table no. 117, and p. 80, Table no. 120.

52. "Safety Group Cites Fatalities Linked to Work," *Wall Street Journal,* August 31, 1990, p. B8; and Sally Squires, "Study Traces More Deaths to Working than Driving," *Washington Post,* August 31, 1990, p. A7.

53. BJS, *Criminal Victimization, 1991,* p. 5.

54. Susan Q. Stranahan, "Why 115,000 Workers Will Die This Year," *Boston Sunday Globe,* March 21, 1976, p. A4.

55. National Safety Council, *Accident Facts* 1992, pp. 34–35.

56. Philip J. Hilts, "U.S. Fines Mine Companies for False Air Tests," *New York Times,* April 5, 1991, p. A12. The fines, by the way, amounted to a total of $5 million distributed among 500 mining companies found to have tampered with the coal dust samples used to test for the risk of black lung disease.

57. Joan Claybrook and the Staff of Public Citizen, *Retreat from Safety: Reagan's Attack on America's Health* (New York: Pantheon, 1984), p. 83. Chronic brown lung is a severely disabling occupational respiratory disease. For a description of its impact on its victims, see Robert Johnson, "Labored Breathing: Living with Brown Lung," paper presented at the Annual Meeting of the American Society of Criminology, Fall 1982, Toronto, Canada. See also Page and O'Brien, *Bitter Wages*, p. 18.

58. Claybrook, *Retreat From Safety*, p. 97. See also Page and O'Brien, *Bitter Wages*, p. 23; and Scott, *Muscle and Blood*, p. 196.

59. Scott, *Muscle and Blood*, pp. 45–46; cf. Page and O'Brien, *Bitter Wages*, p. 25.

60. Page and O'Brien, *Bitter Wages*, p. 37.

61. Ibid., p. 45.

62. "Is OSHA Falling Down on the Job?" pp. A1, A6.

63 Don J. Lofgren, *Dangerous Premises: An Insider's View of OSHA Enforcement* (Ithaca, N.Y.: ILR Press/Cornell University, 1989), p. 223.

64. Frank Swoboda, "More for Wildlife Than for Workers," *Washington Post*, April 28, 1992, p. A13.

65. Anthony Robbins, "Can Reagan Be Indicted for Betraying Public Health?" *American Journal of Public Health* 73, no. 1 (January 1983), p. 13.

66. *Challenge*, p. 52 (emphasis added). See also p. 3 for then-prevailing homicide rates.

67. *Washington Post*, July 16, 1975, p. A3.

68. George A. Silver, "The Medical Insurance Disease," *Nation*, 222, no. 12 (March 27, 1976), p. 369.

69. Ibid., p. 371.

70. *Newsweek*, March 29, 1976, p. 67. Lest anyone think this is a new problem, compare this passage written in a popular magazine over 40 years ago:

> *In an editorial on medical abuse, the* Journal of the Medical Association of Georgia *referred to "surgeons who paradoxically are often cast in the role of the supreme hero by the patient and family and at the same time may be doing the greatest amount of harm to the individual."*
>
> *Unnecessary operations on women, stemming from the combination of a trusting patient and a split fee, have been so deplored by honest doctors that the phrase "rape of the pelvis" has been used to describe them. The American College of Surgeons, impassioned foe of fee-splitting, has denounced unnecessary hysterectomies, uterine suspensions, Caesarian sections. [Howard Whitman, "Why Some Doctors Should Be in Jail,"* Colliers, *October 30, 1953, p. 24.]*

71. *StatAbst-1988*, p. 97, Table no. 153; and American Hospital Association, *Hospital Statistics 1992–93*, p. xlv.

72. *UCR-1991*, p. 17.

73. Paul Weiler, Howard Hiatt, Joseph Newhouse, William Johnson, Troyen Brennan, and Lucian Leape, *A Measure of Malpractice: Medical Injury, Malpractice Litigation and Patient Compensation* (Cambridge, Mass.: Harvard University Press, 1993), p. 137. The data given here come from the Harvard Medical Practice Study. See also Christine Russell, "Human Error: Avoidable Mistakes Kill 100,000 Patients a Year," *Washington Post Health*, February 18, 1992, p. 7.

74. Silver, "The Medical Insurance Disease," p. 369. Silver's estimates are extremely conservative. Some studies suggest that between 30,000 and 160,000 individuals die as a result of drugs prescribed by their doctors. See Boyce Rensberger, "Thousands a Year Killed by Faulty Prescriptions," *New York Times,* January 28, 1976, p. A1, A17. If we assume with Silver that at least 20 percent are unnecessary, this puts the annual death toll from unnecessary prescriptions at between 6,000 and 32,000 persons. For an in-depth look at the recklessness with which prescription drugs are put on the market and the laxness with which the Food and Drug Administration exercises its mandate to protect the public, see the series of eight articles by Morton Mintz, "The Medicine Business," *Washington Post,* June 27–30, July 1–4, 1976.
75. Weiler et al., *A Measure of Malpractice: Medical Injury, Malpractice Litigation and Patient Compensation,* p. 54.
76. "More Crime in the Drug and Device Industry," *Health Letter,* October 1988, p. 12.
77. Rate of increase of medical costs is calculated from StatAbst-1992, p. 104, Table no. 151. Note that the assumption that the *number* of unnecessary operations and prescriptions has remained the same between 1974 and 1991 is a conservative assumption in that it effectively assumes that the rate of these practices relative to the population has declined because population has increased in the period.
78. Lewis Regenstein, *America the Poisoned* (Washington, D.C.: Acropolis Books, 1982), pp. 246–47; and National Institutes of Health, *NCI 1995 Budget Estimate,* September 1993, p. 3.
79. National Institutes of Health, *NCI Fact Book 1992,* p. 57.
80. Gloria Borger, "Figuring the Cost of War," *U.S. News and World Report,* February 4, 1991, pp. 45–47.
81. Morton Mintz, "Cancer Scientist Quits in Policy Split," *Washington Post,* April 30, 1976, p. A2.
82. "The New War on Cancer, Part I," *Washington Star,* May 23, 1976, p. A10.
83. Morton Mintz, "3 Lawyers Leave EPA in Protest," *Washington Post,* February 6, 1976, p. A1. The three lawyers are Jeffrey H. Howard, Frank J. Sizemore III, and William E. Reukauf. All were assigned to regulation of pesticides and toxic substances.
84. Walter A. Rosenbaum, "The Clenched Fist and the Open Hand: Into the 1990s at EPA," in N. Vig and M. Kraft, eds., *Environmental Policy in the 1990s: Toward a New Agenda* (Washington, D.C.: CQ Press [a division of Congressional Quarterly Inc.], 1994), p. 123.
85. Paul Cotton, "'Best Data Yet' Say Air Pollution Kills Below Levels Currently Considered Safe," *Journal of the American Medical Association* 269, no. 24 (June 23/30, 1993), p. 3087.
86. J. Michael McGinnis and William H. Foege, "Actual Causes of Death in the United States," *Journal of the American Medical Association* 270, no. 18 (November 10, 1993), p. 2209.
87. Quoted in Stuart Auerbach, "N.J.'s Chemical Belt Takes Its Toll: $4 Billion Industry Tied to Nation's Highest Cancer Death Rate," *Washington Post,* February 8, 1976, p. A1.

88. Bill Richards, "Arsenic: A Dark Cloud Over 'Big Sky Country,'" *Washington Post,* February 3, 1976, pp. A1, A5.

89. Quotations in this paragraph are from Auerbach, "N.J.'s Chemical Belt Takes Its Toll," p. A1.

90. Lester B. Lave and Eugene P. Seskin, "Air Pollution and Human Health," *Science* 169, no. 3947 (August 21, 1970), pp. 723–33, especially p. 728.

91. Michael Weisskopf, "Particles in Air Help Kill 60,000 a Year, Study Says," *Washington Post,* May 13, 1991, p. A13.

92. Reported in Rosenbaum, "The Clenched Fist and the Open Hand," pp. 121–22.

93. "Toxic Chemicals and Public Protection," A Report to the President by the Toxic Substances Strategy Committee, Council on Environmental Quality, Washington, D.C. (May 1980), p. 6; quoted by Regenstein, *America the Poisoned,* p. 184. See also p. 170 in Regenstein.

94. Michael Edelstein, *Contaminated Communities: The Social and Psychological Impacts of Residential Toxic Exposure* (Boulder: Westview Press, 1988), p. 3.

95. *StatAbst-1992,* p. 215, Table no. 357.

96. Jay M. Gould, *Quality of Life in American Neighborhoods: Levels of Affluence, Toxic Waste, and Cancer Mortality in Residential Zip Code Areas* (Boulder: Westview Press, 1986), pp. 22 and 28.

97. Joan Claybrook, *Retreat from Safety,* pp. 117–29.

98. Rosenbaum, "The Clenched Fist and the Open Hand," p. 132.

99. Rebecca Perl, "30 Years After the Surgeon General's Report, Cigarettes Still Kill More Than 1,000 Americans a Day . . . And Make Money for More Than Just the Tobacco Companies," *Washington Post Health,* January 11, 1994, p. 11. The number of lung cancers is computed using the National Cancer Institute's estimate of 168,000 new lung and bronchus cancers in 1992. See *NCI Fact Book* 1992, p. 46.

100. McGinnis and Foege, "Actual Causes of Death in the United States," p. 2207; see also Perl, "30 Years After the Surgeon General's Report, Cigarettes Still Kill More than 1,000 American's a Day . . . ," p. 11.

101. Edward Sondik, "Progress in Cancer Prevention and Control," in Russell Maulitz, ed., *Unnatural Causes: Three Leading Killer Diseases in America* (New Brunswick: Rutgers, 1988, 1989), p. 117.

102. "The Price of Tobacco: The Basics," *New York Times,* March 23, 1993, p. A14.

103. Robbins, "Can Reagan Be Indicted?" p. 12.

104. "U.S. Urged to Escalate Tobacco War," *Washington Post,* January 12, 1994, p. A17.

105. Larry Tye, "Tobacco Firm Hid Cancer Risks, Smoking Foes Say," *Boston Globe,* July 23, 1989, p. 29.

106. "U.S. Urged to Escalate Tobacco War," p. A17.

107. Geoffrey Cowley, "Poison at Home and at Work: A New Report Calls Secondhand Smoke a Killer," *Newsweek,* June 29, 1992, p. 55.

108. McGinnis and Foege, "Actual Causes of Death in the United States," p. 2208.

109. Hunter, *The Mirage of Safety,* p. 4.

110. Quoted in ibid., p. 2.

111. Ibid., pp. 40–41, 64–65, 85, 148–51, inter alia.

112. Ibid., p. 119.

113. Ibid., pp. 123–24.
114. Ibid., pp. 127–40.
115. Ibid., pp. 102–3.
116. Ibid., pp. 162–76.
117. Public Voice for Food and Health Policy, *A Blueprint for Pesticide Policy* (Washington, D.C., 1989), p. 22.
118. "Pesticide Plan Could Uproot U.S. Farming," *New York Times,* October 10, 1993, p. A6.
119. Philip Landrigan, "Commentary: Environmental Disease—A Preventable Epidemic," *American Journal of Public Health* 82, no. 7 (July 1992), p. 942.
120. Landrigan, "Commentary: Environmental Disease—A Preventable Epidemic," p. 942.
121. Regenstein, *America the Poisoned,* p. 253.
122. At the very least, "we" includes all those who earn considerably above the median income for the nation (around $35,000 for a family in 1990) and who resist, or vote for candidates who resist, moves to redistribute income significantly.
123. *StatAbst-1992,* p. 456, Tables nos. 717, 718; see also Karen Pennar, "The Rich Are Richer—and America May Be the Poorer," *Business Week,* November 18, 1991, pp. 85–88.
124. "Poverty in America," *Scholastic Update,* March 23, 1987, pp. 4–8; "Family Income Up Slightly; Poverty Rate Unchanged," *Washington Post,* September 1, 1988; and "8-Nation Study Ranks U.S. Highest in Child Poverty," *Washington Post,* October 27, 1988, p. A1.
125. Aaron Antonovsky, "Class and the Chance for Life," in *Inequality and Justice,* ed., Lee Rainwater (Chicago: Aldine, 1974), p. 177.
126. McGinnis and Foege, "Actual Causes of Death in the United States," p. 2211.
127. Peter A. Margolis et al., "Lower Respiratory Illness in Infants and Low Socioeconomic Status," *American Journal of Public Health* 82, no. 8 (August 1992), p. 1119.
128. *StatAbst-1992,* p. 123, Table no. 188.
129. Guy Gugliotta, "Number of Poor Americans Rises for 3rd Year," *Washington Post,* October 5, 1993, p. A6.
130. David Stipp, "The Tattered Safety Net," *Wall Street Journal,* April 22, 1988, p. 27R; see also Dan Goodgame, "Ready to Operate," *Time,* September 20, 1993, p. 55.
131. *StatAbst-1992,* p. 80, Table no. 109.
132. Robbins, "Can Reagan Be Indicted?" pp. 12–13. See also, "Infant Mortality Down; Race Disparity Widens," *Washington Post,* March 12, 1993, p. A11.
133. United Nations Development Programme, *Human Development Report 1990* (New York: Oxford University Press, 1990), p. 147.
134. Sonia Nazario, "Curing Doctors of Bedside Bias," *International Herald Tribune,* December 23, 1993, p. 8.
135. Alan M. Gittelsohn et al., "Income, Race, and Surgery in Maryland," *American Journal of Public Health* 81, no. 11 (November 1991), p. 1435.
136. *StatAbst-1992,* p. 129, Table no. 200.

137. National Institutes of Health, Cancer Patient Survival Experience (June 1980), pp. 4–5.

138. Ann Gibbons, "Does War on Cancer Equal War on Poverty?" *Science* 253 (July 19, 1991), p. 260.

139. Barbara L. Wells and John W. Horm, "Stage at Diagnosis in Breast Cancer: Race and Socioeconomic Factors," *American Journal of Public Health* 82, no. 10 (October 1992), p. 1383.

140. Gibbons, "Does War on Cancer Equal War on Poverty?" p. 260.

141. *StatAbst-1992*, p. 76, Table no. 103. Richard Allen Williams reports that "there is no reason why the life span of the White should differ from that of the Black," in his *Textbook of Black-Related Diseases* (New York: McGraw-Hill, 1975), p. 2.

142. McGinnis and Foege, "Actual Causes of Death in the United States," p. 2211.

143. Julian E. Keil et al., "Does Equal Socioeconomic Status in Black and White Men Mean Equal Risk of Mortality?" *American Journal of Public Health* 82, no. 8 (August 1992), p. 1133.

3

. . . and the Poor Get Prison

When we come to make an intelligent study of the prison at first hand . . . we are bound to conclude that after all it is not so much crime in its general sense that is penalized, but that it is poverty which is punished.

Take a census of the average prison and you will find that a large majority of people are there not so much because of the particular crime they are alleged to have committed, but for the reason that they are poor and . . . lacked the money to engage the services of first class and influential lawyers.

Eugene V. Debs, *Walls and Bars*

Laws are like spiders' webs: they catch the weak and the small, but the strong and the powerful break through them.

Scythian, one of the Seven Wise Men of Ancient Greece

Weeding Out the Wealthy

The offender at the end of the road in prison is likely to be a member of the lowest social and economic groups in the country.[1]

This statement in the *Report of the President's Commission on Law Enforcement and Administration of Justice* is as true today as it was over two decades ago when it was written. Our prisons are indeed, as Ronald

Goldfarb has called them, the "national poorhouse."[2] To most citizens this comes as no surprise—recall the Typical Criminal and the Typical Crime. Dangerous crimes they think, are mainly committed by poor people. Seeing that prison populations are made up primarily of the poor only makes them surer of this. They think, in other words, that the criminal justice system gives a true reflection of the dangers that threaten them.

In my view, it also comes as no surprise that our prisons and jails predominantly confine the poor. This is not because these are the individuals who most threaten us. It is because the criminal justice system effectively weeds out the well-to-do, so that at *the end of the road in prison,* the vast majority of those we find there come from the lower classes. This weeding out process starts before the agents of law enforcement go into action. In Chapter 2, I argued that our very definition of crime *excludes* a wide variety of actions at least as dangerous as those included and often worse. Is it any accident that the kinds of dangerous actions excluded are the kinds most likely to be performed by the affluent in America? Even before we mobilize our troops in the war on crime, we have already guaranteed that large numbers of upper-class individuals will never come within their sights.

This process does not stop at the definition of crime. It continues throughout each level of the criminal justice system. At each step, from arresting to sentencing, the likelihood of being ignored or released or lightly treated by the system is greater the better off one is economically. As the late U.S. senator Philip Hart wrote:

> *Justice has two transmission belts, one for the rich and one for the poor. The low-income transmission belt is easier to ride without falling off and it gets to prison in shorter order.*
>
> *The transmission belt for the affluent is a little slower and it passes innumerable stations where exits are temptingly convenient.*[3]

This means that the criminal justice system functions from start to finish in a way that makes certain that "the offender at the end of the road in prison is likely to be a member of the lowest social and economic groups in the country."

For the same criminal behavior, the poor are more likely to be arrested; if arrested, they are more likely to be charged; if charged, more likely to be convicted; if convicted, more likely to be sentenced to prison; and if sentenced, more likely to be given longer prison terms than members of the middle and upper classes.[4] In other words, the image of the criminal population one sees in our nation's jails and prisons is distorted by the shape of the criminal justice system itself. It is the face of evil reflected in a carnival mirror, but it is no laughing matter.

The face in the criminal justice carnival mirror is also, as we have already noted, very frequently a black face. Although blacks do not make up the majority of the inmates in our jails and prisons, they make up a proportion that far outstrips their proportion in the population.[5] Here, too, the image we see is distorted by the processes of the criminal justice system itself. Edwin Sutherland and Donald Cressey write in their widely used textbook *Criminology* that

> *numerous studies have shown that African-Americans are more likely to be arrested, indicted, convicted, and committed to an institution than are whites who commit the same offenses, and many other studies have shown that blacks have a poorer chance than whites to receive probation, a suspended sentence, parole, commutation of a death sentence, or pardon.*[6]

William Wilbanks has attacked this conclusion in *The Myth of a Racist Criminal Justice System.*[7] He uses as "perhaps the most important criticism" of the charge that there is discrimination against blacks in arrests the work of Michael Hindelang, which compares the rate at which respondents to the National Crime Survey report being victimized by assailants perceived to be black with the rate at which blacks are arrested for the relevant crimes according to the UCR, and finds "that the racial gap in *offending* for robbery, assault, and rape (whether or not an arrest occurred) was almost equal to that found for *arrest* statistics." Wilbanks concludes, "these results indicate that police select black and white arrestees in approximately the same proportion as they are found in the pool of offenders," and thus "argue against police bias in the arrest process."[8] Recent statistics, however, suggest quite the opposite. Consider the following:

In 1991, respondents to the National Criminal Victimization Survey reported that approximately 28 percent of their assailants in violent victimizations (rape, robbery, simple and aggravated assault) were perceived to be black. That same year, the UCR indicates that 37.8 percent of the individuals arrested for these crimes were black. If we drop out simple assault on the assumption that it is less often reported to the police than the other violent crimes, the figures change only slightly: 36 percent of violent victimizers are perceived to be black, whereas 44 percent of those arrested for rape, robbery, and aggravated assault are black. These figures indicate that police are arresting blacks about 30 percent more frequently than the occurrence of their perceived offenses.[9] Because arrest determines the pool from which charged, convicted, and imprisoned individuals are selected, this suggests that deep bias persists throughout the criminal justice system.

I am aware that there are various problems with comparing UCR and NCVS statistics and various possible explanations for the divergence of black-white arrest rates from the rates at which blacks and whites are perceived offenders. Thus, I do not claim that the results just presented prove definitively the presence of racism. Nonetheless, because they come from the statistics that Wilbanks uses as "the most important criticism" of the discrimination thesis, I think they suffice to cast significant doubt on Wilbanks's claim. Thus, I shall treat his thesis as currently unsubstantiated and continue to follow the majority of researchers in holding that the criminal justice system is widely marked by racial discrimination as well as by economic bias.[10] Moreover, I shall shortly present the results of numerous studies that demonstrate this point.

Curiously enough, statistics on differential treatment of races are available in greater abundance than are statistics on differential treatment of economic classes. For instance, although the FBI tabulates arrest rates by race (as well as by sex, age, and geographical area), it omits class or income. Similarly, both the President's Crime Commission Report and Sutherland and Cressey's *Criminology* have index entries for race or racial discrimination but none for class or income of offenders. It would seem that both independent and government data gatherers are more willing to own up to America's racism than to its class bias. Nevertheless, it does not pay to look at these as two independent forms of bias. It is my view that, at least as far as criminal justice is concerned, racism is simply one powerful form of economic bias. I use evidence on differential treatment of blacks as evidence of differential treatment of members of the lower classes. There are five reasons:

1. First and foremost, black Americans are disproportionately poor. In 1991, while one out every ten white Americans received income below the poverty line, three out every ten black Americans did.[11] The picture is even worse when we shift from income to wealth (property such as a home, land, stocks): In 1988, black households owned one-tenth the median net worth of white households.[12] Unemployment figures give a similarly dismal picture: In 1991, 6 percent of white workers were unemployed and 12.4 percent of blacks were. Among those in the crime-prone ages of 16 to 19, 16.4 percent of white youngsters and 36.3 (more than one of every three) black youngsters were jobless.[13]
2. The factors most likely to keep one out of trouble with the law and out of prison, such as a suburban living room instead of a tenement alley to gamble in or legal counsel able to devote time to one's case instead of an overburdened public defender, are the kinds of things that money can buy regardless of one's race, creed, or national origin.
3. Blacks who travel the full route of the criminal justice system and end up in jail or prison are close in economic condition to whites who do. In 1978, 53 percent of black jail inmates had pre-arrest incomes below $3,000, compared with 44 percent of whites.[14] In 1983, the median pre-arrest income of black jail inmates was $4,067 and that of white jail inmates was

$6,312. About half of blacks in jail were unemployed before arrest and 44 percent of whites were.[15]

4. Some studies suggest that race works to heighten the effects of economic condition on criminal justice outcomes, so that "being unemployed *and* black substantially increase[s] the chances of incarceration over those associated with being either unemployed or black."[16] This means that racism will produce a kind of selective economic bias, making a certain segment of the unemployed even more likely to end up behind bars.
5. Finally, it is my belief that the economic powers that be in America have sufficient power to end or drastically reduce racist bias in the criminal justice system. To the extent that they allow it to exist, it is not unreasonable to assume that it furthers their economic interests.

For all these reasons, racism will be treated here as either a form of economic bias or a tool that achieves the same end.

In the remainder of this chapter, I show how the criminal justice system functions to *weed out the wealthy* (meaning both middle- and upper-class offenders) at each stage of the process and thus produces a distorted image of the crime problem. Before entering into this discussion, three points are worth noting:

First, it is not my view that the poor are all innocent victims persecuted by the evil rich. The poor do commit crimes, and my own assumption is that the vast majority of the poor who are confined in our prisons are guilty of the crimes for which they were sentenced. In addition, there is good evidence that the poor do commit a greater portion of the crimes against person and property listed in the FBI Index than the middle and upper classes do, relative to their numbers in the national population. What I have already tried to prove is that the crimes in the FBI Index are not the only acts that threaten us nor are they the acts that threaten us the most. What I will try to prove in what follows is that the poor are arrested and punished by the criminal justice system much more frequently than their contribution to the crime problem would warrant—thus the criminals who populate our prisons as well as the public's imagination are disproportionately poor.

Second, the following discussion has been divided into three sections that correspond to the major criminal justice decision points and that also correspond to hypotheses two, three, and four that were stated on page 59 in Chapter 2. As always, such classifications are a bit neater than reality, and so they should not be taken as rigid compartments. Many of the distorting processes operate at all criminal justice decision points. So, for example, while I will primarily discuss the light-handed treatment of white-collar criminals in the section on sentencing, it is also true that white-collar criminals are less likely to be arrested or charged or convicted than are blue-collar criminals. The section in which a given issue is treated is a reflection of the point in the criminal justice process at which the disparities are the most striking. Suffice it to say, however, that the disparities between the treatment of the poor and the nonpoor are to be found at all points of the process.

Third, it must be borne in mind that the movement from arrest to sentencing is a funnelling process, so that discrimination that occurs at any early stage shapes the population that reaches later stages. Thus, for example, some recent studies find little economic bias in sentence length for people convicted of similar crimes.[17] When reading such studies, one should remember that the population that reaches the point of sentencing has already been subject to whatever discrimination exists at earlier stages. If, for example, among people with similar offenses and records, poor people are more likely to be charged and more likely to be convicted, then even if the sentencing of convicted criminals is evenhanded, it will reproduce the discrimination that occurred before.

Arrest and Charging

The problem with most official records of who commits crime is that they are really statistics on who gets arrested and convicted. If, as I will show, the police are more likely to arrest some people than others, these official statistics may tell us more about police than about criminals. In any event, they give us little reliable data about those who commit crime and do not get caught. Some social scientists, suspicious of the bias built into official records, have tried to devise other methods of determining who has committed a crime. Most often, these methods involve an interview or questionnaire in which the respondent is assured of anonymity and asked to reveal whether he or she has committed any offenses for which he or she could be arrested and convicted. Techniques to check reliability of these self-reports also have been devised; however, if their reliability is still in doubt, common sense would dictate that they would understate rather than overstate the number of individuals who have committed crimes and never come to official notice. In light of this, the conclusions of these studies are rather astounding. It would seem that crime is the national pastime. The President's Crime Commission conducted a survey of 10,000 households and discovered that "91 percent of all Americans have violated laws that could have subjected them to a term of imprisonment at one time in their lives."[18]

A number of other studies support the conclusion that serious criminal behavior is widespread among middle- and upper-class individuals, although these individuals are rarely, if ever, arrested. Some of the studies show that there are no significant differences between economic classes in the incidence of criminal behavior.[19] The authors of a recent review of literature on class and delinquency conclude that "Research published since 1978, using both official and self-reported data suggests . . . that there is no pervasive relationship between SES [socioeconomic status] and delinquency."[20] This conclusion is echoed by Jensen and Thompson, who argue that

> *The safest conclusion concerning class structure and delinquency is the same one that has been proposed for several decades: class, no matter how defined, contributes little to explaining variation in self-reports of common delinquency.*[21]

Others conclude that while lower-class individuals do commit more than their share of crime, arrest records overstate their share and understate that of the middle and upper classes.[22] Still other studies suggest that some forms of serious crime—forms usually associated with lower-class youth—show up *more frequently* among higher-class persons than among lower.[23] For instance, Empey and Erikson interviewed 180 white males aged 15 to 17 who were drawn from different economic strata. They found that "virtually all respondents reported having committed not one but a variety of different offenses." Although youngsters from the middle classes constituted 55 percent of the group interviewed, they admitted to 67 percent of the instances of breaking and entering, 70 percent of the instances of property destruction, and an astounding 87 percent of all the armed robberies admitted to by the entire sample.[24] Williams and Gold studied a national sample of 847 males and females between the ages of 13 and 16.[25] Of these, 88 percent admitted to at least one delinquent offense.

Even those who conclude "that more lower status youngsters commit delinquent acts more frequently than do higher status youngsters"[26] also recognize that lower-class youth are significantly overrepresented in official records. Gold writes that "about five times more lowest than highest status boys appear in the official records; if records were complete and unselective, we estimate that the ratio would be closer to 1.5:1." [27] The simple fact is that for the same offense, *a poor person is more likely to be arrested and, if arrested charged, than a middle- or upper-class person.*[28]

This means, first of all, that poor people are more likely to come to the attention of the police. Furthermore, even when apprehended, the police are more likely to formally charge a poor person and release a higher-class person *for the same offense.* Gold writes that

> *boys who live in poorer parts of town and are apprehended by police for delinquency are four to five times more likely to appear in some official record than boys from wealthier sections who commit the same kinds of offenses. These same data show that, at each stage in the legal process from charging a boy*

> *with an offense to some sort of disposition in court, boys from different socio-economic backgrounds are treated differently, so that those eventually incarcerated in public institutions, that site of most of the research on delinquency, are selectively poorer boys.*[29]

From a study of self-reported delinquent behavior, Gold finds that when individuals were apprehended, "if the offender came from a higher status family, police were more likely to handle the matter themselves without referring it to the court."[30]

Terence Thornberry reached a similar conclusion in his study of 3,475 delinquent boys in Philadelphia. Thornberry found that among boys arrested *for equally serious offenses* and who had *similar prior offense records,* police were more likely to refer the lower-class youths than the more affluent ones to juvenile court. The police were more likely to deal with the wealthier youngsters informally, for example, by holding them in the station house until their parents came rather than instituting formal procedures. Of those referred to juvenile court, Thornberry found further that for *equally serious offenses* and with *similar prior records,* the poorer youngsters were more likely to be institutionalized than were the affluent ones. The wealthier youths were more likely to receive probation than the poorer ones. As might be expected, Thornberry found the same relationships when comparing the treatment of black and white youths apprehended for equally serious offenses.[31]

Recent studies continue to show similar effects. For example, Sampson found that, for the same crimes, juveniles in lower-class neighborhoods were more likely to have some police record than those in better-off neighborhoods. Again, for similar crimes, lower-class juveniles were more likely to be referred to court than better-off juveniles. If you think these differences are not so important because they are true only of young offenders, remember that this group accounts for much of the crime problem. Moreover, other studies not limited to the young tend to show the same economic bias. McCarthy found that, in metropolitan areas, for similar suspected crimes, unemployed people were more likely to be arrested than employed.[32]

As I indicated above, racial bias is but another form in which the bias against the poor works. And blacks are more likely to be suspected or arrested than whites. A 1988 *Harvard Law Review* overview of studies on race and the criminal process concludes that "most studies. . . reveal what many police officers freely admit: that police use race as an independently significant, if not determinative, factor in deciding whom to follow, detain, search, or arrest."[33] But racially discriminatory police behavior isn't limited to these functions. Numerous studies of police use of deadly force show that blacks are considerably more likely than whites or Hispanics to be shot by the police. For example, using data from Memphis, Tennessee, covering the years from 1969 through 1974, James Fyfe found that blacks were 10 times more likely than whites to have been shot at unsuccessfully by police, 18 times more likely to have been wounded, and 5 times more likely to have been killed."[34] A nation that has watched the brutal treatment meted out to Rodney King by California police officers will not find this surprising. Does anyone think this would have happened if King were a white man?

Any number of reasons can be offered to account for the differences in police treatment of poor versus well-off citizens. Some argue that they reflect that the poor have less privacy.[35] What others can do in their living rooms or backyards the poor do on the street. Others argue that a police officer's decision to book a poor youth and release a middle-class youth reflects either the officer's judgment that the higher-class youngster's family will be more likely and more able to discipline him or her than the lower-class youngster's or differences in the degree to which poor and middle-class complainants demand arrest. Others argue that police training and police work condition police officers to be suspicious of certain kinds of people, such as lower-class youth, blacks, Mexicans, and so on,[36] and thus more likely to detect their criminality. Still others hold that police mainly arrest those with the least political clout, [37] those who are least able to focus public attention on police practices or bring political influence to bear, and these happen to be the members of the lowest social and economic classes.

Regardless of which view one takes, and probably all have some truth in them, one conclusion is inescapable: One of the reasons the offender "at the end of the road in prison is likely to be a member of the lowest social and economic groups in the country" is that the police officers who guard the access to the road to prison make sure that more poor people make the trip than well-to-do people.

Likewise for prosecutors. A recent study of prosecutors' decisions shows that lower-class individuals are more likely to have charges pressed against them than upper-class individuals.[38] Racial discrimination also characterizes prosecutors' decisions to charge. The *Harvard Law Review* overview of studies on race and the criminal process asserts, "Statistical studies indicate that prosecutors are more likely to pursue full prosecution, file more severe charges, and seek more stringent penalties in cases involving minority defendants than in cases involving nonminority defendants."[39] One study of whites, blacks, and Hispanics arrested in Los Angeles on suspicion of having committed a felony found that, among defendants with equally serious charges and prior records, 59 percent of whites had their charges dropped at the initial screening, compared with 40 percent of blacks and 37 percent of Hispanics.[40]

The *weeding out of the wealthy* starts at the very entrance to the criminal justice system: The decision about whom to investigate, arrest, or charge is not made simply on the basis of the offense committed or the danger posed.

It is a decision distorted by a systematic economic bias that works to the disadvantage of the poor.

This economic bias is a two-edged sword. Not only are the poor arrested and charged out of proportion to their numbers for the kinds of crimes poor people generally commit—burglary, robbery, assault, and so forth—but when we reach the kinds of crimes poor people almost never have the opportunity to commit, such as antitrust violations, industrial safety violations, embezzlement, and serious tax evasion, the criminal justice system shows an increasingly benign and merciful face. The more likely that a crime is the type committed by middle- and upper-class people, the less likely that it will be treated as a criminal offense. When it comes to crime in the streets, where the perpetrator is apt to be poor, he or she is even more likely to be arrested and formally charged. When it comes to crime in the suites, where the offender is apt to be affluent, the system is most likely to deal with the crime noncriminally, that is, by civil litigation or informal settlement. Where it does choose to proceed criminally, as we will see in the section on sentencing, it rarely goes beyond a slap on the wrist. Not only is the main entry to the road to prison held wide open to the poor but the access routes for the wealthy are largely sealed off. Once again, we should not be surprised at whom we find in our prisons.

Many writers have commented on the extent and seriousness of "white-collar crime," so I will keep my remarks to a minimum. Nevertheless, for those of us trying to understand how the image of crime is created, four points should be noted.

1. White-collar crime is costly; it takes far more dollars from our pockets than all the FBI Index crimes combined.
2. White-collar crime is widespread, probably much more so than the crimes of the poor.
3. White-collar criminals are rarely arrested or charged; the system has developed kindlier ways of dealing with the more delicate sensibilities of its higher-class clientele.
4. When the white-collar criminals are prosecuted and convicted, their sentences are either suspended or very light when judged by the cost their crimes have imposed on society.

The first three points will be discussed here, and the fourth will be presented in the section on sentencing below.

Everyone agrees that the cost of white-collar crime is enormous. In 1985, *U.S. News and World Report* reported that "Experts estimate that white-collar criminals rake in a minimum of $200 billion annually."[41] Marshall Clinard also cites the $200 billion estimate in his recent book, *Corporate*

Corruption: The Abuse of Corporate Power.[42] Nonetheless, $200 billion probably understates the actual cost. Tax evasion alone has been estimated to cost from 5 to 7 percent of the gross national product. For 1989, that would be between $260 and $364 billion.[43]

In some areas of the economy, white-collar crime is growing dramatically. For example, the North American Securities Administrators Association conducted a survey of state enforcement actions and found that $400 million had been lost to investors as a result of fraud and abuse in the financial planning industry during the period from 1986 to 1988. Most striking, however, was their finding that "the number of state actions against financial planners rose 155 percent and the amount of lost investor funds climbed 340 percent" since their previous survey in 1985.[44] Then of course there is the recent news about fraud in the savings and loan industry, which we look at later in this chapter.

All we need is a rough estimate of the cost of white-collar crime so that we can compare its impact with that of the crimes reported on by the FBI. For this purpose, we can use the conservative estimates in the U.S. Chamber of Commerce's *A Handbook on White-Collar Crime.*[45] Because the *Handbook* was issued in 1974, we will have to adjust its figures to take into account both inflation and growth in population to compare these figures with losses reported for 1991 by the FBI. (In light of the avalanche of statistics the government puts out on street crimes, it's worth wondering why the Chamber has not seen fit to revise its nearly 20-year-old figures, and why no other private or public institution—neither the FBI nor the U.S. Department of Commerce—keeps up-to-date statistics on the costs of white-collar crime.) In some categories, I shall modify the Chamber's figures in light of more recent estimates. As usual, I use conservative estimates where there is a choice. The result will be a rough estimate of the costs of different categories of white-collar crime, as well as of the overall total.

First, the modifications. As might be expected, the cost of computer crime is far beyond the $0.1 billion estimated by the Chamber in 1974. Current estimates run from $3 to $6 billion annually.[46] I will use the $3 billion estimate. Government revenue loss has also outstripped the Chamber's estimate of $12 billion annually. The IRS "estimates that tax cheaters in legitimate business skim as much as $50 billion a year from the tax collector."[47] Since this doesn't include defense and other procurement fraud, we can take it as a conservative estimate. Credit card fraud has also exceeded the Chamber's expectations, with several sources estimating its annual cost at over $1 billion, a figure we can safely use.[48] The cost of pilferage must be increased as well. "The Bureau of National Affairs estimates total employee theft at $15 billion to $25 billion, while the U.S. Chamber of Commerce [recently] says it may be as high as $20 billion to $40 billion. And that's not including theft by government workers, which can be significant.[49] I'll use the low end of the range recently given by the Chamber. Insurance fraud has also gone far beyond the Chamber's 1974 estimates. The National Insurance Crime Bureau estimates the cost of claim fraud at $17.5 billion. Others in the insurance industry estimate the annual cost of fraud to be $67 billion.[50] I will use the $17.5 billion figure. Finally, it will also be no surprise after the era of Boesky and Milken that security thefts and frauds have far outstripped the Chamber's 1974 estimate of $4 billion. The North American Securities Administrators Association estimates that investors lost $40 billion in 1987.[51]

For the remainder of the Chamber's figures, I will assume that the rate of white-collar crime relative to the population has remained constant from 1974 to 1991 and that its real dollar value has remained constant as well (two conservative assumptions in light of the evidence just cited that shows considerable growth in many white-collar crimes). Thus, I will simply adjust these figures to reflect the growth in population and inflation since 1974. Between 1974 and 1991, the population of the United States increased 20 percent, and the consumer price index increased 176 percent. (That is, 1991's population is 120 percent of 1974's, and 1991's prices are 276 percent of 1974's.) Thus, we can bring the Chamber of Commerce's figures up to date by multiplying them by 3.3 (1.20 x 2.76 = 3.312). This, taken together with the modifications indicated in the previous paragraph, gives us an estimated total cost of white-collar crime in 1991 of *$197.76 billion* (about five times higher than the Chamber's 1974 estimated total cost of $41.78 billion). (See Table 4 for the total cost and the breakdown into costs per category of white-collar crime.) The figure $197.76 billion jibes with the estimates of $200 billion quoted earlier, but it is surely on the conservative side. Nonetheless, it is almost *6,000 times* the total amount taken in all bank robberies in the United States in 1991 and more than *eleven times* the total amount stolen in all thefts reported in the FBI *Uniform Crime Reports* for that year.[52]

In addition to fraud and tax evasion by individuals, corporate crime is also rampant. Sutherland, in a study published in 1949 that has become a classic, analyzed the "behavior" of 70 of the 200 largest U.S. corporations over a period of some 40 years:

> *The records reveal that every one of the seventy corporations had violated one or more of the laws, with an average of about thirteen adverse decisions per corporation and a range of from one to fifty adverse decisions per corporation. . . . Thus, generally, the official records reveal that these corporations violated the trade regulations with great frequency. The "habitual criminal" laws of some states impose severe penalties on criminals convicted the third or fourth time. If this criterion were used here, about 90 percent of the large corporations studied would be considered habitual white-collar criminals.*[53]

TABLE 4

The Cost of White-Collar Crime (in Billions of Dollars)

Bankruptcy fraud		$0.26
Bribery, kickbacks, and payoffs		9.90
Computer-related crime		3.00
Consumer fraud, illegal competition, deceptive practices		79.70
Consumer victims	$18.15	
Business victims	11.55	
Government revenue loss	50.00	
Credit card and check fraud		4.30
Credit card	1.00	
Check	3.30	
Embezzlement and pilferage		29.90
Embezzlement (cash, goods, services)	9.90	
Pilferage	20.00	
Insurance fraud		19.15
Insurer victims	17.50	
Policyholder victims	1.65	
Receiving stolen property		11.55
Securities thefts and frauds		40.00
	Total (billions)	$197.76

SOURCE: Chamber of Commerce of the United States, *A Handbook on White-Collar Crime,* 1974 (figures adjusted for inflation and population growth through 1991; and supplemented from other sources documented in text).

Nevertheless, corporate executives almost never end up in jail, where they would find themselves sharing cells with poorer persons who had stolen less from their fellow citizens. What Sutherland found in 1949 continues up to the present. In his 1990 book, *Corporate Corruption: The Abuse of Power,* Marshall Clinard writes:

> *Many government investigations, both federal and state, have revealed extensive law violations in such industries as oil, autos, and pharmaceuticals. . . . [O]ver one two-year period, the federal government charged nearly two-thirds of the Fortune 500 corporations with law violations; half were charged with a serious violation. . . . According to a 1982* U.S. News and World Report *study, more than one out of five of the Fortune 500 companies had been convicted of at least one major crime or had paid civil penalties for serious illegal behavior between 1970 and 1979.*[54]

A recent study of offenders convicted of federal white-collar crimes found "that white-collar criminals are often repeat offenders."[55] As for the treatment of these repeat offenders, Clinard says "a large-scale study of sanctions imposed for corporate law violations found that administrative [that is, noncriminal] penalties were employed in two-thirds of serious corporate law violations, and that slightly more than two-fifths of the sanctions . . . consisted simply of a warning to the corporation not to commit the offense again."[56]

The continued prevalence of these practices is confirmed in a recent study of white-collar crime prosecutions by Susan Shapiro, titled "The Road Not Taken: The Elusive Path to Criminal Prosecution for White-Collar Offenders." Focusing on the enforcement practices of the Securities and Exchange Commission (SEC), Shapiro writes that,

> *while criminal dispositions are often appropriate, they are rarely pursued to the sentencing stage. Out of every 100 suspects investigated by the SEC, 93 have committed securities violations that carry criminal penalties. Legal action is taken against 46 of them, but only 11 are selected for criminal treatment. Six of these are indicted; 5 will be convicted and 3 sentenced to prison. Thus, for Securities and Exchange Commission enforcement, criminal prosecution most often represents the road not taken. Of those found to have engaged in securities fraud, 88 percent never have to contend with the criminal justice system at all.*[57]

With upper-class lawbreakers, the authorities prefer to sue in civil court for damages or for an injunction rather than treat the wealthy as common criminals. Judges have on occasion stated in open court that they would not make criminals of reputable businessmen. One would think it would be up to the businessmen to make criminals of themselves by their actions, but alas, *this* privilege is reserved for the lower classes.

Examples of reluctance to use the full force of the criminal process for crimes not generally committed by the poor can be multiplied ad infinitum. We shall see later that a large number of potential criminal cases arising out of the savings and loan scandals have been dismissed by Federal law enforcement agencies because they lack the labor power to pursue them—even as we prepare to hire 100,000 new police officers to fight street crime.

Let me close with one final example that typifies this particular distortion of criminal justice policy. Embezzlement is the crime of misappropriating money or property entrusted to one's care, custody, or control. Because the poor are rarely entrusted with tempting sums of money or valuable property, this is predominantly a crime of the middle and upper classes. The U.S. Chamber of Commerce estimate of the annual economic cost of embezzlement, adjusted for 1991, is $9.9 billion—more than half the total value of all property and money stolen in all FBI Index property crimes in 1991. Thus, it is fair to conclude that embezzlement imposes a cost on society comparable to that imposed by the Index property crimes. (Don't be fooled into thinking that this cost is imposed only on the rich or on big companies with lots of resources. They pass on their losses—and their increased insurance costs—to consumers in the form of higher prices. Embezzlers take money out of the very same pockets that muggers do: yours!) Nevertheless, the FBI reports that in 1991, when there were 2,252,500 arrests for property crimes, there were 14,000 arrests for embezzlement nationwide.[58] Although their cost to society is comparable, the number of arrests for property crimes was *161 times greater* than the number of arrests for embezzlement. Roughly, this means there was one property crime arrest for every $7,000 stolen, and one embezzlement arrest for every $707,000 "misappropriated.": Note that even the language becomes more delicate as we deal with a "better" class of crook.

The clientele of the criminal justice system forms an exclusive club. Entry is largely a privilege of the poor. The crimes they commit are the crimes that qualify one for admission—and they are admitted in greater proportion than their share of those crimes. Curiously enough, the crimes the affluent commit are not the kind that easily qualify one for membership in the club.

And as we have seen, the reluctance to use the full force of the criminal justice system in pursuit of white-collar criminals is matched by a striking reluctance to use the full force of current public and private research organizations to provide up-to-date estimates of its cost. This coincidence is worth pondering by anyone interested in how criminal justice policy gets made and in how research and statistics function in the process.

Conviction

Between arrest and imprisonment lies the crucial process that determines guilt or innocence. Studies of individuals accused of similar offenses and with similar prior records show that the poor defendant is more likely to be adjudicated guilty than is the wealthier defendant.[59] In the adjudication process the only thing that *should* count is whether the accused is guilty and whether the prosecution can prove it beyond a reasonable doubt. Unfortunately, at least two other factors that are irrelevant to the question of guilt or innocence significantly affect the outcome: One is the ability of the accused to be free on bail prior to trial, and the second is access to legal counsel able to devote adequate time and energy to the case. Because both bail and high-quality legal counsel cost money, it should come as no surprise that here as elsewhere the poor do poorly.

Being released on bail is important in several respects. First and foremost is that those not released on bail are kept in jail like individuals who have been found guilty. They are thus punished while they are still legally innocent. In 1972, 51,000 (out of a total of 142,000) inmates of local jails were confined while awaiting trial. Their average pretrial or presentence confinement was three months, and 60 percent of the nation's jails do not separate pretrial defendants from convicted offenders. In 1978, out of 158,000 inmates of local jails, 67,000 had not yet been convicted. In 1990, there were

403,019 adult jail inmates, of whom 207,358 were unconvicted.[60] Beyond the obvious ugliness of punishing people before they are found guilty, confined defendants suffer from other disabilities. Specifically, they cannot actively aid in their own defense by seeking out witnesses and evidence. Several studies have shown that among defendants accused of the same offenses, those who make bail are more likely to be acquitted than those who do not.[61] In a recent study of unemployment and punishment, Chiricos and Bales found that "after the effects of other factors [seriousness of crime, prior record, etc.] were controlled, an unemployed defendant was 3.2 times more likely to be incarcerated before trial than his employed counterpart."[62]

Furthermore, because the time spent in jail prior to adjudication of guilt may count as part of the sentence if one is found guilty, the accused are often placed in a ticklish position. Let us say the accused believes he or she is innocent, and let us say also that he or she has been in the slammer for two months awaiting trial. Along comes the prosecutor to offer a deal: If you plead guilty to such-and-such (usually a lesser offense than has been charged, say, possession of burglar's tools instead of burglary), the prosecutor promises to ask the judge to sentence you to two months. In other words, plead guilty and walk out of jail today (free, but with a criminal record that will make finding a job hard and insure a stiffer sentence next time around)—or maintain your innocence, stay in jail until trial, and then be tried for the full charge instead of the lesser offense! In fact, not only does the prosecutor threaten to prosecute for the full charge, but this is often accompanied by the implied but very real threat to press for the most severe penalty as well—for taking up the court's time.

Plea bargaining such as this is an everyday occurrence in the criminal justice system. Contrary to the Perry Mason image, the vast majority of criminal convictions in the United States are reached without a trial. It is estimated that between 70 and 95 percent of convictions are the result of a negotiated plea,[63] that is, a bargain in which the accused agrees to plead guilty (usually to a lesser offense than he or she is charged with or to one offense out of many he or she is charged with) in return for an informal promise of leniency from the prosecutor with the tacit consent of the judge. If you were the jailed defendant offered a deal like this, how would you choose? Suppose you were a poor black man not likely to be able to retain F. Lee Bailey or Edward Bennett Williams for your defense.

The advantages of access to adequate legal counsel during the adjudicative process are obvious but still worthy of mention. In 1963, the U.S. Supreme Court handed down the landmark *Gideon v. Wainwright* decision, holding that the states must provide legal counsel to the indigent in all felony cases. As a result, no person accused of a serious crime need face his or her accuser without a lawyer. However, the Supreme Court has not held that the

Constitution entitles individuals to lawyers able to devote equal time and resources to their cases. Even though *Gideon* represents significant progress in making good on the constitutional promise of equal treatment before the law, we still are left with two transmission belts of justice: one for the poor and one for the affluent. There is an emerging body of case law on the right to effective assistance of counsel;[64] however, this is yet to have any serious impact on the assembly-line legal aid handed out to the poor.

Indigent defendants, those who cannot afford to retain their own lawyers, will be defended either by a public defender or by a private attorney assigned by the court. Because the public defender is a salaried attorney with a case load much larger than that of a private criminal lawyer,[65] and because court-assigned private attorneys are paid a fixed fee that is much lower than they charge their regular clients, neither is able or motivated to devote much time to the indigent defendant's defense. Both are strongly motivated to bring their cases to a close quickly by negotiating a plea of guilty. Because the public defender works in day-to-day contact with the prosecutor and the judge, the pressures on him or her to negotiate a plea as quickly as possible, instead of rocking the boat by threatening to go to trial,[66] are even greater than those that work on court-assigned counsel. In an essay aptly titled "Did You Have a Lawyer When You Went to Court? No, I Had a Public Defender," Jonathan Casper reports the perceptions of this process from the standpoint of the defendants:

> *Most of the men spent very little time with their public defender. In the court in which they eventually plead guilty, they typically reported spending on the order of five to ten minutes with their public defender. These conversations usually took place in the bull-pen of the courthouse or in the hallway.*
>
> *The brief conversations usually did not involve much discussion of the details surrounding the alleged crime, mitigating circumstances or the defendants' motives or backgrounds. Instead, they focused on the deal, the offer the prosecution was likely to make or had made in return for a cop out. Often the defendants reported that the first words the public defender spoke (or at least the first words the defendants recalled) were, "I can get you . . . , if you plead guilty."*[67]

As might be expected, with less time and fewer resources to devote to the cause, public defenders and assigned lawyers cannot devote as much time and research to preparing the crucial pretrial motions that can often lead to dismissal of charges against the accused. A recent study of 28,315 felony defendants in various county and city jurisdictions in Tennessee, Virginia, and Kentucky shows that public defenders got cases dropped for 11.3 percent of their defendants, and private attorneys got dismissals for *48 percent of their defendants*. As also might be expected, the overall acquittal rate for privately retained counsel is considerably better than that for public defenders. The same study shows that public defenders achieved either dismissal of charges or a finding of not guilty in 11.4 percent of the indictments they handled, and private attorneys got their clients off the hook in *56 percent of their cases.* The superior record of private attorneys held good when comparisons were made among defendants accused of similar offenses and with similar prior records.[68] The picture that emerges from federal courts is not much different.[69]

The problem of adequate legal representation may be particularly acute in capital cases. According to Robert Johnson, "Most attorneys in capital cases are provided by the state. Defendants, as good capitalists, routinely assume that they will get what they pay for: next to nothing." Their perceptions, he concludes, "may not be far from right." Indeed, Stephen Gettinger maintains that an inadequate defense was "the single outstanding characteristic" of the condemned persons he studied. The result: Capital defendants appeared in court as "creatures beyond comprehension, virtually gagged and masked in preparation for the execution chamber."[70] Writes Linda Williams in the *Wall Street Journal,*

> *The popular perception is that the system guarantees a condemned person a lawyer. But most states provide counsel only for the trial and the automatic review of the sentence by the state appeals court. Indigent prisoners—a description that applies to just about everybody on death row—who seek further review must rely on the charity of a few private lawyers and on cash-starved organizations like the Southern Prisoners Defense Committee.*[71]

A recent *Time* magazine article on this topic is entitled "You Don't Always Get Perry Mason." Says the author, "Because the majority of murder defendants are . . . broke. . . , many of them get court-appointed lawyers who lack the resources, experience or inclination to do their utmost. . . . Some people go to traffic court with better prepared lawyers than many murder defendants get."[72]

Needless to say, the distinct legal advantages that money can buy become even more salient when we enter the realm of corporate and other white-collar crime. Indeed, it is often precisely the time and cost involved in bringing to court a large corporation with its army of legal eagles that is offered as an excuse for the less formal and more genteel treatment accorded to corporate crooks. This excuse is, of course, not equitably distributed to all economic classes, any more than quality legal service is. This means that regardless of actual innocence or guilt, one's chances of beating the rap increase as one's income increases. Regardless of what fraction of crimes are committed by the poor, the criminal justice system is distorted so that an even greater fraction of those convicted will be poor. And with conviction comes sentencing.

Sentencing

On June 28, 1990, the House Subcommittee on Financial Institutions Supervision, Regulation and Insurance met in the Rayburn House Office Building to hold hearings on the prosecution of savings and loan criminals. The chairman of the subcommittee, Congressman Frank Annunzio, called the meeting to order and said:

> *The American people are furious with the slow pace of prosecutions involving savings and loan criminals. These crooks are responsible for 1/3, 1/2, or maybe even more, of the savings and loan cost. The American taxpayer will be forced to pay $500 billion or more over the next 40 years, largely because of these crooks. For many Americans, this bill will not be paid until their grandchildren are old enough to retire.*
>
> *We are here to get an answer to one question: "When are the S&L crooks going to jail?"*
>
> *The answer from the administration seems to be: "probably never."*
>
> *Frankly, I don't think the administration has the interest in pursuing Gucci-clad, white-collar criminals. These are hard and complicated cases, and the defendants often were rich, successful prominent members of their upper-class communities. It is far easier putting away a sneaker-clad high school dropout who tries to rob a bank of a thousand dollars with a stick-up note, than a smooth talking S&L executive who steals a million dollars with a fraudulent note.*

Later in the hearing, Chairman Annunzio questioned the administration's representative:

> *You cited, Mr. Dennis, several examples in your testimony of successful convictions with stiff sentences, but the average sentence so far is actually about 2 years, compared to an average sentence of about 9 years for bank robbery. Why do we throw the book at people who rob a bank in broad daylight but we coddle people who . . . rob the bank secretly?*[73]

The simple fact is that the criminal justice system reserves its harshest penalties for its lower-class clients and puts on kid gloves when confronted with a better class of crook.

We will come back to the soft treatment of the S&L crooks shortly. For the moment, note that the tendency to treat higher-class criminals more leniently than lower-class criminals has been with us for a long time. In 1972, the *New York Times* did a study on sentencing in state and federal courts. The *Times* stated that "crimes that tend to be committed by the poor get tougher sentences than those committed by the well-to-do," that federal "defendants who could not afford private counsel were sentenced nearly twice as severely as defendants with private or no counsel," and that a "study by the Vera Institute of Justice of courts in the Bronx indicates a similar pattern in the state courts."[74]

Looking at federal and state courts, Stuart Nagel concluded that

> *not only are the indigent found guilty more often, but they are much less likely to be recommended for probation by the probation officer, or to be granted probation or suspended sentences by the judge.*

Further, that

> *the federal data show that this is true also of those with no prior record: 27 percent of the indigent with no prior record were not recommended for probation, against 16 percent of the non-indigent; 23 percent indigent did not receive suspended sentences or probation, against 15 percent non-indigent. Among those of both groups with "some" prior record the spread is even greater.*[75]

Eugene Doleschal and Nora Klapmuts report as "typical of American studies" Thornberry's analysis of "3,475 Philadelphia delinquents that found that blacks and members of lower socioeconomic groups were likely to receive more severe dispositions than whites and the more affluent even when the appropriate legal variables [i.e., offense, prior record, and so on] were held constant."[76] Later, applying more sophisticated statistical techniques to the data upon which his Philadelphia study was based, Thornberry concluded, "When the variable of race was suppressed . . . , SES [socioeconomic status] was found to be significantly related to dispositions such that lower SES subjects were treated more severely than their high SES counterparts."[77] Studying the experiences of 798 burglary and larceny defendants in North Carolina, Clarke and Koch found that "other things being equal, the low-income defendant had a greater chance than the higher-income defendant of emerging from the criminal court with an active prison sentence."[78] Analyzing data from Chicago trial courts, Lizotte concluded that, "other factors being equal, laborers and nonwhites are given longer prison sentences than higher SES groups."[79]

More recently, D'Alessio and Stolzenberg studied a random sample of 2,760 offenders committed to the custody of the Florida Department of Corrections during fiscal year 1985. Although they found no greater sentence severity for poor offenders found guilty of property crimes, they found that poor offenders did receive longer sentences for violent crimes, such as manslaughter, and for morals offenses, such as narcotics possession. Nor, by the way, did sentencing guidelines reduce this disparity.[80] A study of individuals convicted of drunk driving found that increased education (taken as an indicator of higher occupational status) "increase[d] the rate of movement from case filing to probation and decrease[d] the rate of movement to prison." And though when probation was given, more-educated offenders got longer probation, they also got shorter prison sentences, if sentenced to prison at all.[81]

Chiricos and Bales found that, for individuals guilty of similar offenses and with similar prior records, unemployed defendants were more likely to be incarcerated while awaiting trial, and for longer periods, than employed defendants. They were more than twice as likely as their employed counterparts to be incarcerated upon a finding of guilt. And defendants with public defenders experienced longer periods of jail time than those who could afford private attorneys.[82] McCarthy noted a similar link between unemployment and greater likelihood of incarceration.[83] In his study of 28,315 felony defendants in Tennessee, Virginia, and Kentucky, Champion also found that offenders who could afford private counsel had a greater likelihood of probation, and received shorter sentences when incarceration was imposed.[84] A study of the effects of implementing Minnesota's determinate sentencing program shows that socioeconomic bias is "more subtle, but no less real" than before the new program.[85]

Tillman and Pontell examined the sentences received by individuals convicted of Medicaid provider fraud in California. Because such offenders normally have no prior arrests and are charged with grand theft, their sentences were compared with the sentences of other offenders convicted of grand theft and who also had no prior records. While 37.7 percent of the Medicaid defrauders were sentenced to some jail or prison time, 79.2 percent of the others convicted of grand theft were sentenced to jail or prison. This was so even though the median dollar loss due to the Medicaid frauds was $13,000, more than ten times the median loss due to the other grand thefts ($1,149). Tillman and Pontell point out that most of the Medicaid defrauders were health professionals, while most of the others convicted of grand theft had low-level jobs or were unemployed. They conclude that "differences in the sentences imposed on the two samples are indeed the result of the different social statuses of their members."[86]

As usual, data on racial discrimination in sentencing tell the same story of the treatment of those who cannot afford the going price of justice. A study of offender processing in New York State counties found that, for offenders with the same arrest charge and the same prior criminal records, minorities were incarcerated more often than comparably situated whites.[87] A study of sentencing in Miami concludes that when case-related attributes do not clearly point to a given sentence, sentencing disparities are more likely to be based on race.[88] Most striking perhaps is that, in 1990, more than 46 percent of the inmates in federal and state prisons were black, whereas blacks make up only 35 percent of those arrested for serious (FBI Index) crimes. Furthermore, when we look only at federal prisons, where there is reason to believe that racial and economic discrimination is less prevalent than in state institutions, we find that in 1986, nonwhite inmates were sentenced, on average, 33 more months for burglary than white inmates and 22 more months for income tax evasion. In 1989, the average federal sentence for blacks found guilty of violent offenses was 10 months longer than that for whites.[89]

This, too, has been going on for quite some time. An extensive study by the *Boston Globe* of 4,500 cases of armed robbery, aggravated assault, and rape found that "blacks convicted in the superior courts of Massachusetts receive harsher penalties than whites for the same crimes."[90] The authors of a study of almost 1,200 males sentenced to prison for armed robbery in a southeastern state found that "in 1977 whites incarcerated for armed robbery had a greater than average chance of receiving the least severe sentence, while nonwhites had a greater than average chance of receiving a moderately severe sentence."[91] A study of 229 adjudicated cases in a Florida judicial district yielded the finding that "whites have an 18 percent greater chance in the predicted probability of receiving probation than blacks when all other things are equal.[92] A recent study of criminal justice systems in California, Michigan, and Texas by Petersilia confirms the continuation of this trend. "Controlling for the factors most likely to influence sentencing and parole decisions," she writes, "the analysis still found that blacks and Hispanics are less likely to be given probation, more likely to receive *prison* sentences, more likely to receive longer sentences, and more likely to serve a greater portion of their original time."[93] Myers found that "harsher treatment of persons with fewer resources (e.g., female, unemployed, unmarried, black) is . . . pronounced in highly unequal counties."[94]

The federal government has recently introduced sentencing guidelines and minimum mandatory sentences that might be expected to eliminate discrimination, and many states have followed suit. The effect of this, however, has been not to eliminate discretion but to transfer it from those who sentence to those who decide what to charge—that is, from judges to prosecutors. Prosecutors can charge in a way that makes it likely that the offender will get less than the mandatory minimum sentence. And discrimination persists. To examine the effects of mandatory minimum sentences, Barbara Meierhoefer studied 267,178 offenders sentenced in federal courts from January 1984 to June 1990. She found that whites were consistently more likely than blacks to be sentenced below the minimum sentence. The disparity varied from year to year, reaching a high point in 1988, when blacks were 30 percent more likely than whites to receive at least the minimum. Hispanics fared even worse than blacks. Concludes Meierhoefer,

> *despite the laws' emphasis on offense behavior, sentences still vary by offender characteristics. . . . Further, both black and Hispanic offenders now receive notably more severe sentences than their white counterparts.*
>
> *The latter trend suggests that there may be questions to be considered concerning the impact of shifting discretion affecting sentencing from the court to the prosecutor's office.*[95]

There is considerable evidence that *double discrimination*—by race of the victim and of the offender—affects death penalty sentencing. In Florida, for example, blacks "who kill whites are nearly forty times more likely to be sentenced to death than those who kill blacks." Moreover, among "killers of whites, blacks are five times more likely than whites to be sentenced to death." This pattern of double discrimination was also evidenced, though less pronouncedly, in Texas, Ohio, and Georgia, the other states surveyed. Together, these four states "accounted for approximately 70 percent of the nation's death sentences" between 1972 and 1977.[96]

More recent studies have shown the same pattern. It was on the basis of such research that what may have been the last constitutional challenge to the death penalty was raised and rejected. In the 1987 case of *McCleskey v. Kemp,* evidence of discrimination on the basis of the victim's race was provided by a study by Professor David Baldus, of the University of Iowa, who examined 2,484 Georgia homicide cases that occurred between 1973 (when the current capital murder law was enacted) and 1979 (a year after McClesky received his death sentence).[97] After controlling for all legitimate nonracial factors—such as severity of crime, presence of aggravating factors—Baldus found that "murderers of white victims are still being sentenced to death 4.3 times more often than murderers of black victims."[98] The justices of the Supreme Court acknowledged the systemic disparities, but a majority held that the disparities would not invalidate death penalty convictions unless discrimination could be shown in the individual case at hand.

A 1990 report of the General Accounting Office to the Senate and House Committees on the Judiciary reviewed 28 studies on racial disparities in death penalty sentencing and concluded that race of the victim strongly influenced the likelihood of a death penalty: "those who murdered whites were found to be more likely to be sentenced to death than those who murdered blacks."[99] Note that all these discriminatory sentences were rendered under statutes that had passed constitutional muster and were therefore presumed free of the biases that led the Supreme Court to invalidate death penalty statutes in *Furman v. Georgia* in 1972.

Another study has shown that among blacks and whites on death row, whites are more likely to have their sentences commuted. Also, blacks or whites who have private counsel are more likely to have their execution commuted than condemned persons defended by court-appointed attorneys.[100]

As I have already pointed out, justice is increasingly tempered with mercy as we deal with a better class of crime. The Sherman Antitrust Act is a criminal law. It was passed in recognition of the fact that one virtue of a free enterprise economy is that competition tends to drive consumer prices down, so agreements by competing firms to refrain from price competition is the equivalent of stealing money from the consumer's pocket.

Nevertheless, although such conspiracies cost consumers far more than lower-class theft, price fixing was a misdemeanor until 1974.[101] In practice, few conspirators end up in prison, and when they do, the sentence is a mere token, well below the maximum provided in the law.

In the historic *Electrical Equipment* cases in the early 1960s, executives of several major firms secretly met to fix prices on electrical equipment to a degree that is estimated to have cost the buying public well over a billion dollars. The executives involved knew they were violating the law. They used plain envelopes for their communications, called their meetings "choir practice," and referred to the list of executives in attendance as the "Christmas card list." This case is rare and famous because it was one in which the criminal sanction was actually imposed. Seven executives received and served jail sentences. In light of the amount of money they had stolen from the American public, however, their sentences were more an indictment of the government than of themselves: *thirty days in jail!*

Speaking about the record of federal antitrust prosecution, Clinard and Yeager write that

> *even in the most widespread and flagrant price conspiracy cases, few corporate executives are ever imprisoned; of the total 231 cases with individual defendants from 1955 to 1975, prison sentences were given in only 19 cases. Of a total of 1,027 individual defendants, only 49 were sentenced to prison.*[102]

There is some (slight) indication of a toughening in the sentences since antitrust violations were made a felony in 1974 and penalties were increased. "In felony cases prosecuted under the new penalties through March 1978, 15 of 21 sentenced individuals (71 percent) were given terms averaging 192 days each."[103] Nevertheless, when the cost to society is reckoned, even such penalties as these are hardly severe.

After the "anything goes" attitude of the Reagan era, which brought us such highly publicized white-collar skulduggery as the multibillion dollar savings and loan scandal, the 1990s have seen a kind a backlash, with the government under pressure to up the penalties for corporate offenders. Here too, however, progress follows a slow and zigzagging course. Consider, for example, the following series of titles of articles from the *Washington Post:* March 2, 1990: "Criminal Indictments: Training Bigger Guns on Corporations"; April 1, 1990: "Going Soft on Corporate Crime"; April 28, 1990: "Justice Dept. Shifts on Corporate Sentencing" ("Attorney General Dick Thornburgh last month withdrew the Justice Department's longstanding support for tough mandatory sentences for corporate criminals following an intense lobbying campaign by defense contractors, oil companies and other *Fortune* 500 firms."); April 27, 1991: "Corporate Lawbreakers May Face Tougher Penalties."[104] Lest this last one be taken as truly reversing the trend to leniency, note that it reports new sentencing guidelines approved by the U.S. Sentencing Commission, and it points out, "The only penalties set forth by the guidelines are fines and probation because the defendants in such cases are not individuals. " Compare this with a statement from Ira Reiner, Los Angeles district attorney, quoted in the first of the articles just listed: "A fine, no matter how substantial, is simply a cost of doing business for a corporation. But a jail term for executives is different. What we are trying to do is to change the corporate culture." Good luck, Ira.

Studies have shown that even though corporate and white-collar lawbreakers are being more frequently brought to justice and more frequently being sanctioned, they still receive more lenient sentences than do those who are sentenced for common property crimes.[105] A study by Hagan and Palloni, which focuses particularly on the differences between pre- and post-Watergate treatment of white-collar offenders, concludes that likelihood of prosecution after Watergate was increased, but that the effect of this was canceled out by the leniency of the sentences meted out:

> *the new incarcerated white-collar offenders received relatively light sentences that counterbalanced the increased use of imprisonment. Relative to less-educated common criminals, white-collar offenders were more likely to be imprisoned after Watergate than before, but for shorter periods.*[106]

Even after the heightened public awareness of white-collar crime that came in the wake of Watergate and the S&L scandals, it remains the case that the crimes of the poor receive stiffer sentences than the crimes of the well-to-do (see Table 5). Keep in mind while looking at these figures that *each* of the "crimes of the affluent" costs the public more than *all* of the "crimes of the poor" put together.

I do not deny that there has been some toughening of the treatment of white-collar offenders in recent years. Nonetheless, this toughening has been relatively mild, especially when compared with the treatment dealt out to lower-class offenders. Before turning to the "great" scandals of Watergate and the savings and loans industry, here are two "small" cases that illustrate the new developments.

In September 1991, a fire destroyed a chicken-processing plant in Hamlet, North Carolina. When the 100 employees in the plant tried to escape, they found that the company executives had ordered the doors locked "to keep out insects and to keep employees from going outside for coffee breaks, or stealing chickens." Twenty-five workers died in the fire, some were found burned to death at the doors they couldn't open. Another 50 people were injured. The owner of the company and two plant managers were charged with involuntary manslaughter. The outcome: The owner pleaded guilty and was sentenced to 19 years and 11 months in prison. You

TABLE 5

Sentences for Different Classes of Crime

	Percent Sentenced to Prison	*Average Sentence (in months)*	*Average Time Served (in months)*
Crimes of the poor			
Robbery	99%	101.1	60.2
Burglary	82%	62.8	26.0
Larceny/theft	39%	17.9	15.2
Crimes of the affluent			
Fraud[a]	48%	22.2	15.6
Tax law violation[b]	43%	25.2	11.6
Embezzlement	31%	15.7	11.0

SOURCE: *Sourcebook-1992* (Compiled from Tables 5.20, 5.22, 5.37).

[a] Does not include tax fraud.

[b] Includes tax fraud.

may or may not think this is severe as a punishment for someone responsible for 25 very painful deaths, but note two revealing facts. First, as part of the plea agreement, the involuntary manslaughter cases against the two plant managers were dismissed, though they surely knew that the doors were locked and what the risks were. And second, the sentence is "believed to be the harshest judgment ever handed out for a workplace safety violation."[107]

Consider the case I referred to briefly at the beginning of Chapter 2. It occurred earlier but was decided later than the chicken-processing plant fire. In September 1989, "the worst American mining accident in nearly a decade occurred . . . at the William Station Mine near Madisonville," Kentucky. Ten workers were killed in a methane explosion. "The grand jury found that supervisors at the William Station Mine had falsified daily and weekly safety reports, including those that recorded methane levels." Other violations were cited as well, "including requiring miners to work under unsupported roofs, historically the leading causes of death in mines." On February 20, 1993, the company that operates the mine "pleaded guilty to a pattern of safety misconduct there and agreed to pay the Government a fine of $3.75 million," said to be "the largest criminal fine ever imposed for violations of the Mine Safety Act." Is this severe for ten deaths? Was this an accident, if it resulted from intentional falsification of safety records? Note that there was the possibility of a prison sentence for this. "James H. Tichenor, who was acting foreman at the mine, pleaded guilty to charges of falsifying records of methane levels. . . . Prosecutors said that Mr. Tichenor [who was the only individual charged] was cooperating in the investigation and that they had agreed to recommend he receive a minimum sentence. Under Federal guidelines, the minimum sentence for his violations could be probation to six months in prison."[108]

We turn now to the greatest examples of upper-class crime in our era, the savings and loan debacle and the Watergate scandals. The federally insured system of savings and loans banks (also known as "thrifts") was created in the 1930s to promote the building and sales of new homes during the Great Depression. The system had built into it important limitations on the kinds of loans that could be made and was subject to federal supervision to prevent the bank failures that came in the wake of the depression of 1929. Starting in the 1970s and speeding up in the early 1980s, this entire system of regulation and supervision was, first, loosened, and then essentially dismantled, as part of the Reagan administration's policy of deregulation. Although S&L's could now make riskier investments, their deposits were still insured by the Federal Savings and Loan Insurance Corporation (FSLIC). Translation: The S&Ls could take risky investments shooting for windfall profits, with the taxpayers picking up the tab for losses. This combination proved to be financial dynamite. The thrifts made high-risk investments, and many failed. By 1982, the bill to the FSLIC for bailing out insolvent thrifts was over $2.4 billion. By 1986, the FSLIC was itself insolvent![109] One current estimate of the cost to the American taxpayer of the S&L debacle is *$1 trillion.*[110]

Not all this loss is due to crime. Some is due to foolish but legal investments, some is due to inflation, and some is due to foot dragging by federal agencies that allowed interest to accumulate. Nonetheless, there is evidence that fraud was a central factor in 70 to 80 percent of the S&L failures.[111] Much of this fraud took the form of looting of bank funds for the personal gain of bank officers at the expense of the institution. The commissioner of the California Department of Savings and Loans is quoted as saying in 1987, "The best way to rob a bank is to own one."[112] Says *Fortune* magazine, "Though yet perceived only in hazy outline, today's S&L fraud dwarfs every previous carnival of white-collar crime in America."[113]

In response to the enormity of this scandal, American public opinion has hardened toward white-collar crime, and federal law enforcement agencies have been prosecuting, fining, and even jailing offenders at unprecedented rates. Nonetheless, considering the size of the scandal and the far-reaching damage it had done to the American economy, the treatment is still light-handed compared with that of even nonviolent "common" crime. According to a recent report of the General Accounting Office, of $84,000,000 in court-ordered fines and repayments (itself but a fraction of the total loss), only $365,000 has been collected. As of the close of 1991, 2,654 persons had been charged in major fraud cases. The conviction rate is 96 percent, and many are going to jail. However, the average prison sentence is 18 months![114] Even these represent just a small fraction of the crooks involved in the S&L looting. One observer points out that "from 1987 to 1992, Federal bank and thrift regulators filed a staggering 95,045 criminal referrals with the FBI. The volume was so large that more than 75 percent of these referrals have been dropped without prosecution."[115] At the same time, the Justice Department advised against funding for 425 new agents requested by the FBI and 231 new assistant U.S. attorneys, and the administration recommended against increasing funds authorized by Congress for the S&L investigations from $50 million to $75 million.[116] And yet we now find the president and the Congress ready to spend $23 billion on criminal justice and hire 100,000 new police officers to keep our streets safe!

To give you a concrete idea of what some of the S&L crooks did and the treatment they are getting, I have culled, from various sources, a roughly representative "rogues gallery" (see Table 6). In looking at these rogues, their acts and their punishments, keep in mind the treatment meted out to the Typical Criminal when he steals a fraction of what they did.

The Watergate scandal was a different sort of affair. Rather than seeking to rob money, former President Richard Nixon's henchmen sought to steal the 1972 presidential election by burglarizing, wire tapping, and generally disrupting the opposing party. Nixon himself was never indicted. He was forced to resign the presidency in disgrace, and "sentenced" to (what was recently) a $148,000 a year federal pension (plus office, staff, and other perks, costing the taxpayer an additional $335,000 a year).[117] His underlings did occasionally go to jail. Nonetheless, considering that their crime involved an attempt to undermine the constitutional processes of the American republic, their treatment must also be regarded as lenient (see Table 7).

We have seen in this chapter and the one before that the criminal justice system is triply biased against the poor. First, there is the economic class bias *between harmful acts* as to which get labeled crimes and which are treated as regulatory matters, as we saw in the previous chapter. Second, there is economic class bias *between crimes* that we have already seen in this chapter. The crimes that poor people are likely to commit carry harsher sentences than the "crimes in the suites" committed by well-to-do people. Third, *among defendants convicted of the same crimes,* the poor receive less probation and more years of confinement than well-off defendants, assuring us once again that the vast majority of those put behind bars are from the lowest social and economic classes in the nation. On either side of the law, the rich get richer . . .

TABLE 6

The Savings and Loan Roster

Michael Hellerman aka Michael Rapp	Defrauded a Flushing Federal S&L (New York) of $8.4 million and Florida Center Bank out of $7.5 million.	Sentenced to 32 years for Florida theft and 15 years for N.Y. theft, plus $1.75 million fine. Reduced on appeal to 15 years and a fine of $100,000. Released on parole in 1992 after serving 5 1/2 years; has not paid any of fine, but lawyer claims $100 a month is being deducted from Hellerman/Rapp's salary.
Charles Bazarian	Convicted for "swindling $20 million from two California S&Ls and skimming at least $100,000 from a low-income H.U.D.project." Also convicted with Rapp in Florida case.	Sentenced to 2 years and $100,000 fine in Florida case; sentenced to 2 years in prison, 3 years probation, and $10,000 fine for other incidents. Served less than 2 years for cooperating with authorities and has paid $18,000.
Mario Renda	As partner in a brokerage business, he stole about $16 million.	Sentenced to prison, ordered to pay $9.9 million in restitution and $125,000 in criminal fines; was given early parole after serving 21 months. As of April 1992, he had paid $950 of the fine and only about $500,000 of the restitution.
Herman Beebe	Involved in widespread loan fraud involving more than $30 million.	Pleaded guilty to two counts under a bargain in which he received a sentence of 1 year and 1 day. Served 10 months and is immune from prosecution for fraud charges in Louisiana and Texas.
Richard Mariucci	As branch manager of Gibraltar Federal (California), stole $3.4 million, which he spent on gambling and raising racehorses.	Sentenced to 2 years and 3 months.

Walter Vladovich	Video store owner, defrauded Westlake Thrift and Loan (California) out of $4 million and bribed First United Federal (California) vice president to approve a $556,269 loan, which he pocketed.	Sentenced to 4 years and $50,000 fine.
Arthur Kick	President of North Chicago Federal S&L, stole$1.2 million by misappropriating loans.	Sentenced to full restitution and 3 years probation.
Jack Lee Odon	President of Sioux Valley Savings (Iowa), stole $1 million, took kickbacks from developers, and set up a slush fund to hide bad loans from examiners.	Sentenced to 6 years.
Edward Jolly, Jr.	Assistant regional vice president and consumer loan manager at First Federal Savings and Loan (South Carolina), stole $4.5 million through fictitious loan applications and lost all the money playing the futures market.	Sentenced to 2 years and 9 months
Ted Musacchio	President of Columbus Marin S&L (California), stole $9.3 million and lied about it on federal disclosure forms.	Sentenced January 1990 to 5 years probation and immediate restitution of $9.3 million, but as of April 1992 no restitution had been paid.
Gina Loren	Investment manager, together with stockbroker Daniel Burkhart and attorney Charles Lusin, "conned California thrifts, individuals, and an order of nuns out of $4.1 million."	Sentenced to 6 years (Lusin sentenced to 5 years and Burkhart to 4 years).

SOURCE: Stephen Pizzo and Paul Muolo, "Take the Money and Run: A Rogues Gallery of Some Lucky S & L Thieves," *New York Times Magazine,* May 9, 1993; Alan Fomhan, "S&L Felons," *Fortune,* November 5, 1990, p. 93; "Former Columbus President Guilty of Misapplying Funds," *American Banker,* December 26, 1989; and "Why S&L Crooks Have Failed to Pay Millions of Dollars In Court-Ordered Restitution: Nineteen Case Studies," A *Staff Report for the Subcommittee on Financial Institutions Supervision, Regulation and Insurance of the Committee on Banking, Finance and Urban Affairs, House of Representatives,*102nd Congress, Second session, April 1992.

TABLE 7

The Watergate Roster

Richard M. Nixon	Unindicted co-conspirator	Pardoned	
Dwight L.Chapin	Convicted of lying to a grand jury	Sentenced to serve 10 to 30 months	Served 8 months
Charles W. Colson	Pleaded guilty to obstruction of justice and fined $5,000	Sentenced to serve 1 to 3 years	Served 7 months
John W. Dean III	Pleaded guilty to conspiracy to obstruct justice	Sentenced to serve 1 to 4 years	Served 4 months
John D. Ehrlichman	Convicted of conspiracy to obstruct justice, conspiracy to violate civil rights, and perjury	Sentenced to serve concurrent terms of 20 months to 8 years	Served 18 months
H.R. Haldeman	Convicted of conspiracy to obstruct justice and perjury	Sentenced to serve 30 months to 8 years	Served 18 months
E.Howard Hunt	Pleaded guilty to conspiracy, burglary, and wiretapping	Sentenced to serve 30 months to 8 years and fined $10,000	Served 33 months
Herbert W. Kalmbach	Pleaded guilty to violation of the Federal Corrupt Practices Act and promising federal employment as a reward for political activity	Sentenced to serve 6 to 18 months and fined $10,000	Served 6 months
Richard G. Kleindienst	Pleaded guilty to refusal to answer pertinent questions before a Senate committee	Sentenced to 30 days and fined $100	Sentence suspended
Egil Krogh, Jr.	Pleaded guilty to conspiracy to violate civil rights	Sentenced to serve 2 to 6 years (all but 6 months were suspended)	Served 4 1/2 months
Frederick C. LaRue	Pleaded guilty to conspiracy to obstruct justice	Sentenced to serve 1 to 3 years (all but 6 months were suspended)	Served 5 1/2 months

G.Gordon Liddy	Convicted of conspiracy, conspiracy to violate civil rights, burglary, and wiretapping	Sentenced to serve 6 years and 8 months to 20 years and fined $40,000	Served 52 months
Jeb S. Magruder	Pleaded guilty to conspiracy to obstruct justice, wiretapping, and fraud	Sentenced to serve 10 months to 4 years	Served 7 months
John N. Mitchell	Convicted of conspiracy to obstruct justice and perjury	Sentenced to serve 30 months to 8 years	Served 19 months
Donald H. Segretti	Pleaded guilty to campaign violations and conspiracy	Sentenced to serve 6 months	Served 4 1/2 months
Maurice H. Stans	Pleaded guilty to five misdemeanor violations of the Federal Elections Campaign Act	Fined $5,000	
James W. McCord, Jr.	Convicted of conspiracy, burglary, wiretapping, and unlawful possession of intercepting devices	Sentenced to serve 1 to 5 years	Served 4 months
Bernard L. Barker	Pleaded guilty to conspiracy, burglary, wiretapping, and unlawful possession of intercepting devices	Sentenced to serve 18 months to 6 years	Served 12 months
Virgilio R. Gonzalez	Pleaded guilty to conspiracy, burglary, wiretapping, and unlawful possession of intercepting devices	Sentenced to serve 1 to 4 years	Served 15 months
Eugenio R. Martinez	Pleaded guilty to conspiracy, burglary, wiretapping, and unlawful possession of intercepting devices	Sentenced to serve 1 to 4 years	Served 15 months
Frank A. Sturgis	Pleaded guilty to conspiracy, burglary, wiretapping, and unlawful possession of intercepting devices	Sentenced to serve 1 to 4 years	Served 13 months

SOURCE: *Washington Post*, June 17, 1982.

. . . and the Poor Get Prison

At 9:05 A.M. on the morning of Thursday, September, 9, 1971, a group of inmates forced their way through a gate at the center of the prison, fatally injured a guard named William Quinn, and took 50 hostages. The Attica uprising had begun. It lasted four days, until 9:43 A.M. on the morning of Monday, September 13, when corrections officers and state troopers stormed the prison and killed 29 inmates and 10 hostages.[118] During those four days the nation saw the faces of its captives on television—the hard black faces of young men who had grown up on the streets of Harlem and other urban ghettos. Theirs were the faces of crime in America. The television viewers who saw them were not surprised. Here were faces of dangerous men who should be locked up. Nor were people outraged when the state launched its murderous attack on the prison, killing many more inmates and guards than did the prisoners themselves. Maybe they were shocked—but not outraged. Neither were they outraged when two grand juries refused to indict any of the attackers, nor when the mastermind of the attack, Gov. Nelson Rockefeller, was named to be vice president of the United States three years after the uprising and massacre.[119]

They were not outraged because the faces they saw on the TV screens fit and confirmed their beliefs about who is a deadly threat to American society—and a deadly threat must be met with deadly force. How did those men get to Attica? How did Americans get their beliefs about who is a dangerous person? These questions are interwoven. People get their notions about who is a criminal at least in part from the occasional television or newspaper picture of who is inside our prisons. The individuals they see there have been put in prison because people believe certain kinds of individuals are dangerous and should be locked up.

I have argued in this chapter that this is not a simple process of selecting the dangerous and the criminal from among the peace-loving and the law-abiding. It is also a process of *weeding out the wealthy* at every stage, so that the final picture—a picture like that that appeared on the TV screen on September 9, 1971—is not a true reflection of the real dangers in our society but a distorted image, the kind reflected in a carnival mirror.

It is not my view that the inmates in Attica were innocent of the crimes that sent them there. I am willing to assume they and just about all the individuals in prisons in America are probably guilty of the crime for which they were sentenced and maybe more. My point is that people who are equally or more dangerous, equally or more criminal, are not there; that the criminal justice system works systematically not to punish and confine the dangerous and the criminal *but to punish and confine the poor who are dangerous and criminal.*

It is successful at all levels. In 1973, there were 204,211 individuals in state and federal prisons, or 96 prisoners for every 100,000 individuals (of all ages) in the general population. By 1979, state and federal inmates numbered 301,470, or 133 per 100,000 Americans. By mid-1992, there were 855,958 persons in state and federal prisons, a staggering 342 for every 100,000 individuals in the general population. Add to this the 426,479 inmates of local jails (as of mid-1991), and you have over 1,128,000 men and women currently behind bars in America: 513 prisoners for every 100,000 persons (of all ages and both sexes) in the U.S. population. However, of the 1,128,000 prisoners, at least 1 million are men, virtually all above the age of 18. Because the adult male population in the United States is 88.6 million, *this means that more than one out of every 100 American adult men is behind bars!*[120] This enormous number of prisoners is, of course, predominantly from the bottom of society.

Of the estimated 711,643 people in state prisons in June 1991, 33 percent were not employed at all (full or part time) prior to their arrests. About half of these were looking for work and half were not. Another 12 percent had only part-time jobs before prison, making fully 45 percent who were without full-time employment prior to arrest. These statistics represent a general worsening compared with 1986, when 31 percent of state inmates had no pre-arrest employment at all, and 43 percent had no full-time pre-arrest employment. Of those 1991 state inmates who had been free at least a year before arrest, 19 percent had some pre-arrest annual income but less than $3,000; and 50 percent had some pre-arrest annual income but less than $10,000.[121]

To get an idea of what part of society is in prison, we should compare these figures with comparable figures for the general population. Because 95 percent of state inmates are male, we can look at employment and income figures for males in the general society in 1990. Statistics on employment and income for 1990 are close to those for 1988 and 1989, and so will give us a fair sense of the general population from which the current state inmates came:

In 1990, 5.6 percent of males, 16-years-old and above, in the labor force were unemployed and looking for work. This corresponds to half the state inmates who were unemployed before arrest, because the other half who were unemployed was not looking for work. Where 16 percent of state prisoners had been unemployed and still looking for work, only 5.6 percent of males in the general population were in this condition. Thus, prisoners were unemployed at a rate at least three times that of males in the general population. But this doesn't give us the full picture, because it doesn't capture the unemployed prisoners who had not been seeking work. To capture that, let us assume that, as among the prisoners, the number of males in the general population who are unemployed and not looking is equal to the number who are unemployed and looking. (Note that this assumption is high, but for present purposes conservative, as the higher it is the more it will decrease the relative difference between prisoners and general male population.) The 5.6 percent represents approximately 3,799,000 persons. If we double it, we get 7,598,000 as an estimate of the total number of males in the general population who are unemployed, looking for work or not. As a percentage of the total noninstitutionalized population of males 16 and over, this is 8.5 percent. Compare this with the 33 percent of state inmates who were unemployed prior to being arrested. *Then, state prisoners were unemployed at a rate nearly four times that of males in the general population.*[122]

Where 19 percent of prisoners with any pre-arrest income at all earned less than $3,000 a year, 6.8 percent of males in the civilian labor force in 1990 earned between $1 and $2,499 a year, and 12.3 percent earned between $1 and $4,999. Fifty percent of the inmates had annual incomes between $1 and $10,000, while 25 percent of males in the general population earned in that range.[123]

Our prisoners are not a cross-section of America. They are considerably poorer and considerably less likely to be employed than the rest of Americans. Moreover, they are also less educated, which is to say less in possession of the means to improve their sorry situations. Of the state inmates, 36 percent had completed high school at least (about one-third of these, 12 percent, had some college).[124] More than 60 percent were high school dropouts! Compare this with the fact that 78.5 percent of males in the general population have completed at least four years of high school, and 42.5 percent have completed one or more years of college.[125]

The criminal justice system is sometimes thought of as a kind of sieve in which the innocent are progressively sifted out from the guilty, who end up behind bars. I have tried to show that the sieve works another way as well. It sifts the affluent out from the poor, so it is not merely the guilty who end up behind bars, but the *guilty poor.*

With this I think I have proven the hypotheses set forth in Chapter 2, in the section titled "Criminal Justice as Creative Art." The criminal justice system does not simply weed the peace-loving from the dangerous, the law-abiding from the criminal. At every stage, starting with the very definitions of crime and progressing through the stages of investigation, arrest, charging, conviction, and sentencing, the system *weeds out the wealthy.* It refuses to define as "crimes" or as serious crimes the dangerous and predatory acts of the well-to-do—acts that, as we have seen, result in the loss of thousands of lives and billions of dollars. Instead, the system focuses its attention on those crimes likely to be committed by members of the lower classes. Thus, it is no surprise to find that so many of the people behind bars are from the lower classes. The people we see in our jails and prisons are no doubt dangerous to society, but they are not *the danger* to society, not *the gravest danger* to society. Individuals who pose equal or greater threats to our well-being walk the streets with impunity.

In Chapter 1, I argued that the society fails to institute policies that have a good chance of reducing crime. In the present chapter and the previous one, I have argued that the criminal justice system works to make crime appear to be the monopoly of the poor by restricting the label crime to the dangerous acts of the poor and not those of the well off (previous chapter) and by more actively pursuing and prosecuting the poor rather than the well off for the acts labeled crime (present chapter). *The joint effect of all these phenomena is to maintain a real threat of crime that the vast majority of Americans believes is a threat from the poor.* The criminal justice system is a carnival mirror that throws back a distorted image of the dangers that lurk in our midst—and conveys the impression that those dangers are the work of the poor. In Chapter 4, I suggest who benefits from this illusion and how.

Summary

In this chapter, I have mainly tried to document that, *even among those dangerous acts that our criminal justice system labels as crimes,* the system works to make it more likely that those who end up in jail or prison will be from the bottom of society. This works in two broad ways: 1. *For the same crime,* the system is more likely to investigate and detect, arrest and charge, convict and sentence, sentence to prison and for a longer time, a lower-class individual than a middle- or upper-class individual. To support this we reviewed a large number of studies comparing the treatment of high and low socioeconomic offenders and of white and nonwhite offenders, from arrest through sentencing for the same crimes. 2. *Between crimes that are characteristically committed by poor people (street crimes) and those characteristically committed by the well off (white-collar and corporate crimes),* the system treats the former much more harshly than the latter, even when the crimes of the well off take more money from the public or cause more death and injury than the crimes of the poor. To support this we compared the sentences meted out for robbery with those for embezzlement, for grand theft, and Medicaid provider fraud, and we looked at the treatment of those responsible for death and destruction in the workplace as well as those responsible for the savings and loan scandal and the Watergate crimes.

Study Questions

1. Who is in our jails and prisons? How do the people behind bars in America compare with the general population in employment, wealth, and level of education?
2. What is meant by "white-collar crime"? How costly is it compared with the crimes on the FBI's Index?
3. What factors make it likelier that a poor person who commits a crime such as shoplifting or nonaggravated assault will get arrested than a middle-class person who commits the same crime?
4. What factors make it likelier that a middle- or upper-class person charged with a crime will get acquitted than a lower-class person charged with the same crime?
5. Are the people responsible for white-collar crime, including crimes that result in serious injury, more or less blameworthy than muggers? Do we punish white-collar criminals justly?
6. Is the criminal justice system racist? What evidence would establish or refute your view?
7. If killers of whites are more likely to get sentenced to death than killers of blacks, what should we do? Should we abolish the death penalty? Do you agree with the Supreme Court's decision in *McCleskey v. Kemp?* Why?

Additional Readings

CLINARD, MARSHALL. *Corporate Corruption: The Abuse of Power.* New York: Praeger, 1990.

DAY, KATHLEEN. *S & L Hell: The People and the Politics Behind the $1 Trillion Savings and Loan Scandal.* New York: Norton, 1993.

GEIS, GILBERT AND PAUL JESLOW. *White-Collar Crime.* Newbury Park, Calif.: Sage, 1993.

LUSANE, CLARENCE. *Pipe Dream Blues: Racism and the War on Drugs.* Boston: South End Press, 1991.

LYNCH, MICHAEL AND E. BRITT PATTERSON. *Race and Criminal Justice.* New York: Harrow and Heston, 1991.

PIZZO, STEPHEN *et al. Inside Job: The Looting of America's Savings and Loans.* New York: McGraw-Hill, 1989.

SIMON, DAVID AND STANLEY EITZEN. *Elite Deviance,* 4th ed. Boston: Allyn and Bacon, 1993.

TIMMER, DOUG AND STANLEY EITZEN. *Crimes in the Streets and Crimes in the Suites.* Boston: Allyn and Bacon, 1989.

WEISBURD, DAVID *et al. Crimes of the Middle Classes: White-Collar Offenders in the Federal Courts.* New Haven: Yale University Press, 1991.

Notes to Chapter 3

1. *Challenge,* p. 44.
2. Ronald Goldfarb, "Prisons: The National Poorhouse," *New Republic,* November 1, 1969, pp. 15–17.
3. Philip A. Hart, "Swindling and Knavery, Inc.," *Playboy,* August 1972, p. 158.
4. Compare the statement, written more than half a century ago, by Professor Edwin H. Sutherland, one of the major luminaries of twentieth-century criminology:

   > *First, the administrative processes are more favorable to persons in economic comfort than to those in poverty, so that if two persons on different economic levels are equally guilty of the same offense, the one on the lower level is more likely to be arrested, convicted, and committed to an institution. Second, the laws are written, administered, and implemented primarily with reference to the types of crimes committed by people of lower economic levels.* [E. H. Sutherland, *Principles of Criminology* (Philadelphia: Lippincott, 1939), p. 179].

5. For example, in 1991, when blacks made up 12 percent of the national population, they accounted for 46 percent of the U.S. state prison population. BJS, *Survey of State Prison Inmates, 1991,* p. 3.
6. Edwin H. Sutherland and Donald R.Cressey, *Criminology,* 9th ed. (Philadelphia: Lippincott, 1974), p. 133. The following studies are cited in support of this point (p. 133, note 4): Edwin M. Lemert and Judy Roseberg, "The Administration of Justice to Minority Groups in Los Angeles County," University of California Publications in Culture and Society 2, no. 1 (1948), pp. 1–28; Thorsten Sellin, "Race Prejudice in the Administration of Justice," *American Journal of Sociology* 41 (September 1935), pp. 212–217; Sidney Alexrad, "Negro and White Male Institutionalized Delinquents," *American Journal of Sociology* 57 (May 1952), pp. 569–74; Marvin E. Wolfgang, Arlene Kelly, and Hans C. Nolde, "Comparisons of the Executed and the Commuted Among Admissions to Death Row," *Journal of Criminal Law, Criminology, and Police Science* 53 (September 1962), pp. 301–11; Nathan Goldman, *The Differential Selection of Juvenile Offenders for Court Appearance* (New York: National Council on Crime and Delinquency, 1963); Irving Piliavin and Scott Briar, "Police Encounters with Juveniles," *American Journal of Sociology* 70 (September 1964), pp. 206–14; Robert M. Terry, "The Screening of Juvenile

Offenders," *Journal of Criminal Law, Criminology, and Police Science* 58 (June 1967), pp. 173–81. See also Ramsey Clark, *Crime in America* (New York: Simon And Schuster, 1970), p. 51: "Negroes are arrested more frequently and on less evidence than whites and are more often victims of mass or sweep arrests"; and Donald Taft, *Criminology*, 3d ed. (New York: Macmillan, 1956), p. 134:

> *Negroes are more likely to be suspected of crime than are whites. They are also more likely to be arrested. If the perpetrator of a crime is known to be a Negro the police may arrest all Negroes who were near the scene —a procedure they would rarely dare to follow with whites. After arrest Negroes are less likely to secure bail, and so are more liable to be counted in jail statistics. They are more liable than whites to be indicted and less likely to have their case nol prossed or otherwise dismissed. If tried, Negroes are more likely to be convicted. If convicted they are less likely to be given probation. For this reason they are more likely to be included in the count of prisoners. Negroes are also more likely than whites to be kept in prison for the full terms of their commitments and correspondingly less likely to be paroled.*

7. William Wilbanks, *The Myth of a Racist Criminal Justice System* (Monterey, Calif.: Brooks/Cole, 1987).

8. Ibid., pp. 64–65.

9. Computed from *Sourcebook-1992*, p. 287, Table 3.51; and *UCR-1991*, p. 231, Table no. 43.

10. For an overview of this double distortion, see Thomas J. Dolan, "The Case for Double Jeopardy: Black and Poor, " *International Journal of Criminology and Penology* 1 (1973), pp. 129–50.

11. *StatAbst-1992*, p. 456, Tables nos. 717, 718; see also Karen Pennar, "The Rich are Richer—and America May Be the Poorer," *Business Week*, November 18, 1991, pp. 85–88.

12. *StatAbst-1992*, p. 456, Table no. 717; and p. 460, Table no. 726; Carole Shammas, "A New Look at Long-Term Trends in Wealth Inequality in the United States," *American Historical Review* 98, no. 2 (April 1993), pp. 422.

13. *StatAbst-1992*, p. 399, Table no. 635.

14. *Sourcebook-1981*, p. 463.

15. *StatAbst-1988*, p. 175, Table no. 304.

16. Theodore Chiricos and William Bales, "Unemployment and Punishment: An Empirical Assessment, " *Criminology* 29, no. 4 (1991), p. 718.

17. "An offender's socioeconomic status . . . did not impact sentence length for any of the property offenses." Stewart J. D'Alession and Lisa Stolzenberg, "Socioeconomic Status and the Sentencing of the Traditional Offender," *Journal of Criminal Justice* 21 (1993), p. 73. The same study did find lower socioeconomic status offenders received harsher sentences for violent and moral order crimes. Another study that finds no greater likelihood of incarceration based on socioeconomic status is Michael Benson and Esteban Walker, "Sentencing the White-Collar Offender," *American Sociological Review* 53

(April 1988), pp. 294–302. And yet another found higher-status offenders to be more likely to be incarcerated. David Weisburd, Elin Waring, and Stanton Wheeler, "Class, Status, and the Punishment of White Collar Criminals," *Law and Social Inquiry* 15 (1990), pp. 223–41. These last two studies are limited to offenders convicted of white-collar crimes, and so they deal with a sample that has already been subject to whatever discrimination exists in the arrest, charging, and conviction of white-collar offenders.

18. Isidore Silver, "Introduction" to the Avon edition of *The Challenge of Crime in a Free Society* (New York: Avon, 1968), p. 31.

19. This is the conclusion of Austin L. Porterfield, *Youth in Trouble* (Fort Worth: Leo Potishman Foundation, 1946); Fred J. Murphy, M. Shirley, and H.L. Witmer, "The Incidence of Hidden Delinquency," *American Journal of Orthopsychiatry* 16 (October 1946), pp. 686–96; James F. Short Jr., "A Report on the Incidence of Criminal Behavior, Arrests, and Convictions in Selected Groups, " *Proceedings of the Pacific Sociological Society, 1954,* pp. 110–18, published as vol. 22, no. 2 of *Research Studies of the State College of Washington* (Pullman: State College of Washington, 1954); F. Ivan Nye, James F. Short Jr., and Virgil J. Olson, "Socioeconomic Status and Delinquent Behavior," *American Journal of Sociology* 63 (January 1958), pp. 381–89; Maynard L. Erickson and Lamar T. Empey, "Class Position, Peers and Delinquency," *Sociology and Social Research* 49 (April 1965), pp. 268–82; William J. Chambliss and Richard H. Nagasawa, "On the Validity of Official Statistics; A Comparative Study of White, Black, and Japanese High-School Boys," *Journal of Research in Crime and Delinquency* 6 (January 1969), pp. 71–77; Eugene Doleschal, "Hidden Crime," *Crime and Delinquency Literature* 2, no. 5 (October 1970), pp. 546–72; Nanci Koser Wilson, *Risk Ratios in Juvenile Delinquency* (Ann Arbor, Mich.: University Microfilms, 1972); and Maynard L. Erikson, "Group Violations, Socioeconomic Status, and Official Delinquency," *Social Forces* 52, no.1 (September 1973), pp. 41–52.

20. Charles R. Tittle and Robert F. Meier, "Specifying the SES/Delinquency Relationship," *Criminology* 28, no., 2 (1990), p. 292.

21. Gary F. Jensen and Kevin Thompson, "What's Class Got to Do with It? A Further Examination of Power-Control Theory," *American Journal of Sociology* 95, no. 4 (January 1990), p. 1021.

22. This is the conclusion of Martin Gold, "Undetected Delinquent Behavior," *Journal of Research in Crime and Delinquency* 3, no. 1 (1966), pp. 27–46; and of Sutherland and Cressey, *Criminology,* pp. 137, 220.

23. Cf. Larry Karacki and Jackson Toby, "The Uncommitted Adolescent: Candidate for Gang Socialization," *Sociological Inquiry* 32 (1962), pp. 203–15; William R. Arnold, "Continuities in Research—Scaling Delinquent Behavior," *Social Problems* 13, no. 1 (1965), pp. 59–66; Harwin L. Voss, "Socio-economic Status and Reported Delinquent Behavior," *Social Problems,* 13, no. 3 (1966), pp. 314–24; LaMar Empey and Maynard L. Erikson, "Hidden Delinquency and Social Status," *Social Forces* 44, no. 4 (1966), pp. 546–54; Fred J. Shanley, "Middle-class Delinquency As a Social Problem," *Sociology and Social*

Research 51 (1967), pp. 185–98; Jay R. Williams and Martin Gold, "From Delinquent Behavior to Official Delinquency," *Social Problems* 20, no. 2 (1972), pp. 209–29.

24. Empey and Erikson, "Hidden Delinquency and Social Status," pp. 549, 551. Nye, Short, and Olson also found destruction of property to be committed most frequently by upper-class boys and girls, "Socioeconomic Status and Delinquent Behavior," p. 385.

25. Williams and Gold, "From Delinquent Behavior to Official Delinquency," *Social Problems* 20, no. 2 (1972), pp. 209–29.

26. Gold, "Undetected Delinquent Behavior," p. 37.

27. Ibid., p. 44.

28. Comparing socioeconomic status categories "scant evidence is found that would support the contention that group delinquency is more characteristic of the lower-status levels than other socioeconomic status levels. In fact, only arrests seem to be more characteristic of the low-status category than the other categories." Erikson, "Group Violations, Socioeconomic Status and Official Delinquency," p. 15 (emphasis added).

29. Gold, "Undetected Delinquent Behavior," p. 28 (emphasis added).

30. Ibid., p. 38.

31. Terence P. Thornberry, "Race, Socioeconomic Status and Sentencing in the Juvenile Justice System," *Journal of Criminal Law and Criminology* 64, no. 1 (1973), pp. 90–98.

32. Robert Sampson, "Effects of Socioeconomic Context on Official Reaction to Juvenile Delinquency," *American Sociological Review* 51 (December 1986), pp. 876–85; Belinda R. McCarthy, "Social Structure, Crime, and Social Control: An Examination of Factors Influencing Rates and Probabilities of Arrest," *Journal of Criminal Justice* 19, (1991), pp. 19–29.

33. Note, "Developments in the Law—Race and the Criminal Process," *Harvard Law Review* 101 (1988), p. 1496.

34. James Fyfe, "Blind Justice: Police Shootings in Memphis," *Journal of Criminal Law and Criminology* 73 (1982), pp. 707, 718–20.

35. See, for example, D. Chapman, "The Stereotype of the Criminal and the Social Consequences," *International Journal of Criminology and Penology* 1 (1973), p. 24.

36. This view is widely held, although the degree to which it functions as a self-fulfilling prophecy is less widely recognized. Versions of this view can be seen in *Challenge*, p. 79; Jerome Skolnick, *Justice Without Trial* (New York: Wiley, 1966), pp. 45–48, 217–218; and Jessica Mitford, *Kind and Usual Punishment*, p. 53. Piliavin and Briar write in "Police Encounters with Juveniles":

> *Compared to other youths, Negroes and boys whose appearance matched the delinquent stereotype were more frequently stopped and interrogated by patrolmen—often even in the absence of evidence that an offense had been committed—usually were given more severe dispositions for the same violations. Our data suggest, however, that these*

selective apprehension and disposition practices resulted not only from the intrusion of long-held prejudices of individual police officers but also from certain job-related experiences of law-enforcement personnel. First, the tendency of police to give more severe dispositions to Negroes and to youths whose appearance correspond to that which police associated with delinquents partly reflected the fact, observed in this study, that these youths also were much more likely than were other types of boys to exhibit the sort of recalcitrant demeanor which police construed as a sign of the confirmed delinquent. Further, officers assumed, partly on the basis of departmental statistics, that Negroes and juveniles who "look tough" (e.g. who wear chinos, leather jackets, boots, etc.) commit crimes more frequently than do other types of youths. [p. 212]

Cf. Albert Reiss, *The Police and the Public* (New Haven, Conn.: Yale University Press, 1971). Reiss attributes the differences to the differences in the actions of complainants.

37. Richard J. Lundman, for example, found higher arrest rates to be associated with "offender powerlessness." "Routine Police Arrest Practices: A Commonweal Perspective," *Social Problems* 22, no. 1 (October 1974), pp. 127–41.

38. William Bales, "Race and Class Effects on Criminal Justice Prosecution and Punishment Decisions." (unpublished Ph.D. dissertation, Florida State University, 1987).

39. Note, "Developments in the Law—Race and the Criminal Process," *Harvard Law Review* 101 (1988), p 1520.

40. Spohn, Gruhl, and Welch, "The Impact of the Ethnicity and Gender of Defendants on the Decision to Reject or Dismiss Felony Charges," *Criminology* 25 (1987), pp. 175, 180, 185.

41. "Stealing $200 Billion the Respectable Way, " *U.S. News and World Report*, May 20, 1985, p. 83.

42. Marshall B. Clinard, *Corporate Corruption: The Abuse of Corporate Power* (New York: Praeger, 1990), p. 15.

43. Michael Levi, *Regulating Fraud: White-Collar Crime and the Criminal Process* (London: Tavistock, 1987), p. 33; *StatAbst-1992*, p.831, Table no. 1371.

44. North American Securities Administrators Administration, *The NASAA Survey of Fraud and Abuse in the Financial Planning Industry—Report to the U.S. Senate Subcommittee on Consumer Affairs, Committee on Banking, Housing and Urban Affairs* (Washington, D.C., July 1988), pp. 1–2.

45. Chamber of Commerce of the United States, *A Handbook on White Collar Crime* (Washington, D.C., 1974), p. 6. Copyright © 1974 by the Chamber of Commerce of the United States. Table reprinted by permission of the Chamber of Commerce of the United States.

46. Kenneth Rosenblatt quotes the accounting firm of Ernst and Young, which estimates the cost of computer crime at between $3 billion to $5 billion a year.

Roger Doost puts the cost at $6 billion. See Kenneth Rosenblatt, "Deterring Computer Crime," *Technology Review* 93 (February-March 1990), p. 34; and Roger Doost, "Accounting Irregularities and Computer Fraud," *National Public Accountant* 35, no. 5 (May 1990), p. 36.

47. BJS, *Drugs, Crime and the Justice System* (December 1992), p. 62.

48. "At year end 1992, MasterCard International reported worldwide fraud losses of $382.5 million, up 17 percent from 1991. And Visa reported worldwide fraud losses of $719.3 million for the 12 months ending September 30, 1992, a 26.7 percent increase from the same period in 1991." Linda Punch, "Battling Credit Card Fraud," *Bank Management* 69, no. 3 (March 1993), p. 18. These are worldwide figures, not just for the United States. However, they represent only two credit card companies. Another observer maintains that 1989 credit card fraud in the United States exceeded $1 billion. Jerry Godfrey, "The Three 'Rs' of Credit Card Fraud," *Target Marketing* 13, no. 6 (June 1990), p. 28.

49. Robert McGough and Elicia Brown, "Thieves at Work," *Financial World* 159 (December 11, 1990), p. 18.

50. For the National Insurance Crime Bureau estimate, see David Sullivan, "Another Perspective: It Takes Teamwork to Fight Insurance Fraud," *National Underwriter* 96, no. 33 (August 17, 1992), p. 21. See also "Insurance Fraud Costing $67 Billion Annually," *National Underwriter* 96, no. 38 (September 21, 1992), p. 39.

51. Gretchen Morgenson, "Are You a Born Sucker?" *Forbes* 141 (June 27, 1988), p. 270.

52. *UCR-1991,* pp. 6, 26, 27, 36.

53. Sutherland and Cressey, *Criminology,* p. 41 (emphasis added).

54. Marshall B. Clinard, *Corporate Corruption: The Abuse of Power* (New York: Praeger, 1990), p. 15.

55. David Weisburd, Ellen F. Chayet, and Elin J. Waring, "White-Collar Crime and Criminal Careers: Some Preliminary Findings," *Crime & Delinquency* 36, no. 3 (July 1990), p. 352.

56. Clinard, *Corporate Corruption: The Abuse of Power,* p. 15.

57. Susan Shapiro, "The Road Not Taken: The Elusive Path to Criminal Prosecution for White-Collar Offenders," *Law and Society Review* 19, no. 2 (1985), p. 182.

58. *UCR-1991,* p. 213.

59. See, for example, Theodore G. Chiricos, Philip D. Jackson, and Gordon P. Waldo, "Inequality in the Imposition of a Criminal Label," *Social Problems* 19, no. 4 (Spring 1972), pp. 553–572.

60. *Sourcebook-1981,* p. 462; and BJS, *Correctional Populations in the United States, 1990,* p. 8, Table no. 2.2. The figures from 1990 come from the *Annual Survey of Jails,* which may overestimate the number of unconvicted inmates. Some facilities do not distinguish between unconvicted inmates and those convicted but awaiting sentence, both of which are counted as unconvicted.

61. See, for example, C. E. Ares, A. Rankin, and J .H. Sturz, "The Manhattan Bail Project: An Interim Report on the Use of Pre-trial Parole," *NYU Law Review* 38 (1963), p. 67; C. Foote, "Compelling Appearances in Court-Administration of Bail in Philadelphia," *University of Pennsylvania Law Review* 102 (1954), pp. 1031–1079; and C. Foote, "A Study of the Administration of Bail in New York City," *University of Pennsylvania Law Review* 106 (1958), p. 693. For statistics on persons held in jail awaiting trial, see U.S. Bureau of the Census, *The Social and Economic Status of the Black Population in the U.S.,* 1974 (Washington, D.C.: U.S. Government Printing Office, 1975), p. 171; and USLEAA *Survey of Inmates in Local Jails 1972—Advance Report* (Washington, D.C.: U.S. Government Printing Office, 1974), pp. 5, 8.

62. Theodore Chiricos and William Bales, "Unemployment and Punishment: An Empirical Assessment," *Criminology* 29, no. 4 (1991), p. 712.

63. Blumberg, *Criminal Justice,* pp. 28–29; *Challenge,* p. 134; and Donald J. Newman, *Conviction: The Determination of Guilt or Innocence without Trial* (Boston: Little, Brown, 1966), p. 3.

64. A good summary of these developments can be found in Joel Jay Finer, "Ineffective Assistance of Counsel," *Cornell Law Review* 58, no. 6 (July 1973), pp. 1077–1120.

65. See, for example, Dallin H. Oaks and Warren Lehman, "Lawyers for the Poor," in *Law and Order: The Scales of Justice,* ed., A. Blumberg, pp. 92–93; also Jerome H. Skolnick, "Social Control in the Adversary System," in *Criminal Justice: Law and Politics,* ed., George Cole (Belmont, Calif.: Duxbury, 1972), pp. 266. "The National Legal Aid and Defender Association has suggested that experienced attorneys handle no more than 150 felony cases per year, rather than the case load of over 500 felony cases per attorney with which some public defender offices in major cities are burdened." Finer, "Ineffective Assistance of Counsel," p. 1120.

66. In several essays, Abraham S. Blumberg has described the role of the public defender as an officer of the court bureaucracy rather than as a defender of the accused. See his "Lawyers with Convictions," in *Law and Order: The Scales of Justice,* pp. 51–67; "The Practice of Law as Confidence Game: Organizational Cooptation of a Profession," in *Criminal Law in Action,* ed., William J. Chambliss (Santa Barbara, Calif.: Hamilton, 1975), pp. 262–75; and his book *Criminal Justice* (Chicago: Quadrangle, 1967), especially pp. 13–115.

67. Jonathan D. Casper, "Did You Have a Lawyer When You Went to Court? No, I Had a Public Defender," in *Criminal Justice: Law and Politics,* ed., Cole, pp. 239–40.

68. Dean J. Champion, "Private Counsels and Public Defenders: A Look at Weak Cases, Prior Records, and Leniency in Plea Bargaining," *Journal of Criminal Justice* 17, no. 4 (1989), pp. 253–63.

69. Of those defendants convicted in U.S. district courts in 1971, 46 percent had assigned lawyers (including public defenders); of those acquitted, 37.5 percent had assigned counsel; and of those dismissed, only 33.3 percent had assigned counsel. *Sourcebook-1974,* p. 388.

70. Robert Johnson, *Condemned to Die: Life Under Sentence of Death* (New York: Elsevier, 1981), p. 138; Stephen Gettinger, *Sentenced to Die: The People, the Crimes, and the Controversy* (New York: Macmillan, 1979), p. 261.

71. "Death-Row Inmates Often Lack Help for Appeals, But Few Lawyers Want to Do Distasteful Work," *Wall Street Journal,* August 27, 1987, p. 48.
72. Richard Lacayo, "You Don't Always Get Perry Mason," *Time,* June 1, 1992, pp. 38–39.
73. "When Are the Savings and Loan Crooks Going to Jail?" *Hearing before the Subcommittee on Financial Institutions Supervision, Regulation and Insurance of the Committee on Banking, Finance and Urban Affairs, House of Representatives, 101st Congress, 2d Session, June 28, 1990* (Washington, D.C.: U.S. Government Printing Office, 1990), pp. 1, 21.
74. Lesley Oelsner, "Wide Disparities Mark Sentences Here," *New York Times,* September 27, 1972, p. 1.
75. Nagel, "The Tipped Scales of American Justice," p. 39.
76. Doleschal and Klapmuts, "Toward a New Criminology," *Crime and Delinquency Literature* 5 (December 1973), p. 613; reporting the findings of Terence Patrick Thornberry, *Punishment and Crime: The Effect of Legal Dispositions on Subsequent Criminal Behavior* (Ann Arbor, Mich.: University Microfilms, 1972).
77. Terence P. Thornberry, "Sentencing Disparities in the Juvenile Justice System," *Journal of Criminal Law and Criminology* 70, no. 2 (Summer 1979), pp. 164–71, especially p. 170.
78. Steven H. Clarke and Gary G. Koch, "The Influence of Income and Other Factors on Whether Criminal Defendants Go to Prison," *Law and Society Review* (Fall 1976), pp. 57–92, especially pp. 81, 83–84.
79. Alan J. Lizotte, "Testing the Conflict Model of Criminal Justice," *Social Problems* 25, no. 5 (1978), pp. 564–80, especially p. 564.
80. Stewart J. D'Alession and Lisa Stolzenberg, "Socioeconomic Status and the Sentencing of the Traditional Offender," *Journal of Criminal Justice* 21 (1993), pp. 71–74.
81. Barbara C. Nienstedt, Marjorie Zatz, and Thomas Epperlein, "Court Processing and Sentencing of Drinking Drivers," *Journal of Quantitative Criminology* 4, no. 1 (1988), pp. 39–59.
82. Theodore Chiricos and William Bales, "Unemployment and Punishment: An Empirical Assessment," *Criminology* 29, no. 4 (1991), pp. 701–24.
83. Belinda R. McCarthy, "A Micro-Level Analysis of Social Control: Intrastate Use of Jail and Prison Confinement," *Justice Quarterly* 7, no. 2 (June 1990), pp. 334–35.
84. Dean J. Champion, "Private Counsels and Public Defenders: A Look at Weak Cases, Prior Records, and Leniency in Plea Bargaining," p. 143.
85. T. Miethe and C. Moore, "Socioeconomic Disparities Under Determinate Sentencing Systems: A Comparison of Preguideline and Postguideline Practices in Minnesota," *Criminology* 23, no. 2 (1985), p. 358.
86. Robert Tillman and Henry Pontell, "Is Justice 'Collar-Blind'?: Punishing Medicaid Provider Fraud," *Criminology* 30, no. 4 (1992), pp. 547–73, quote from p. 560.
87. James F. Nelson, "Hidden Disparities in Case Processing: New York State, 1985–1986," *Journal of Criminal Justice* 20 (1992), pp. 181–200.

88. Unnever and Hembroff, "The Prediction of Racial/Ethnic Sentencing Disparities," *Journal of Research in Crime and Delinquency* 25 (1988), p. 53.

89. BJS, *Correctional Populations in the United States, 1990,* p. 50; *UCR-1991,* p. 231; *Sourcebook-1987,* pp. 376, 491, 518; *Sourcebook-1992,* p. 492, Table no. 5.21.

90. "Blacks Receive Stiffer Sentences," *Boston Globe*, April 4, 1979, pp. 1, 50f.

91. Randall Thomson and Matthew Zingraff, "Detecting Sentencing Disparity: Some Problems and Evidence," *American Journal of Sociology* 86, no. 4 (1981), pp. 869–80, especially p. 875.

92. J. Unnever, C. Frazier, and J. Henretta, "Race Differences in Criminal Sentencing," *Sociological Quarterly* 21 (Spring 1980), pp. 197–205, especially p. 204.

93. J. Petersilia, "Racial Disparities in the Criminal Justice System: A Summary," *Crime & Delinquency* 31, no. 1 (1985), p. 28. See also G. Bridges and R. Crutchfield, "Law, Social Standing and Racial Disparities in Imprisonment," *Social Forces* 66, no. 3 (1988), pp. 699–724.

94. M. Myers, "Economic Inequality and Discrimination in Sentencing," *Social Forces* 65, no. 3 (1987), p. 761.

95. Barbara S. Meierhoefer, *The General Effect of Mandatory Minimum Prison Terms: A Longitudinal Study of Federal Sentences Imposed* (Washington, D.C.: Federal Judicial Center, 1992), especially pp. 1, 20, 25. Between October 1989 and 1990, 46 percent of whites received federal sentences below the mandatory minimum, but 32 percent of blacks did. *Sourcebook-1991,* p. 542, Table no. 5.43

96. William J. Bowers and Glenn L. Pierce, "Racial Discrimination and Criminal Homicide Under Post-Furman Capital Statutes," in *The Death Penalty in America,* ed., H. A. Bedau (New York: Oxford University Press, 1982), pp. 206–24.

97. *McCleskey v. Kemp,* 107 S. Ct. 1756 (1987). The research central to this case was that of David Baldus, reported in D. Baldus, C. Pulaski, and G. Woodworth, "Comparative Review of Death Sentences: An Empirical Study of the Georgia Experience," *Journal of Criminal Law and Criminology* 74 (1983), pp. 661–725. Other studies that support the notion of discrimination in capital sentencing based on race of victim are R. Paternoster, "Race of Victim and Location of Crime: The Decision to Seek the Death Penalty in South Carolina," *Journal of Criminal Law and Criminology* 74, no. 3 (1983), pp. 754–88; R. Paternoster, "Prosecutorial Discretion in Requesting the Death Penalty: A Case of Victim Based Racial Discrimination," *Law and Society Review* 18 (1984), pp. 437–78; S. Gross and R. Mauro, "Patterns of Death: An Analysis of Racial Disparities in Capital Sentencing and Homicide Victimization," *Stanford Law Review* 37 (1984), pp. 27–120; Radelet and Pierce, "Race and Prosecutorial Discretion in Homicide Cases," *Law and Society Review* 19 (1985), pp. 587, 615–19.

98. Anthony G. Amsterdam, "Race and the Death Penalty," in S. Gold, ed., *Moral Controversies* (Belmont, Calif.: Wadsworth, 1993), pp. 268–69.

99. United States General Accounting Office, Report to the Senate and House Committees on the Judiciary, *Death Penalty Sentencing: Research Indicates Pattern of Racial Disparities* (February 1990), especially p. 5.
100. Marvin E. Wolfgang, Arlene Kelly, and Hans C. Nolde, "Comparison of the Executed and the Commuted Among Admissions to Death Row," in *Crime and Justice in Society,* ed., Quinney, pp. 508, 513.
101. "Antitrust: Kauper's Last Stand," *Newsweek,* June 21, 1976, p. 70. On December 21, 1974, the "Antitrust Procedures and Penalty Act" was passed, striking out the language of the Sherman Antitrust Act, which made price fixing a misdemeanor punishable by a maximum sentence of one year in prison. According to the new law, price fixing is a felony punishable by up to three years in prison. Because prison sentences were a rarity under the old law and usually involved only 30 days in jail when actually imposed, there is little reason to believe the new law will strike fear in the hearts of corporate crooks.
102. Clinard and Yeager, *Corporate Crime,* pp. 291–92.
103. Ibid., p. 153.
104. *Washington Post,* March 2, 1990, pp. A1, A20; April 1, 1990, p. C3; April 28, 1990, pp. A1, A14; April 27, 1991, p. A6.
105. K. Johnson, "Federal Court Processing of Corporate, White Collar, and Common Crime Economic Offenders over the Past Three Decades," *Mid-American Review of Sociology* 11, no. 1 (1986), pp. 25–44.
106. J. Hagan and A. Palloni, "Club Fed' and the Sentencing of White-Collar Offenders Before and After Watergate," *Criminology* 24, no. 4 (1986), pp. 616–17. See also J. Hagan and P. Parker, "White-Collar Crime and Punishment: The Class Structure and Legal Sanctioning of Securities Violations," *American Sociological Review* 50 (1985), pp. 302–16.
107. Laurie Grossman, "Owner Sentenced to Nearly 20 Years Over Plant Fire," *Wall Street Journal,* September 15, 1992, p. A10.
108. "Company in Mine Deaths Set to Pay Big Fine," *New York Times,* February 21, 1993, p. 19.
109. This summary of the history leading up to the S&L debacle is based on Henry Pontell and Kitty Calavita, "White-Collar Crime in the Savings and Loan Scandal," *Annals of the American Academy of Political and Social Science* 525 (January 1993), pp. 31–45.
110. See Kathleen Day, *S&L Hell: The People and the Politics Behind the Savings and Loan Scandal* (New York: Norton, 1993).
111. Pontell and Calavita, "White-Collar Crime in the Savings and Loan Scandal," p. 32, citing: U.S. General Accounting Office, *Failed Thrifts: Internal Control Weaknesses Create an Environment Conducive to Fraud, Insider Abuse and Related Unsafe Practices,* Statement of Frederick D. Wolf, Assistant Comptroller General, before the subcommittee on Criminal Justice, Committee on the Judiciary, House of Representatives, March 22, 1989; and U.S. Congress, House, Committee on Government Operations, *Combatting Fraud, Abuse and Misconduct in the Nation's Financial Institutions,* 72d report by the Committee on Government Operations, October 13, 1989.

112. Pontell and Calavita, "White-Collar Crime in the Savings and Loan Scandal," p. 37.

113. Alan Fornham "S&L Felons," *Fortune,* November 5, 1990, p. 92.

114. Susan Schmidt, "Tiny Portion of S&L Fines Recovered," *Washington Post,* February 7, 1992, p. A1.

115. Stephen Pizzo and Paul Muolo, "Take the Money and Run: A Rogues Gallery of Some Lucky S&L Thieves," *New York Times Magazine,* May 9, 1993, p. 26.

116. "When Are the Savings and Loans Crooks Going to Jail?," p. 2.

117. "House Votes to End Subsidies to ex-Presidents,"*Washington Times,* June 19, 1993, p. A4. Actually, the House didn't vote to end all subsidies, only to cut back on some of the perks.

118. Tom Wicker, *A Time to Die* (New York: Quadrangle, 1975), pp. 311, 314.

119. Ibid., p. 310.

120. *Sourcebook-1987,* p. 486; BJS, *Correctional Populations in the United States, 1985,* p. 10, Table no. 2.6; *StatAbst-1988,* p. 13. Table no. 13; BJS, *National Update,* January 1993, pp. 8, 10.

121. BJS, *Survey of State Prison Inmates, 1991,* p. 3.

122. *StatAbst-1992,* p. 383, Table no. 612.

123. *StatAbst-1992,* p. 453, Table no. 711.

124. BJS, *Survey of State Prison Inmates, 1991,* p. 3. Another 25 percent had obtained a general equivalency diploma (GED), technically equivalent to a high school diploma but practically not as useful in getting employment.

125. *StatAbst-1992,* p. 144, Table no. 221.

4

To the Vanquished Belong the Spoils: Who is Winning the Losing War Against Crime?

In every case the laws are made by the ruling party in its own interest; a democracy makes democratic laws, a despot autocratic ones, and so on. By making these laws they define as "just" for their subjects whatever is for their own interest, and they call anyone who breaks them a "wrongdoer" and punish him accordingly.

Thrasymachus, in Plato's *Republic*

Why Is the Criminal Justice System Failing?

The streams of my argument flow together at this point in a question: *Why is it happening?* I have shown how it is no accident that "the offender at the end of the road in prison is likely to be a member of the lowest social and economic groups in the country."[1] I have shown that this is not an accurate group portrait of who threatens society—it is a picture of whom the criminal justice systems *selects* for arrest and imprisonment from among those who threaten society. It is an image distorted by the shape of the criminal justice carnival mirror. This much we have seen and now we want to know why: *Why is the criminal justice system allowed to function in a fashion that neither protects society nor achieves justice? Why is the criminal justice system failing?*

My answer to these questions will require looking at who benefits from this failure and who suffers from it. More particularly, I will argue that the rich and powerful in America, those who derive the greatest advantage from the persistence of the social and economic system as it is currently organized, reap benefits from the failure of criminal justice that has been documented in this book. However—as I cautioned early on—this should not lead the reader to think that my explanation for the current shape of the criminal justice system is a "conspiracy theory."

A conspiracy theory would argue that the rich and the powerful, seeing the benefits to be derived from the failure of criminal justice, consciously set out to use their wealth and power to make it fail. There are many problems with such a theory. First, it is virtually impossible to prove. If the conspiracy succeeds, then this is possible only to the extent that it is kept secret. Thus, evidence for a conspiracy would be as difficult to obtain as the conspiracy was successful. Second, conspiracy theories strain credibility precisely because the degree of secrecy they would require seems virtually impossible in a society as open and fractious as our own. If there is a "ruling elite" in the United States that comprises a group as small as the richest *one thousandth of 1 percent* of the population, it would still be made up of more than 2,000 people. To think that a conspiracy to make the criminal justice system fail in the way it does could be kept secret among this number of people in a country like ours is just unbelievable. Third, conspiracy theories are not plausible because they do not correspond to the way most people act most of the time. Although there is no paucity of conscious mendacity and manipulation in our politics, most people most of the time seem sincerely to believe that what they are doing is right. Whether this is a tribute to human beings' creative capacities to rationalize what they do or just a matter of shortsightedness, it seems a fact. For all these reasons, it is not plausible that so fateful and harmful a policy as the failure of criminal justice could be purposely maintained by the rich and powerful. Rather, we need an explanation that is compatible with believing that policymakers, on the whole, are simply doing what they sincerely believe is right.

To understand how the Pyrrhic defeat theory explains the current shape of our failing criminal justice policy, note that this failure is really *three* failures that work together. First, there is the failure to implement policies that stand a good chance of reducing crime and the harm it causes. (This was argued in Chapter 1). Second, there is the failure to identify as crimes the harmful acts of the rich and powerful. (This is the first of the hypotheses listed on page 59 in Chapter 2 and it is confirmed by the evidence presented in Chapter 2.) Third, there is the failure to eliminate economic bias in the criminal justice system, so that the poor continue to have a substantially greater chance than better-off people of being arrested, charged, convicted, and penalized for committing the acts that are treated as crimes. (This corresponds to the second through fourth hypotheses listed on page 59 in Chapter 2 and is confirmed by the evidence presented in Chapter 3.) The effect of the first failure is that there remains a large amount of crime—even if crime rates occasionally dip as a result of factors outside the control of the criminal justice system, such as the decline in the number of 15- to 24-year-olds. The effect of the second failure is that the acts identified as crimes are predominantly done by the poor. The effect of the third failure is that the individuals who are arrested and convicted for crimes are predominantly poor people. The effect of the three failures working together is that we are largely unprotected against the harmful acts of the well off, while at the same time we are confronted on the streets and in our homes with a real and large threat of crime and in the courts and prisons with a large and visible population of poor criminals. In short, the effect of current criminal justice policy is at once to narrow the public's conception of what is dangerous to acts of the poor *and* to present a convincing embodiment of this danger.

The Pyrrhic defeat theory aims to explain the *persistence* of this failing criminal justice policy, rather than its origins. The criminal justice system we have originated as a result of complex historical factors that have to do with the development of the common law tradition in England, the particular form in which this was transplanted on American soil, and the zigzagging course of reform and reaction that has marked our history since the English colonies were transformed into an independent American nation. The study of these factors would surely require another book longer than this one—but, more important, for our purposes it would be unnecessary because it is not the origin of criminal justice policy and practices that is puzzling. The focus on one-on-one harm reflects the main ways in which people harmed each other in the days before large-scale industrialization; the refusal to implement policies that might reduce crime (such as gun control or legalization of heroin or amelioration of poverty) reflects a defensive and punitive response to crime that is natural and understandable, if not noble and farsighted; and the existence of economic bias in the criminal justice system reflects the real economic and political inequalities that characterize the society in which that system is embedded. What is puzzling, then, is not how these policies came to be what they are but why they persist in the face of their failure to achieve either security of justice. The explanation I shall offer for this persistence I call "historical inertia."

The historical inertia explanation argues that current criminal justice policy persists because it fails in a way that does not give rise to an effective demand for change, for two reasons: First, this failing system provides benefits for those with the power to make changes, while it imposes costs on those without such power. Second, because the criminal justice system shapes the public's conception of what is dangerous, it creates the impression that the harms it is fighting are *the real* threats to society— thus, even when people see that the system is less than a roaring success, they generally do no more than demand more of the same: more police, more prisons, longer prison sentences, and so on.

Consider first the benefits that the system provides for those with wealth and power. I have argued that the triple failure of criminal justice policy diverts attention from the harmful (noncriminal) acts of the well off and confronts us in our homes and on our streets with a real substantial threat of crime and in the courts and prisons with a large and visible population of poor criminals. This in turn conveys a vivid image to the American people, namely, that *there is a real threat to our lives and limbs, and it is a threat from the poor.* This image provides benefits to the rich and powerful in America. It carries an *ideological message* that serves to protect their wealth and privilege. Crudely put, the message is this:

- *The threat to "law-abiding Middle America" comes from below them on the economic ladder, not above them.*
- *The poor are morally defective, and thus their poverty is their own fault, not a symptom of social or economic injustice.*

The effect of this message is to funnel the discontent of middle Americans into hostility toward, and fear of, the poor. It leads Americans to ignore the ways in which they are injured and robbed by the acts of the affluent (as catalogued in Chapter 2) and leads them to demand harsher doses of "law and order" aimed mainly at the lower classes. Most important, it nudges middle Americans toward a *conservative* defense of American society with its large disparities of wealth, power, and opportunity—and nudges them away from a progressive demand for equality and an equitable distribution of wealth and power.

On the other hand, but equally important, is that those who are mainly victimized by the "failure" to reduce crime are by and large the poor themselves. The people who are hurt the most by the failure of the criminal justice system are those with the least power to change the system. The Department of Justice's *National Criminal Victimization Survey* says of 1991, "In general, persons from households with low incomes experienced higher violent crime victimization rates than did persons from wealthier households. Persons from households with an income under $7,500 had significantly higher rates of robbery and assault than persons in most other income groups, particularly those from households earning $50,000 or more."[2] For 1991, households with less than $7,500 had 59.4 crimes of violence per 1,000 persons aged 12 and older. The rate was 25.0 for families earning $30,000 to $49,999; families above $50,000 had a rate of 19.9 per 1,000.

For 1991, the rate of completed robberies with injury for those with family income less than $7,500 was 2.4 per 1,000 persons age 12 and over; for those with family income of $30,000 to $49,999, it was 0.5; and for those with $50,000 or more, it was 0.7 (the estimates in these two upper brackets are based on ten or fewer sample cases). Attempted robbery with injury adds another 2.2 victimizations to the poor group; for the $30,000 to $49,000 group it adds 0.3 (based on ten or fewer cases), and 0.8 for the $50,000 and above group. There were 8.3 aggravated assaults with injury per 1,000 persons age 12 and over in households earning less than $7,500; 2.3 per 1,000 in households earning from $25,000 to $29,999; 2.2 per 1,000 in households earning from $30,000 to $49,999 and 1.2 per 1,000 in households earning $50,000 and above. There were 61.6 completed burglaries per 1,000 households with income less than $7,500. This group is victimized 63 percent more frequently than those who make $25,000 to $29,999 (rate: 37.8 per 1,000). They are victimized 86 percent more frequently than those who make $30,000 to $49,999 (rate: 33.1 per 1,000). And they are victimized 77 percent more frequently than those with a family income of $50,000 or more (rate: 34.9 per 1,000).[3]

The difference in the rates of property crime victimization between rich and poor understates the difference in the harms that result. The poor are far less likely than the affluent to have insurance against theft, and because they have little to start with, what they lose to theft takes a much deeper bite out of their ability to meet their basic needs. Needless to add, the various noncriminal harms documented in Chapter 2 (occupational hazards, pollution, poverty, and so on) also fall more harshly on workers and those at the bottom of society than on those at the top.

To summarize, those who suffer most from the failure to reduce crime (and the failure to treat noncriminal harms as crimes) are not in a position to change criminal justice policy. Those who are in a position to change the policy are not seriously harmed by its failure—indeed, there are actual benefits to them from that failure. Note that I have not said that criminal justice policy is created to achieve this distribution of benefits and burdens. Instead, my claim is that the criminal justice policy that has emerged piecemeal over time and usually with the best of intentions happens to produce this distribution of benefits. And because criminal justice policy happens to

produce this distribution, there is no inclination to change the criminal justice system among people with the power to do so. Moreover, because the criminal justice system shapes the public's conception of what is dangerous, it effectively limits its conception of how to protect itself to more of the same. Thus, though it fails, it persists.

My argument in the remainder of this chapter takes the following form. In the section titled "The Poverty of Criminals and the Crime of Poverty," I spell out the content of the ideological message broadcast by the failure of the criminal justice system. In the section titled "Ideology, or How to Fool Enough of the People Enough of the Time," I discuss the *nature* of ideology in general and the *need* for it in America. For those who doubt that our legal system could function in such questionable ways, I also present evidence on how the criminal justice system has been used in the past to protect the rich and powerful against those who would challenge their privileges or their policies. These sections, then, flesh out the historical inertia explanation of the failure of criminal justice by showing the ideological benefits that that failure yields and to whom.

Ultimately, the test of the argument in this chapter is whether it provides a plausible explanation of the failure of criminal justice and draws the arguments of the previous chapters together into a coherent theory of contemporary criminal justice policy and practice.

The Poverty of Criminals and the Crime of Poverty

Criminal justice is a very visible part of the American scene. As fact and fiction, countless images of crime and the struggle against it assail our senses daily, even hourly. In every newspaper, in every TV or radio newscast, there is at least one criminal justice story and often more. It is as if we live in an embattled city, besieged by the forces of crime and bravely defended by the forces of the law, and as we go about our daily tasks, we are always conscious of the war raging not very far away. Newspapers bring us daily and newscasts bring us hourly reports from the "front." Between reports, we are vividly reminded of the stakes and the desperateness of the battle by fictionalized portrayals of the struggle between the forces of the law and the breakers of the law. There is scarcely an hour on television without some dramatization of the struggle against crime. (A report to the Federal Communications Commission estimates that by the time the average American child reaches age 14, he or she has seen 13,000 human beings killed by violence on television. Although a few of these are killed by science fiction monsters, the figure still suggests that the extent of the impact of the televised portrayal of crime and the struggle against it on the imaginations of Americans is nothing short of astounding—particularly on children: As of 1990, American children aged 2 to 5 were watching on average 27 hours of TV a week.)[4] In the mid-1980s, it was estimated that "detective, police, and other criminal justice-related programs accounted for some eighty percent of prime-time TV viewing."[5] If we add to this the news accounts, the panel discussions, the movies, the novels, the comic books, and the TV cartoon shows that imitate the comics, as well as the political speeches about crime, there can be no doubt that as fact or fantasy or both, criminal justice is vividly present in the imaginations of most Americans.

This is no accident. Everyone can relate to criminal justice in personal and emotional terms. Everyone has some fear of crime, and as we saw in Chapter 3, just about everyone has committed some. Everyone knows the primitive satisfaction of seeing justice done and the evildoers served up their just deserts. Furthermore, in reality or in fiction, criminal justice is naturally dramatic. It contains the acts of courage and cunning, the high risks and high stakes, and the life-and-death struggle between good and evil missing from the routine lives so many of us lead. To identify with the struggle against crime is to expand one's experience vicariously to include the danger, the suspense, the triumphs, the meaningfulness—in a word, the drama—often missing in ordinary life. How else can we explain the seemingly bottomless appetite Americans have for the endless repetition, in only slightly altered form, of the same theme: the struggle of the forces of law against the forces of crime? Criminal justice has a firm grip on the imaginations of Americans and is thus in a unique position to convey a message to Americans and to convey it with drama and with conviction.

Let us now look at this message in detail. Our task falls naturally into two parts. There is an ideological message supportive of the status quo, built into *any* criminal justice system by its very nature. Even if the criminal justice system were not failing, even if it were not biased against the poor, it would still—by its very nature—broadcast a message supportive of established institutions. This is the *implicit ideology of criminal justice.* Beyond this, there is an additional ideological message conveyed by the *failure* of the system and by its *biased* concentration on the poor. I call this the *bonus of bias.*

The Implicit Ideology of Criminal Justice

Any criminal justice system like ours conveys a subtle yet powerful message in support of established institutions. It does this for two interconnected reasons: first, because it concentrates on *individual* wrongdoers. This means that *it diverts our attention away from our institutions, away from consideration of whether our institutions themselves are wrong or unjust or indeed "criminal."*

Second, the criminal law is put forth as the *minimum neutral ground rules* for any social living. We are taught that no society can exist without rules against theft and violence, and thus the criminal law seems to be politically neutral, the minimum requirements for *any* society, the minimum obligations that any individual owes his or her fellows to make social life of any decent sort possible. Thus, it not only diverts our attention away from the possible injustice of our social institutions, but the criminal law bestows upon those institutions the mantle of its own neutrality.

Because the criminal law protects the established institutions (e.g., the prevailing economic arrangements are protected by laws against theft, and so on), attacks on those established institutions become equivalent to violations of the minimum requirements for any social life at all. In effect, the criminal law enshrines the established institutions as equivalent to the minimum requirements for *any* decent social existence—and it brands the individual who attacks those institutions as one who has declared war on *all* organized society and who must therefore be met with the weapons of war.

This is the powerful magic of criminal justice. By virtue of its focus on *individual* criminals, it diverts us from the evils of the social order. By virtue of its presumed neutrality, it transforms the established social (and economic) order from being merely *one* form of society open to critical comparison with others into the conditions of *any* social order and thus immune from criticism. Let us look more closely at this process.

What is the effect of focusing on individual guilt? Not only does this divert our attention from the possible evils in our institutions but it puts forth half the problem of justice as if it were the *whole* problem. To focus on individual guilt is to ask whether the individual citizen has fulfilled his or her obligations to his or her fellow citizens. *It is to look away from the issue of whether the fellow citizens have fulfilled their obligations to him or her.* To look only at individual responsibility is to look away from social responsibility. Writing about her stint as a "story analyst" for a prime-time TV "real crime" show based on videotapes of actual police busts, Debra Seagal describes the way focus on individual criminals deflects attention away from the social context of crime, and how television reproduces this effect in millions of homes daily:

> *By the time our 9 million viewers flip on their tubes, we've reduced fifty or sixty hours of mundane and compromising video into short, action-packed segments of tantalizing, crack-filled, dope-dealing, junkie-busting cop culture. How easily we downplay the pathos of the suspect; how cleverly we breeze past the complexities that cast doubt on the very system that has produced the criminal activity in the first place.*[6]

Seagal's description illustrates as well how a television program that shows nothing but videos of actual events, that uses no reenactments whatsoever, can distort reality by selecting and recombining pieces of real events.

To look only at individual criminality is to close one's eyes to social injustice and to close one's ears to the question of whether our social institutions have exploited or violated the individual. *Justice is a two-way street—but criminal justice is a one-way street.* Individuals owe obligations to their fellow citizens because their fellow citizens owe obligations to them. Criminal justice focuses on the first and looks away from the second. *Thus, by focusing on individual responsibility for crime, the criminal justice system literally acquits the existing social order of any charge of injustice!*

This is an extremely important bit of ideological alchemy. It stems from the fact that the same act can be criminal or not, unjust or just, depending on the circumstances in which it takes place. Killing someone is ordinarily a crime, but if it is in self-defense or to stop a deadly crime, it is not. Taking property by force is usually a crime, but if the taking is retrieving what has been stolen, then no crime has been committed. Acts of violence are ordinarily crimes, but if the violence is provoked by the threat of violence or by oppressive conditions, then, like the Boston Tea Party, what might ordinarily be called criminal is celebrated as just. This means that when we call an act a crime, *we are also making an implicit judgment about the conditions in response to which it takes place.* When we call an act a crime, we are saying that the conditions in which it occurs are not themselves criminal or deadly or oppressive or so unjust as to make an extreme response reasonable or justified or noncriminal. This means that when the system holds an individual responsible for a crime, *it implicitly conveys the message that the social conditions in which the crime occurred are not responsible for the crime,* that they are not so unjust as to make a violent response to them excusable.

Judges are prone to hold that an individual's responsibility for a violent crime is diminished if it was provoked by something that might lead a "reasonable man" to respond violently and that criminal responsibility is eliminated if the act was in response to conditions so intolerable that any "reasonable man" would have been likely to respond in the same way. In this vein, the law acquits those who kill or injure in self-defense and treats leniently those who commit a crime when confronted with extreme provocation. The law treats understandingly the man who kills his wife's lover and the woman who kills her brutal husband, even when neither has acted directly in self-defense. By this logic, when we hold an individual completely responsible for a crime, we are saying that the conditions in which it occurred are such that a "reasonable man" should find them tolerable. In other words, by focusing on individual responsibility for crimes, *the criminal justice system broadcasts the message that the social order itself is reasonable and not intolerably unjust.*

Thus, the criminal justice system focuses moral condemnation on individuals and deflects it away from the social order that may have either violated the individual's rights or dignity or literally pushed him or her to the brink of the crime. This not only serves to carry the message that our social institutions are not in need of fundamental questioning, but it further suggests that the justice of our institutions is obvious, not to be doubted. Indeed, because it is deviations from these institutions that are crimes, the established institutions become the implicit standard of justice from which criminal deviations are measured.

This leads to the second way in which a criminal justice system always conveys an implicit ideology. It arises from the presumption that the criminal law is nothing but the politically neutral minimum requirements of any decent social life. What is the consequence of this? As already suggested, this presumption transforms the prevailing social order into justice incarnate and all violations of the prevailing order into injustice incarnate. This process is so obvious that it may be easily missed.

Consider, for example, the law against theft. It does seem to be one of the minimum requirements of social living. As long as there is scarcity, any society—capitalist or socialist—will need rules preventing individuals from taking what does not belong to them. The law against theft, however, is more: It is a law against stealing what individuals *presently* own. *Such a law has the effect of making present property relations a part of the criminal law.*

Because stealing is a violation of the law, this means that present property relations become the implicit standard of justice against which criminal deviations are measured. Because criminal law is thought of as the minimum requirements of any social life, this means that present property relations become the equivalent to the minimum requirements of *any* social life. The criminal who would alter the present property relations becomes nothing less than someone who is declaring war on all organized society. The question of whether this "war" is provoked by the injustice or brutality of the society is swept aside. Indeed, this suggests yet another way in which the criminal justice system conveys an ideological message in support of the established society.

Not only does the criminal justice system acquit the social order of any charge of injustice; it specifically cloaks the society's own crime-producing tendencies. I have already observed that by blaming the individual for a crime, the society is acquitted of the charge of injustice. I would like to go further now and argue that by blaming the individual for a crime, the society is acquitted of the charge of *complicity* in that crime. This is a point worth developing, because many observers have maintained that modern competitive societies such as our own have structural features that tend to generate crime. Thus, holding the individual responsible for his or her crime serves the function of taking the rest of society off the hook for their role in sustaining and benefiting from social arrangements that produce crime. Let us take a brief detour to look more closely at this process.

Cloward and Ohlin argued in their book *Delinquency and Opportunity*[7] that much crime is the result of the discrepancy between social goals and the legitimate opportunities available for achieving them. Simply put, in our society everyone is encouraged to be a success, but the avenues to success are open only to some. The conventional wisdom of our free-enterprise democracy is that anyone can be a success if he or she has the talent and the ambition. Thus, if one is not a success, it is because of one's own shortcomings: laziness or lack of ability or both. On the other hand, opportunities to achieve success are not equally open to all. Access to the best schools and the best jobs is effectively closed to all but a few of the poor and becomes more available only as one goes up the economic ladder. The result is that many are called but few are chosen. Many who have taken the bait and accepted the belief in the importance of success and the belief that achieving success is a result of individual ability must cope with feelings of frustration and failure that result when they find the avenues to success closed. Cloward and Ohlin argue that one method of coping with these stresses is to develop alternative avenues to success. Crime is such an alternative avenue.

Crime is a means by which people who believe in the American dream pursue it when they find the traditional routes barred. Indeed, it is plain to see that the goals pursued by most criminals are as American as apple pie. I suspect one of the reasons that American moviegoers enjoy gangster films—movies in which gangsters such as Al Capone, Bonnie and Clyde, or Butch Cassidy and the Sundance Kid are the heroes, as distinct from police and detective films whose heroes are defenders of the law—is that even where we deplore the hero's methods, we identify with his or her notion of success, because it is ours as well, and we respect the courage and cunning displayed in achieving that success.

It is important to note that the discrepancy between success goals and legitimate opportunities in America is not an aberration. It is a structural feature of modern competitive industrialized society, a feature from which many benefits flow. Cloward and Ohlin write that

> *a crucial problem in the industrial world is to locate and train the most talented persons in every generation, irrespective of the vicissitudes of birth, to occupy technical work roles. Since we cannot know in advance who can best fulfill the requirements of the various occupational roles, the matter is presumably settled through the process of competition. But how can men throughout the social order be motivated to participate in this competition?*
>
> *One of the ways in which the industrial society attempts to solve this problem is by defining success-goals as potentially accessible to all, regardless of race, creed, or socioeconomic position.*[8]

Because these universal goals are urged to encourage a competition to select the best, there are necessarily fewer openings than seekers. Also, because those who achieve success are in a particularly good position to exploit their success to make access for their own children easier, the competition is rigged to work in favor of the middle and upper classes. As a result, "many lower-class persons are the victims of a contradiction between the goals toward which they have been led to orient themselves and socially structured means of striving for these goals."[9]

> *[The poor] experience desperation born of the certainty that their position in the economic structure is relatively fixed and immutable—a desperation made all the more poignant by their exposure to a cultural ideology in which failure to orient oneself upward is regarded as a moral defect and failure to become mobile as a proof of it.*[10]

The outcome is predictable. "Under these conditions, there is an acute pressure to depart from institutional norms and to adopt illegitimate alternatives."[11]

This means that the very way in which our society is structured to draw out the talents and energies that go into producing our high standard of living has a costly side effect: It produces crime. By holding individuals responsible for this crime, those who enjoy that high standard of living can have their cake and eat it too. They can reap the benefits of the competition for success and escape the responsibility of paying for the costs of the competition. By holding the poor crook legally and morally guilty, the rest of society not only passes the costs of competition on to the poor but they effectively deny that they (the affluent) are the beneficiaries of an economic system that exacts such a high toll in frustration and suffering.

William Bonger, the Dutch Marxist criminologist, maintained that competitive capitalism produces egotistic motives and undermines compassion for the misfortunes of others and thus makes human beings literally *more capable of crime*—more capable of preying on their fellows without moral inhibition or remorse—than earlier cultures that emphasized cooperation rather than competition.[12] Here again, the criminal justice system relieves those who benefit from the American economic system of the costs of that system. By holding criminals morally and individually responsible for their crimes, we can forget that the motives that lead to crime—the drive for success at any cost, linked with the beliefs that success means outdoing others and that violence is an acceptable way of achieving one's goals—are the *same motives* that powered that drive across the American continent and that continue to fuel the engine of America's prosperity.

David Gordon, a contemporary political economist, maintains "that nearly all crimes in capitalist societies represent perfectly *rational* responses to the structure of institutions upon which capitalist societies are based."[13] Like Bonger, Gordon believes that capitalism tends to provoke crime in all economic strata. This is so because most crime is motivated by a desire for property or money and is an understandable way of coping with the pressures of inequality, competition, and insecurity, all of which are essential ingredients of capitalism. Capitalism depends, Gordon writes,

> *on basically competitive forms of social and economic interaction and upon substantial inequalities in the allocation of social resources. Without inequalities, it would be much more difficult to induce workers to work in alienating environments. Without competition and a competitive ideology, workers might not be inclined to struggle to improve their relative income and status in society by working harder. Finally, although rights of property are protected, capitalist societies do not guarantee economic security to most of their individual members. Individuals must fend for themselves, finding the best available opportunities to provide for themselves and their families. Driven by the fear of economic insecurity and by a competitive desire to gain some of the goods unequally distributed throughout the society, many individuals will eventually become "criminals."*[14]

To the extent that a society makes crime a reasonable alternative for a large number of its members from all classes, that society is itself not very reasonably or humanely organized and bears some degree of responsibility for the crime it encourages. Because the criminal law is put forth as the minimum requirements that can be expected of any "reasonable man," its enforcement amounts to a denial of the real nature of the social order to which Gordon and the others point. Here again, by blaming the individual criminal, the criminal justice system serves implicitly but dramatically to acquit the society of its criminality.

The Bonus of Bias

We now consider the additional ideological bonus derived from the criminal justice system's bias against the poor. This bonus is a product of the association of crime and poverty in the popular mind. This association, the merging of the "criminal classes" and the "lower classes" into the "dangerous classes," was not invented in America. The word *villain* is derived from the Latin *villanus,* which means a farm servant. The term *villein* was used in feudal England to refer to a serf who farmed the land of a great lord and who was literally owned by that lord.[15] In this respect, our present criminal justice system is heir to a long tradition.

The value of this association was already seen when we explored the average citizen's concept of the Typical Criminal and the Typical Crime.

It is quite obvious that throughout the great mass of Middle America, far more fear and hostility are directed toward the predatory acts of the poor than toward the acts of the rich. Compare the fate of politicians in recent history who call for tax reform, income redistribution, prosecution of corporate crime, and any sort of regulation of business that would make it better serve American social goals with that of politicians who erect their platform on a call for "law and order," more police, fewer limits on police power, and stiffer prison sentences for criminals—and consider this in light of what we have already seen about the real dangers posed by corporate crime and "business as usual."

It seems clear that Americans have been effectively deceived as to what are the greatest dangers to their lives, limbs, and possessions. The very persistence with which the system functions to apprehend and punish poor crooks and ignore or slap on the wrist equally or more dangerous individuals is testimony to the sticking power of this deception. That Americans continue to tolerate the comparatively gentle treatment meted out to white-collar criminals, corporate price fixers, industrial polluters, and political-influence peddlers while voting in droves to lock up more poor people faster and longer indicates the degree to which they harbor illusions as to who most threatens them. It is perhaps also part of the explanation for the continued dismal failure of class-based politics in America. American workers rarely seem able to forget their differences and unite to defend their shared interests against the rich whose wealth they produce. Ethnic divisions serve this divisive function well, but undoubtedly the vivid portrayal of the poor—and, of course, the blacks—as hovering birds of prey waiting for the opportunity to snatch away the workers' meager gains serves also to deflect opposition away from the upper classes. A politician who promises to keep working-class communities free of blacks and their prisons full of them can get their votes even if the major portion of his or her policies amount to continuation of the favored treatment of the rich at their expense. The sensationalistic use, in the 1988 presidential election, of photos of Willie Horton (a convicted black criminal who committed a brutal rape while out of prison on a furlough) suggests that such tactics are still effective politics.

The most important "bonus" derived from the identification of crime and poverty is that it paints the picture that the threat to decent middle Americans comes from those below them on the economic ladder, not those above. For this to happen the system must not only identify crime and poverty, but *it must also fail to reduce crime so that it remains a real threat.* By doing this, it deflects the fear and discontent of middle Americans, and their possible opposition, away from the wealthy.

There are other bonuses as well. For instance, if the criminal justice system sends out a message that bestows legitimacy on present property relations, the dramatic impact is greatly enhanced if the violator of the present arrangements is without property. In other words, the crimes of the well-to-do "redistribute" property among the haves. In that sense, they do no pose a symbolic challenge to the larger system in which some have much and many have little or nothing. If the criminal threat can be portrayed as coming from the poor, then the punishment of the poor criminal becomes a morality play in which the sanctity and legitimacy of the system in which some have plenty and others have little or nothing is dramatically affirmed. It matters little whom the poor criminals really victimize. What counts is that middle Americans come to fear that those poor criminals are out to steal what they own.

There is yet another bonus for the powerful in America, produced by the identification of crime and poverty. It might be thought that the identification of crime and poverty would produce sympathy for the criminals. My suspicion is that it produces or at least reinforces the reverse: *hostility toward the poor.*

There is little evidence that Americans are very sympathetic to poor criminals. Very few Americans believe poverty to be a cause of crime (6 percent of those questioned in a 1981 survey, although 21 percent thought unemployment was a cause). Other surveys find that most Americans believe that the police should be tougher than they are now in dealing with crime (83 percent of those questioned in a 1972 survey); that courts do not deal harshly enough with criminals (80 percent of those questioned in 1991); that a majority of Americans would like to see the death penalty for convicted murderers (76 percent of those questioned in 1991); and that most would be more likely to vote for a candidate who advocated tougher sentences for lawbreakers (83 percent of those questioned in a 1972 survey).[16] Indeed, the experience of Watergate seems to suggest that sympathy for criminals begins to flower only when we approach the higher reaches of the ladder of wealth and power. For some poor ghetto youth who robs a liquor store, five years in a penitentiary is our idea of tempering justice with mercy. When a handful of public officials try to walk off with the U.S. Constitution, a few months in a minimum security prison will suffice. If the public official is high enough, say president of the United States, resignation from office and public disgrace tempered with a $148,000-a-year pension is punishment enough.

My view is that, because the criminal justice system, in fact and fiction, deals with *individual legal and moral guilt,* the association of crime with poverty does not mitigate the image of individual moral responsibility for crime, the image that crime is the result of an individuals poor character. It does the reverse: It generates the association of poverty and individual moral failing and thus *the belief that poverty itself is a sign of poor or weak char-*

acter. The clearest evidence that Americans hold this belief is to be found in the fact that attempts to aid the poor are regarded as acts of charity, rather than as acts of justice. Our welfare system has all the demeaning attributes of an institution designed to give handouts to the undeserving and none of the dignity of an institution designed to make good on our responsibilities to our fellow human beings. If we acknowledged the degree to which our economic and social institutions themselves breed poverty, we would have to recognize our own responsibilities toward the poor. If we can convince ourselves that the poor are poor because of their own shortcomings, particularly moral shortcomings like incontinence and indolence, then we need acknowledge no such responsibility to the poor. Indeed, we can go further and pat ourselves on the back for our generosity in handing out the little that we do, and, of course, we can make our recipients go through all the indignities that mark them as the undeserving objects of our benevolence. By and large, this has been the way in which Americans have dealt with their poor.[17] It is a way that enables us to avoid asking the question of why the richest nation in the world continues to produce massive poverty. It is my view that this conception of the poor is subtly conveyed by the way our criminal justice system functions.

Obviously, no ideological message could be more supportive of the present social and economic order than this. It suggests that poverty is a sign of individual failing, not a symptom of social or economic injustice. It tells us loud and clear that massive poverty in the midst of abundance is not a sign pointing toward the need for fundamental changes in our social and economic institutions. It suggests that the poor are poor because they deserve to be poor or at least because they lack the strength of character to overcome poverty. When the poor are seen to be poor in character, then economic poverty coincides with moral poverty and the economic order coincides with the moral order. As if a divine hand guided its workings, capitalism leads to everyone getting what he or she morally deserves!

If this association takes root, then when the poor individual is found guilty of a crime, the criminal justice system acquits the society of its responsibility not only for crime *but for poverty as well.*

With this, the ideological message of criminal justice is complete. The poor rather than the rich are seen as the enemies of the majority of decent middle Americans. Our social and economic institutions are held to be responsible for neither crime nor poverty and thus are in need of no fundamental questioning or reform. The poor are poor because they are poor of character. The economic order and the moral order are one. To the extent that this message sinks in, the wealthy can rest easily—even if they cannot sleep the sleep of the just.

We can understand why the criminal justice system is allowed to create the image of crime as the work of the poor and fails to reduce it so that the threat of crime remains real and credible. The result is ideological alchemy of the highest order. The poor are seen as the real threat to decent society. The ultimate sanctions of criminal justice dramatically sanctify the present social and economic order, and *the poverty of criminals makes poverty itself an individual moral crime!*

Such are the ideological fruits of a losing war against crime whose distorted image is reflected in the criminal justice carnival mirror and widely broadcast to reach the minds and imaginations of America.

Ideology, or How to Fool Enough of the People Enough of the Time

What is Ideology?

The view that the laws of a state or nation are made to serve the interests of those with power, rather than to promote the well-being of the whole society, is not a new discovery made in the wake of Watergate. It is a doctrine with a pedigree older even than Christianity itself. Writing during the fourth century B.C., virtually at the dawn of Western thought, Plato expressed this view through the lips of Thrasymachus.[18] A more contemporary and more systematic formulation of the idea is found in the works of Karl Marx, written during the nineteenth century, not long after the dawn of Western industrialism. Marx wrote in *The Communist Manifesto* that the bourgeoisie—the class of owners of businesses and factories, the class of capitalists—has

> *conquered for itself, in the modern representative State, exclusive political sway. The executive of the modern State is but a committee for managing the common affairs of the whole bourgeoisie.*[19]

Anyone who thinks this is a ridiculous idea ought to look at the backgrounds of our political leaders. The vast majority of the president's cabinet, the administrators of the federal regulatory agencies, and the members of the two houses of Congress come from the ranks of business or are lawyers who serve business. Many still maintain their business ties or law practices, with no sense of a conflict of interest with their political role.[20] Even those who start from humble beginnings are usually quite rich by the time they finally make it into office. If either Thrasymachus or Marx is right, there *is* no conflict with their political role because that role is to protect and promote the interests of business.

It is clear that the most powerful criminal justice policymakers come from the have-plenties, not from the have-littles. It is no surprise that legislators and judges—those who make the laws that define criminality and those who interpret those laws—are predominantly members of the upper classes, if not at birth then surely by the time they take office. One study of justices appointed to the U.S. Supreme Court between 1933 and 1957 found that 81 percent were sons of fathers with high social–status occupations and that 61 percent had been educated in schools of high standing. Richard Quinney compiled background data on key members of criminal justice policymaking and policy-advising committees and agencies, such as the President's Commission on Law Enforcement and Administration of Justice, the National Advisory Commission on Civil Disorders, the National Commission on the Causes and Prevention of Violence, the Senate Judiciary Committee's Subcommittee on Criminal Laws and Procedures (the subcommittee had a strong hand in shaping the Omnibus Crime Control and Safe Streets Act of 1968), the Law Enforcement Assistance Administration, the Federal Bureau of Investigation, and, last but not least, the U.S. Department of Justice. With few exceptions, Quinney's report reads like a *Who's Who* of the business, legal, and political elite. For instance, 63 percent of the members of the President's Crime Commission had business and corporate connections.[21]

Further, there is considerable evidence that the American criminal justice system has been used throughout its history in rather unsubtle ways to protect the interests of the powerful against the lower classes and political dissenters. The use of the FBI and local police forces to repress dissent by discrediting, harassing, and undermining dissident individuals and groups has been recently revealed. The FBI, often with active cooperation or tacit consent of local police, has engaged in literally hundreds of illegal burglaries of the offices of law-abiding left-wing political parties,[22] and in political sabotage against the Black Panthers (e.g., "a Catholic priest, the Rev. Frank Curran, became the target of FBI operations because he permitted the Black Panthers to use his church for serving breakfasts to ghetto children").[23] It conducted a campaign to discredit the late Martin Luther King Jr. ("the FBI secretly categorized King as a "Communist months before it ever started investigating him").[24] Directors of the FBI have said that the bureau is "truly sorry" for these past abuses and that they are over. Later reports indicate that abuses continue.[25]

These acts of repression are only the latest in a long tradition. The first organized uniformed police force in the English-speaking world was established in London in 1829. They came to be called "bobbies" because of the role played by Sir Robert Peel in securing passage of the London Metropolitan Police Act, which established the force. The first full-time uniformed police force in the United States was set up in New York City in 1845.[26] It was also in the period from the 1820s to the 1840s that the movement to build penitentiaries to house and reform criminals began in New York and Pennsylvania and spread rapidly through the states of the young nation.[27] That these are also the years that saw the beginnings of a large industrial working class in the cities of England and America is a coincidence too striking to ignore.

The police were repeatedly used to break strikes and harass strikers.[28] The penitentiaries were mainly used to house the laborers and foreigners (often one and the same) whom the middle and upper classes perceived as a threat.[29] Throughout the formative years of the American labor movement, public police forces, private police such as the Pinkertons, regular army troops, and the National Guard were repeatedly used to protect the interests of capital against the attempts of labor to organize in defense of its interests. The result was that "the United States has had the bloodiest and most violent labor history of any industrialized nation in the world"—with most of the casualties on the side of labor.[30]

Marx, of course, went further. Not only are the laws of a society made to protect the interests of the most powerful economic class, but also, Marx argued, the prevailing ways of thinking about the world—from economic theory to religion to conventional moral ideas about good and evil, guilt and responsibility—are shaped in ways that promote the belief that the existing society is the best of all possible worlds. Marx wrote that

> *the ideas of the ruling class are in every epoch the ruling ideas: i.e. the class which is the ruling material force of society, is at the same time its ruling intellectual force. The class which has the means of material production at its disposal, has control at the same time over the means of mental production.*[31]

Because those who have economic power own the newspapers, endow the universities, finance the publication of books and journals, and (in our own time) control the television and radio industries, they have a prevailing say in what is said, heard, and thought by the millions who get their ideas—their picture of reality—from these sources. This does not mean that the controllers of the "means of mental production" consciously deceive or manipulate those who receive their message. What it means is that the picture of reality held by these controllers—believed by them, no doubt sincerely, to be an accurate representation of reality—will be largely the picture of reality that fills the heads of the readers and viewers of the mass media. Recognizing this involves no disrespect of the so-called common person. It is simply a matter of facing reality. The average man or woman is almost wholly occupied with the personal tasks of earning a living, piloting a family, and the like. He or she lacks the time (and usually the training) necessary to seek out and evaluate alternative sources of information. They are lucky when they have the time to catch a bit of news on television or in the papers. Moreover, except when there is division of opinion among those who control the media, the average person is so surrounded by unbroken "consensus" that he or she takes it simply as the way things are, with no particular reason even to consider the possibility that there are other sides of the issue to be considered, much less to seek these out. Then, even if people do come up with alternative sources of information, there are no general forums available for the sharing of views among members of the public. What we call mass communication is communication *to* the masses, not among them.

Consequently, the vast majority of people will accept, as a true picture of reality, the picture held by those who control the media. This is likely to be a distorted picture, even if those who create it act with the best of intentions and sincerity. The point is that, for a wide variety of reasons, people will tend to view the world in ways that make their own role in it (particularly the advantages and privileges they have in it) seem morally just, indeed, part of the best of all possible worlds. Thus, without any intention to deceive at all, those who control the content of the mass media are virtually certain to convey a picture of reality that supports the existing social order.

As a result, even in a society such as ours, where freedom of expression has reached a level probably unparalleled in history, there is almost never any *fundamental* questioning of our political-economic institutions in the mass media, that is, television and radio, the major newspapers, or the news weeklies such as *Time* or *Newsweek*. There is much criticism of individuals and of individual policies. How often, though, does one find the mass media questioning whether the free enterprise system is really the best choice for America, or whether our political and legal arrangements systematically promote the domination of society by the owners of big business? These issues are rarely, if ever, raised. Instead, it is taken for granted that, although they need some reform tinkering from time to time, our economic institutions are the most productive, our political institutions the freest, and our legal institutions the most just that *there can be.*

In other words, even in a society as free as ours, the ides that fill the heads of most Americans and shape their picture of reality either explicitly or implicitly convey the message that our leaders are pursuing the common good (with only occasional lapses into personal venality—note how we congratulate ourselves on how "the system is working" when we expose these "aberrations" and then return to business as usual). Thus, we are told that the interests of the powerful coincide with the common interests of us all[32]—that "what's good for General Motors is good for the country." Where this picture of reality shows up some blemishes, they will always be portrayed as localized problems that can be remedied without fundamental overhaul of the entire social order, aberrations in an otherwise well-functioning social system. Indeed, the very willingness to publicize these blemishes "proves" there is nothing fundamentally wrong with the social system, because if the media are free, willing, and able to portray the blemishes, they would surely portray fundamental problems with the social system if there were any—and because they do not, there must not be any! When ideas, however unintentionally, distort reality in a way that justifies the prevailing distribution of power and wealth, hides society's injustices, and thus secures uncritical allegiance to the existing social order, we have what Marx called *ideology*.[33]

Ideology is not conscious deception. People may spout ideology simply because it is all they know or all they have been taught or because they do not see beyond the "conventional wisdom" that surrounds them. This can be just as true of scholars who fail to see beyond the conventional assumptions of their disciplines as it is of laypersons who fail to see beyond the oversimplifications of what is commonly called "common sense." Such individuals do not mouth an ideology out of a willful desire to deceive and manipulate their fellows, but rather because their own view of reality is distorted by untruths and half-truths—and criminal justice is one source of such distortion. One way in which this works without conscious lying is that we have become so used to the criminal justice carnival mirror (described in Chapter 2) that we don't notice its curves. It looks flat, and thus we take it as an accurate picture of who threatens us in society.

It should be noted in passing that not everyone uses the term *ideology* as I have, to point to what is necessarily deceptive. Some writers speak of ideology as if it meant any individual or group's "belief system" or "value system" or *Weltanschauung*, that is, "world view."[34] I do not intend to quibble about semantics. However, such a moral neutralization of the concept of "ideology" strikes me as unnecessarily dulling an instrument than thinkers like Marx and others have sharpened into an effective tool for cutting through the illusions that dog our political life. Such tools are few and hard to find. Once found, they should be carefully preserved, especially when concepts such as "belief system" or "world view" are available to perform the more neutral function.

The Need for Ideology

A simple and persuasive argument can be made for the claim that the rich and powerful in America have an interest in conveying an ideological message to the rest of the nation. The have-nots and have-littles far outnumber the have-plenties. This means, to put it rather crudely, the have-nots and the have-littles could have more if they decided to take it from the have-plenties. This, in turn, means that the have-plenties need the cooperation of the have-nots and the have-littles. Because the have-plenties are such a small minority that they could never *force* this cooperation on the have-nots and have-littles, this cooperation must be voluntary. For the cooperation to be voluntary, the have-nots and the have-littles must believe it would not be right or reasonable to take away what the have-plenties have. In other words, they must believe that for all its problems the present social, political, and economic order, with its disparities of wealth and power and privilege, is about the best that human beings can create. More specifically, the have-nots and have-littles must believe that they are not being exploited by the have-plenties. Now this seems to me to add up to an extremely plausible argument that ours is a social system that requires for its continued operation a set of beliefs necessary to secure the allegiance of the less well-off majority. These beliefs must be in some considerable degree false, because the distribution of wealth and power in the United States is so evidently arbitrary and unjust. Ergo, the need for ideology.

A disquisition on the inequitable distribution of wealth and income in the United States is beyond the scope and purpose of this book. This subject, as well as the existence of a "dominant" or "ruling" class in America, has been documented extensively by others.[35] I will make only two points here. First, there are indeed wide disparities in the distribution of wealth and income in the United States. Second, these disparities are so obviously unjust that it is reasonable to assume the vast majority of people who must struggle to make ends meet put up with them only because they have been sold a bill of goods, that is, an ideology.

In 1990, the richest 20 percent of American families received 44.3 percent of the income received by all families, whereas the poorest 60 percent of American families received 32.0 percent of the total income. In crude terms, this means that while the wealthiest 50 million Americans had almost half of the money pie to themselves, the least wealthy 150 million Americans had to share less than a third of that pie among them. At the outer edges the figures are more extreme: The richest 5 percent of families received 17.4 percent of the total income, more than the poorest 40 percent of families, who receive 15.4 percent. This means that the richest 5 percent—maybe 12 million people—had more money to divide among themselves than the 100 million persons who make up the bottom 40 percent.[36]

The distribution of *wealth* (property such as stocks and land that generate income and tend to give one a say in major economic decisions) is even worse than the distribution of income.[37] A recent study of long-term trends in wealth inequality shows that the top fifth of households has owned three-quarters of the nation's wealth at least over the period from 1962 to 1989. The author writes, "If anything, wealth concentration increased during the 1980s. It is estimated that the top 1 percent of households in 1989 owned 33 percent of household wealth, compared to 30 percent in 1986 and 28 percent in 1983." Looking back over the whole period from colonial times to the present, the author concludes, "at no time has the majority of the U.S. adult population or households managed to gain title to any more than about 10 percent of the nation's wealth." And, she adds, "the governmental policies of the past two decades have been hostile to progressive tax rates and economic measures benefiting workers. Real per capita income began declining in the early 1970s, benefits eroded in the 1980s. . . . This situation suggests that the lower four quintiles' share of total wealth may well shrink in future years."[38]

I offer no complicated philosophical argument to prove that these disparities are unjust, although such arguments abound for those who are interested.[39] It is a scandal that, in a nation as rich as ours, some 33.6 million people (27 million reckoned with the most generous valuation of in-kind benefits) should live below what the government conservatively defines as the poverty level and that many millions more must scramble to make ends meet. It is shameful that more than a third of the individuals below the poverty line are children![40] It is tragic that in our wealthy nation so many millions cannot afford a proper diet, a college education, a decent place to live, and good health care. We know too much about the causes of wealth and poverty to believe that the rich become rich simply because of their talent or contribution to society or that the poor are poor because they are lazy or incapable. Because we are nowhere near offering all Americans a good education and an equal opportunity to get ahead, we have no right to think that the distribution of income reflects what people have truly earned. The distribution of income in America is so fundamentally shaped by factors such as race, educational opportunity, and the economic class of one's parents[41] that few people who are well off can honestly claim they deserve *all* that they have. Those who think they do should ask themselves where they would be today if they had been born to migrant laborers in California or to a poor black family in the Harlem ghetto.

Enough said. I take it, then, as established that the disparities of wealth and income in America are wide and unjustified. For the vast majority, the many millions struggling hard to satisfy basic needs, to acquiesce to the vast wealth of a small minority, it is necessary that the majority come to believe that these disparities are justified, that the present order is the best that human beings can accomplish, and that they are not being exploited by the have-plenties. In other words, the system requires an effective ideology to fool enough of the people enough of the time.

This account of the nature and need for ideology, coupled with the historical inertia explanation of the persistence of criminal justice in its current form and the analysis of the ideological benefits produced by the criminal justice system, adds up to an explanation of the continued failure of criminal justice in America.

Summary

This chapter has presented the "historical inertia" explanation as a way of understanding the triple failure of criminal justice in America (1) to institute policies likely to reduce the incidence of crime, (2) to treat as crime the dangerous acts of the well off, and (3) to eliminate the bias against the poor in the treatment of those acts labeled crimes. It was argued that these failures harm most those who lack the power to change things and benefit those who have that power. They benefit the latter by broadcasting the message that the threat to Americans' well-being comes from below them on the economic ladder, not from above them; and that poverty results not from social causes but from the moral depravity of the poor. It was also argued that aside from these "bonuses of bias," there is an implicit ideological message of any criminal justice system, insofar as such systems, by focusing on individual guilt, implicitly broadcast the message that the social system itself is a just one.

Study Questions

1. What is a conspiracy theory? What are the shortcomings of such a theory? Is the Pyrrhic defeat theory a conspiracy theory?
2. What is meant by ideology? What is the difference between ideology and propaganda? Is ideology needed in the United States?
3. How does any criminal justice broadcast an ideological message supportive of the prevailing social and economic arrangements?
4. What additional ideological benefits result from the bias against the poor in the definition and treatment of crime?
5. Why are poor people in America poor?
6. Now that you have reviewed the historical inertia explanation of criminal justice in America, has the Pyrrhic defeat theory been proven?

Additional Readings

BOX, STEVEN. *Power, Crime and Mystification.* London: Tavistock, 1983.
CHAMBLISS, WILLIAM AND ROBERT SEIDMAN. *Law, Order and Power.* Reading, Mass.: Addison-Wesley, 1982.
CHAMBLISS, WILLIAM AND MILTON MANKOFF. *Whose Law and What Order? A Conflict Approach to Criminology.* New York: Wiley, 1976.
GORDON, DIANA. *The Justice Juggernaut: Fighting Street Crime, Controlling Citizens.* New Brunswick, N.J.: Rutgers University Press, 1990.
HAMOWY, RONALD. *Dealing with Drugs: Consequences of Government Control.* Lexington, Mass.: Lexington Books, 1987.
KAPPELER, VICTOR et al. *The Mythology of Crime and Criminal Justice.* Prospect Heights, Ill.: Waveland, 1993.
LYNCH, MICHAEL AND W. BYRON GROVES. *A Primer in Radical Criminology,* 2d ed. New York: Harrow and Heston, 1989.
TURK, AUSTIN. *Political Criminality: The Defiance and Defense of Authority.* Beverly Hills, Calif.: Sage, 1982.

Notes to Chapter 4

1. *Challenge,* p. 44
2. BJS, *Criminal Victimization,* 1991, p. 6.
3. *Sourcebook-1992,* p. 265, Table no. 3.25; p. 281, Table no. 3.43.
4. See Eve Merriam, "We're Teaching Our Children That Violence Is Fun," in *Violence: An Element of American Life,* eds. K. Taylor and F. Soady Jr. (Boston: Holbrook Press, 1972), p. 155; and Brandon Centerwall, "Television Violence: The Scale of the Problem and Where to Go From Here," *Journal of the American Medical Association* 267, no. 22 (June 10, 1992), pp. 3059, 3062.
5. Graeme R. Newman, "Popular Culture and Criminal Justice: A Preliminary Analysis," *Journal of Criminal Justice* 18 (1990), p. 261.
6. Debra Seagal, "Tales from the Cutting-Room Floor: The Reality of 'Reality-Based' Television," *Harper's Magazine,* November 1993, p. 52.
7. Richard A. Cloward and Lloyd E. Ohlin, *Deliquency and Opportunity: A Theory of Delinquent Gangs* (New York: Free Press, 1960), especially pp. 77–107.
8. Ibid., p. 81.
9. Ibid., p. 10.
10. Ibid., p. 107.
11. Ibid., p. 10.
12. Willem Bonger, *Criminality and Economic Conditions,* abridged and with an introduction by Austin T. Turk (Bloomington: Indiana University Press, 1969), pp. 7–12, 40–47. Willem Adriaan Bonger was born in Holland in 1876 and died by his own hand in 1940 rather than submit to the Nazis. His *Criminalité et con-*

ditions économiques first appeared in 1905. It was translated into English and published in the United States in 1916. Ibid., pp. 3–4.

13. David M. Gordon, "Capitalism, Class and Crime in America," *Crime and Delinquency* (April 1973), p. 174.

14. Ibid.

15. William and Mary Morris, *Dictionary of Word and Phrase Origins,* vol. 2 (New York: Harper and Row, 1967), p. 282.

16. *Sourcebook-1974,* pp. 203, 204, 207, 223; *Sourcebook-1981,* pp. 192, 205, 210–11; *Sourcebook-1987,* pp. 142–43, 160–61; *Sourcebook-1991,* p. 211, Table no. 2.45; *Sourcebook-1992,* p. 197, Table no. 2.45.

17. Historical documentation of this can be found in David J. Rothman, *The Discovery of the Asylum: Social Order and Disorder in the New Republic* (Boston: Little, Brown, 1971); and in Frances Fox Piven and Richard A. Cloward, *Regulating the Poor: The Functions of Public Welfare* (New York: Pantheon, 1971), which carries the analysis up to recent times.

18. *The Republic of Plato,* trans. F. M. Cornford (New York: Oxford University Press, 1945), p. 18 [I. 338]. Plato was born in Athens in the year 428 B.C. (or 427, depending on the reckoning) and died there in 348 B.C. (or 347). Scholars generally agree that at least Book One of *The Republic* (the section in which Thrasymachus speaks) was written between the death of Socrates in 399 B.C. and Plato's first journey to Sicily, from which he returned in 388 B.C. (or 387). See Frederick Copleston, S.J., *A History of Philosophy, volume 1: Greece and Rome* (Westminster, Md.: Newman Press, 1946), pp. 127–141.

19. Karl Marx and Friedrich Engels, *Manifesto of the Communist Party,* in *The Marx-Engels Reader,* ed., Robert C. Tucker (New York: Norton, 1972), p. 337. Marx was born in Trier, Prussia (now in Germany) on May 5, 1818, and died on March 14, 1883. *The Manifesto* was first published in London in February 1848—when Marx was nearly 30 years old. Ibid., pp. xi–xiv.

20. An article on congressional ethics in *Newsweek* (June 14, 1976) makes the point so graphically that it is worth quoting at length:

> *Some of the Hill's most powerful veterans have long earned part of their income from outside business interests—and may be tempted to vote with their own bank accounts in mind when legislation affecting those interests has come before Congress. House whip Thomas P. (Tip) O'Neill is active in real estate and insurance in Massachusetts, Minority Leader John Rhodes of Arizona is a director and vice-president of a life insurance company and scores of other senior members are involved with the banking industry, oil and gas companies and farming operations. Do these connections destroy their judgment? Not necessarily, argues Russell Long of Louisiana, chairman of the powerful Senate Finance Committee and a reliable defender of oil interests—who nevertheless refuses to disclose the size of his personal oil and gas holdings, most of them inherited from his father, former Gov. Huey Long. "A long time ago I became convinced that if you have financial interests completely parallel to your state, then you have no problem," says Long. "If I didn't represent the oil and gas industry, I wouldn't represent the state of Louisiana."*

Even more difficult to trace is the influence of representatives who keep their law practices—and their clients, many of whom do business with the Federal government—when they become members of Congress. [p. 25]

For recent analyses of the marriage of economic and political power, see William Greider, *Who Will Tell the People? The Betrayal of American Democracy* (New York: Touchstone/Simon & Schuster, 1993); Phillip Stern, *Still the Best Congress Money Can Buy,* revised and expanded edition (Washington, D.C. : Regenery Gateway, 1992); John Jackley, *Hill Rat: Blowing the Lid Off Congress* (Washington, D.C.: Regnery Gateway, 1992); Donald Axelrod, *Shadow Government: The Hidden World of Public Authorities— and How they Control Over $1 Trillion of Your Money* (New York: Wiley, 1992); Michael Useem, *The Inner Circle: Large Corporations and the Rise of Business Political Activity in the US and UK* (New York: Oxford University Press, 1984); and Kim McQuaid, *Big Business and Presidential Power: From FDR to Reagan* (New York: Morrow, 1982).

21. J.A. Schmidhauser, "The Justices of the Supreme Court: A Collective Portrait," *Midwest Journal of Political Science* 3 (1959), pp. 2–37, 40–49, cited in William J. Chambliss and Robert B. Seidman, *Law, Order, and Power* (Reading, Mass.: Addison-Wesley, 1971), p. 96; and Richard Quinney, *Critique of Legal Order: Crime Control in Capitalist Society* (Boston: Little, Brown, 1973), pp. 60–82, 86–92.

22. See Ross Gelbspan, *Break-ins, Death Threats and the FBI: The Covert War Against The Central American Movement* (Boston: South End Press, 1991); Margaret Jayko, *FBI on Trial: The Victory in the Socialist Workers Party Suit Against Government Spying* (New York: Pathfinder Press, 1988); "F.B.I. Burglarized Leftist Offices Here 92 times in 1960–66, Official Files Show," *New York Times,* March 29, 1976, p. A1; "Burglaries by FBI Listed in Hundreds," *Washington Post,* July 16, 1975, p. A1. See also *Cointelpro: The FBI's Secret War on Political Freedom,* ed., Cathy Perkus, introduction by Noam Chomsky (New York: Monad Press, 1975).

23. "Hill Panel Raps FBI's Anti-Panthers Tactics," *Washington Post,* May 7, 1976, pp. A1, A22.

24. "FBI Labeled King 'Communist' in '62," *Washington Post,* May 6, 1976, pp. A1, A26; Michael Friedly and David Gallen, *Martin Luther King, Jr: The FBI File* (New York: Carroll & Graf, 1993). See also Carson Clayborne and David Gallen, *Malcom X: The FBI File* (New York: Carroll & Graf, 1991); and Kenneth O'Reilly, *'Racial Matters': The FBI's Secret File on Black America, 1960–1972* (New York: Free Press, 1989).

25. "Kelley Says FBI Is 'Truly Sorry' for Past Abuses, " *Washington Post* May 9, 1976, pp. A1, A14; "FBI Break-Ins Still Go On, Panel Reports," *Washington Post,* May 11, 1976. For more recent accounts, see "FBI Tactics Questioned in Probe of Activists," *Chicago Tribune,* March 2, 1990, p. 1: 5; "Here Come the '60s, With FBI in Tow," *Los Angeles Times,* June 26, 1990, p. A3; Peter Matthiesses, *In the Spirit of Crazy Horse* (New York: Viking, 1983) (FBI and the American Indian

Movement [AIM]; FBI sued author and delayed publication for several years); Rex Weyler, *Blood of the Land: The Government and Corporate War Against First Nations* (Philadelphia: New Society Publishers, 1992) (FBI and AIM). For other agencies of the government see, for example, "Military Spied on King, Other Blacks, Paper Says: Army Reportedly Targeted Southern Churches," *Washington Post,* March 21, 1993, p. A16.

26. James F. Richardson, *Urban Police in the United States* (Port Washington, N.Y.: Kennikat Press, 1974), pp. 8–13, 22. See also Richardson's *The New York Police: Colonial Times to 1901* (New York: Oxford University Press, 1970).

27. Rothman, *The Discovery of the Asylum,* pp. 57–108, especially pp. 79–81. Cf. Michel Foucault, *Discipline and Punish: The Birth of the Prison* (London: Allen Lane, 1977).

28. Richardson, *Urban Police,* pp. 158–61. See also R. Boyer and H. Morais, *Labor's Untold Story* (New York: United Electrical, Radio & Machine Workers of America, 1976).

29. Rothman, *The Discovery of the Asylum,* pp. 253–54.

30. Philip Taft and Philip Ross, "American Labor Violence: Its Causes, Character, and Outcome," in *The History of Violence in America,* eds., H. D. Graham and T. R. Gurr (New York: Bantam, 1969), pp. 281–395, especially pp. 281, 380; and Richard E. Rubenstein, *Rebels in Eden: Mass Political Violence in the United States* (Boston: Little, Brown, 1970), p. 81 inter alia. See also Center for Research in Criminal Justice, *The Iron Fist and the Velvet Glove,* pp. 16–19.

31. Karl Marx, *The German Ideology,* in *The Marx-Engels Reader,* ed., Tucker, p. 136.

32. Each new ruling class "is compelled, merely in order to carry through its aim, to represent its interest as the common interest of all the members of society." Marx, *The German Ideology,* p. 138.

33. Marx was not the first to use the term ideology. The term was coined by the Frenchman Antoine Destutt de Tracy, who was among the intellectuals named in 1795 to direct the researches of the newly founded Institut de France. The idéologues of the Institut generally believed that existing ideas were prejudices rooted in individual psychology or in political conditions and that the path to liberation from these prejudices and thus toward a rational society lay in a science of ideas (literally, an "idea-ology"), which made human beings aware of the sources of their ideas. Thomas Jefferson tried (albeit unsuccessfully) to have Destutt de Tracy's theory made part of the original curriculum of the University of Virginia. See George Lichtheim, "The Concept of Ideology," *History and Theory* 4, no. 2 (1965), pp. 164–195; and *Ideology, Politics, and Political Theory,* ed., Richard H. Cox (Belmont, Calif. : Wadsworth, 1969), pp. 7–8. Needless to say, Marx used the term ideology in ways that neither Destutt de Tracy nor Jefferson anticipated.

34. Lichtheim's essay provides a good discussion of the philosophical antecedents of the gradual separation of the notion of ideology from that of false consciousness.

Undoubtedly, this separation is of a piece with the current wisdom that insists that all views of the world are conditioned and rendered partial by the limits of the viewer's historical and social vantage point, and thus shrinks from trying to say anything true about the human condition. An illuminating contemporary example of this "current wisdom" applied to the criminal justice system is Walter B. Miller, "Ideology and Criminal Justice Policy: Some Current Issues," *Journal of Criminal Law and Criminology* 64, no. 2 (1973), pp. 141–62. I shall use the concept of ideology in the Marxian sense, that is, to include that of false consciousness.

35. What follows is just a smattering of the literature documenting the wide and abiding disparities of wealth in America or the existence of a very small, not necessarily organized, group of individuals who, in addition to being extremely wealthy, make most of the economic and political decisions that shape America's destiny: Douglas Massey and Nancy Denton, (Cambridge, Mass.: Harvard University Press, 1993); Thomas Dye, *Who's Running America: the Bush Era,* 5th ed. (Englewood Cliffs, N.J.: Prentice-Hall, 1990); G. William Domhoff, *The Power Elite and the State: How Policy Is Made in America* (New York: de Gruyter, 1990); Michael Parenti, *Democracy for the Few,* 5th ed. (New York: St Martin's Press, 1988); William Julius Wilson, *The Truly Disadvantaged: The Inner City, the Underclass, and Public Policy* (Chicago: University of Chicago Press, 1987); P. J. Quirk, *Industry and Influence in Federal Regulatory Agencies* (Princeton: Princeton University Press, 1981); Bertram Gross, *Friendly Fascism: The New Face of Power in America* (Boston: South End Press, 1980); G. Willian Domhoff, *The Powers that Be: Processes of Ruling Class Domination in America* (New York: Vintage , 1979); Edward S. Greenberg, *Serving the Few: Corporate Capitalism and the Bias of Government Policy* (New York: Wiley, 1974); Joseph Pechman and Benjamin A. Okner, *Who Bears the Tax Burden?* (Washington, D.C. : Brookings Institution, 1974); Philip M. Stern, *The Rape of the Taxpayer* (New York: Vintage, 1974); Richard C. Edwards, Michael Reich, and Thomas E. Weisskopf, *The Capitalist System: A Radical Analysis of American Society* (Englewood Cliffs, N.J.: Prentice-Hall, 1972); John Kenneth Galbraith, *The New Industrial State* (New York: Signet, 1968); G. William Domhoff, *Who Rules America?* (Englewood Cliffs, N.J.: Prentice-Hall, 1967); Gabriel Kolko, *Wealth and Power in America: An Analysis of Social Class and Income Distribution* (New York: Praeger, 1962); C. Wright Mills, *The Power Elite* (New York: Oxford University Press, 1956)

36. *StatAbst-1992,* p. 450, Table no. 704.

37. Alan S. Blinder, "The Level and Distribution of Economic Well-Being," in *The American Economy in Transition,* ed., Martin Feldstein (Chicago: University of Chicago Press, 1980), p. 466.

38. Carole Shammas, "A New Look at Long-Term Trends in Wealth Inequality in the United States," *American Historical Review* 98, no. 2 (April 1993), pp. 420, 421, 429. See Denis Kessler and Edward N. Wolff, "A Comparative Analysis of Household Wealth Patterns in France and the United States," *Review of Income and Wealth* 37 (1991), pp. 249–66., which concludes: "The major finding of this study is that wealth is distributed more unequally in the U.S. than in France. The differences are considerable" (p. 262).

39. Undoubtedly, the most interesting recent work on this topic is John Rawls's *A Theory of Justice* (Cambridge, Mass.: Harvard University Press, 1971). The noted British philosopher Stuart Hampshire has called it the most important work in moral philosophy since the World War II. It has largely dominated theoretical discussions of political, legal, and economic justice for the last two decades. Rawl's approach is essentially "naturalistic"; that is, he takes the "good" to be that which people rationally desire, and the "moral good" to be that which would best serve all people's rational desires. From this, he takes justice to be those social (legal, political, economic) arrangements that best serve the interests of all. To reach specific principles of justice, he asks for those principles that it would be rational for all people to agree to if each could not use force or influence to tailor the principles to his or her own interest. On the question of the distribution of income or wealth, this way of questioning leads to the principle that economic inequalities are just only if they work to everyone's advantage, for instance, as incentives that work to raise the level of productivity and thus the level of well-being for all. It would be the task of government to rectify inequalities that exceed this point, by means of taxes and transfers. I cannot, of course, do justice here to what Rawls takes 600 pages to explain and defend. However, I offer this short summary to suggest that the disparities of income in America are far from just in the light of contemporary moral philosophy. Clearly, those disparities are far greater than anything that could be claimed to be necessary to increase the well-being of all. Indeed, one would have to be blind not to see that they are not increasing the well-being of all. Robert Nozick has replied to Rawls in a book titled *Anarchy, State and Utopia* (New York: Basic Books, 1974), which no doubt represents the free enterprise system's theory of justice. Nozick holds that no theory (such as Rawls's) that calls for government intervention to rectify income distribution can be just. His argument is that if people acquire their property (including money) legitimately, then they have the right to sell or spend it as they wish. If this leads to disparities in wealth, one cannot alter this outcome without denying that those sellers or spenders had the right to dispose of their property or money as they saw fit. I shall not try to answer Nozick here. It should be noted, however, that his view starts from the assumption that the property or money that is sold or spent was acquired legitimately. In light of the fact that so much American property was stolen at gunpoint form Indians or Mexicans and so much wealth taken from the hides of black slaves, applying Nozick's theory in the American context would require a massive redistribution of wealth to reach the starting point at which we could say that individuals own what they own legitimately. For an extended discussion of these theories of justice, see Jeffrey Reiman, *Justice and Modern Moral Philosophy* (New Haven, Conn.: Yale University Press, 1990).

40. *StatAbst-1992*, p. 456, Tables nos. 717, 718; p. 460, Table no. 726.

41. One study reports that "among high school graduates with equal academic ability, the proportion going on to college averages nearly 25 percentage points lower for males (and nearly 35 for females) in the bottom socioeconomic quarter of the population than in the top quarter." Another indicates that "the sons of families in the top fifth of the socioeconomic pyramid have average incomes 75 percent higher than those coming from the bottom fifth." Arthur M. Okun, *Equality and Efficiency* (Washington, D.C.: Brookings Institution, 1975), pp. 81, 75.

Conclusion: *Criminal* Justice or Criminal *Justice*

What are states without justice but robber-bands enlarged?

St. Augustine, *Confessions*

. . . unjust social arrangements are themselves a kind of extortion, even violence.

John Rawls, *A Theory of Justice*

. . . the policeman moves through Harlem, therefore, like an occupying soldier in a bitterly hostile country; which is precisely what, and where he is, and the reason he walks in twos and threes.

James Baldwin, *Nobody Knows My Name*

The Crime of Justice

Robbers, extortionists, occupying soldiers are terms used to characterize those who enforce an unjust law and an unjust order. It would be a mistake to think this is merely a matter of rhetoric. There is a very real and very important sense in which those who use force unjustly or who use force to protect an unjust social order are no different from a band of criminals or an occupying army. If this isn't understood, you are likely to think that what has been described in the first three chapters and accounted for in the fourth amounts to no more than another call for reform of the criminal justice system to make it more effective and fairer, when in fact it is much more. A criminal justice system that functions like ours—that imposes its penalties on the poor and not equally on all who threaten society, that does not protect us against threats to our lives and possessions equal to or graver than those presently defined as "crimes," and that fails even to do those things that could better protect us against the crimes of the poor—*is morally no better than the criminality it claims to fight.*

At the end of this chapter, I propose some reforms of the system. However, these should not be taken as proposals aimed merely at improving the effectiveness or fairness of American criminal justice. If the argument of this chapter is correct, then these proposals represent the necessary conditions for establishing the moral superiority of criminal justice to criminality. They are the conditions that must be fulfilled if the criminal justice system is to be acquitted of the indictment implicit in the above statements of Baldwin, Rawls, and St. Augustine. Bear in mind that, by the criminal justice system, I do not mean only police, courts, and prisons. I include the entire legal system, from lawmakers to law enforcers.

What is common to the charge implicit in the statements of Baldwin, Rawls, and St. Augustine is the idea that *injustice transforms a legal system into its opposite.* What is common to the robber, the extortionist, and the occupying soldier is that each uses force (or the threat of force) to coerce other people to do things against their own interests. The robber and the extortionist use force to make other people hand over things of value. The occupying soldier uses force to subject one people to domination by another. The injustice at the heart of criminal acts is the forcing of people to serve the interests of others.

A legal system, of course, also uses force. Its defenders, however, maintain that it uses force to protect people's control over the things they value and over their own destinies. They claim that the legal system protects what people possess against robbers and extortionists and protects their autonomy against those who would try to impose their will on them by force. In short, although both a legal system and its opposite, either criminality or military domination, use force, the moral superiority of the legal system lies in the fact that it uses

force to secure the interests of the people subject to its force, whereas criminals and occupation troops use force to subject some people to the interests of others. The moral legitimacy of a legal system and the lack of legitimacy of crime and military domination hinge, then, on the question of whether coercion is being used to enhance people's own interests or the interests of others.

To say that the criminal justice system uses force to coerce people into serving the interests of others at the expense of their own *is to say the same thing about the criminal justice system that we say of crime!* In the absence of some compelling moral reason, force used to coerce people into serving the interests of others at the expense of their own is *morally no better than criminal force.* Because a legal system purports to do the reverse—to use force to protect *everyone's* interest in freedom and security by preventing and rectifying violations of those interests—legal systems call themselves *systems of justice.*[1]

This adds up to something that should be obvious but is not. A criminal justice system is criminal to the extent that it is not a system of justice. To call the criminal justice system a system of justice is to assert that the force used by the criminal justice system is morally opposite from, and morally superior to, the force used by criminals or conquerors. But then we must ask whether this assertion is true. A criminal justice system is a system of justice to the extent that it protects equally the interests and rights of all and to the extent that it punishes equally all who endanger these interests or violate these rights. To the extent that it veers from these goals, the criminal justice system is guilty of the same sacrificing of the interests of some for the benefit of others that it exists to combat. It is, therefore, morally speaking, guilty of crime. Which is it?

The experience of the twentieth century has taught us that we should not take for granted that every legal system is a system of justice. Hitler's Gemany and Stalin's Soviet Union, as well as (happily now changing) South Africa, are testimony to the fact that what is put forth as law may well be outrageously unjust. We have come to recognize that truth implicit in the statements of Baldwin, Rawls, and St. Augustine: What is put forth under color of law may be morally no better than crime or tyranny. Therefore, we can no longer uncritically take for granted that our own legal order is just merely because it is legal. We must subject it to the moral test of whether it serves and protects the interests of all to make sure it is not injustice disguised as justice, criminality wearing the mask of law.

It is, of course, not my aim to place the American legal system on par with that of Hitler's Germany or Stalin's Soviet Union. As I have acknowledged, there is much in the system that is legitimate and many are caught by the system who should be. Rather my claim is this:

- *To the extent that* the American criminal justice system fails to implement policies that could significantly reduce crime and the suffering it produces (as argued in Chapter 1)
- *To the extent that* the American criminal justice system fails to protect Americans against the gravest dangers to their lives and property (as argued in Chapter 2)

- *To the extent that* the American criminal justice system apprehends and punishes individuals, not because they are dangerous, but because they are *dangerous and poor* (as argued in Chapter 3)
- *Then, to that same extent,* the American criminal justice system fails to give all Americans either protection or justice, aids and abets those who pose the greatest dangers to Americans, and uses force in ways that do not serve equally the interests of all who are subject to that force, and *thus its use of force is morally no better than crime itself.*

Rehabilitating Criminal Justice in America

The criminal justice system in America is morally indistinguishable from criminality insofar as it exercises force and imposes suffering on human beings *while violating its own morally justifying ideals: protection and justice.* Once this is understood, the requirements for rehabilitating the system follow rather directly. The system must institute policies that make good on its claim to protect society and to do justice. In the remainder of this chapter I briefly suggest the outlines of a "treatment strategy" for *helping the system go straight.* It cannot be reiterated too frequently that these proposals are not offered as a means of *improving* the system. Nor am I under any illusion that these proposals will be easily adopted or implemented. They are presented as the necessary requirements for establishing the criminal justice system's moral difference from, and moral superiority to, *crime;* and even if not implemented or not likely to be implemented, they stand as a measure against which this moral difference and superiority can be judged. The proposals fall under the headings of the two ideals that justify the existence of a criminal justice system. These ideals are that the criminal justice system protect us against the real dangers that threaten us and that it not be an accomplice to injustice in the larger society. To realize these ideals, it is necessary that the harms and injustices done by the criminal justice system itself be eliminated.

Protecting Society

First, it must be acknowledged that every day that we refuse to implement those strategies that have a good chance of cutting down on the crimes people fear—the crimes on the FBI Index—the system is an accomplice to those crimes and bears responsibility for the suffering they impose. Thus:

We must put an end to the crime-producing poverty in our midst.

Throughout this book I have documented the striking persistence of large-scale poverty in America as well as the link between that poverty and much of the crime people fear the most. The elimination of poverty is the most promising crime-fighting strategy there is, and, in the long run, the most cost-effective. It is sometimes observed that poverty itself doesn't cause crime, because, for example, there was more poverty during the Great Depression than there is now and yet less crime. There is an important truth here, but it is easy to miss it. The truth is that it is not poverty as such that breeds crime, but the things that poverty brings with it in a modern, free, and free-enterprise society like ours: lack of good education (because schools are financed primarily out of local property taxes), lack of parental authority (because unemployed parents easily lose their children's respect), lack of cohesive local community (because those who can, escape the poor inner cities as quickly as possible), and so on. It is these things, rather than lack of money itself, that lead to crime. Investing in our inner cities and providing high-quality education, job-training, and jobs for the unemployed will give us more productive citizens with a stake in playing by the rules. And it will be cheaper than paying for police and prisons to house those who break the rules.

Eliminating the debilitating and crime-producing poverty around us is essential to any serious, long-term effort to protect society from crime. But along with it, we must:

Let the crime fit the harm and the punishment fit the crime.

For the criminal justice system to justify its methods, it must make good on its claim to protect society. This requires that the criminal law be redrawn so that the list of crimes reflects the real dangers that individuals pose to society. Notice here that I am not saying we should start punishing people for things that are currently not crimes. For all that I have said about the harms of occupational hazards, for example, I do not say that we should simply treat the people responsible for them as if they were criminals, if there are not yet criminal laws against what they have done. The traditional prohibition against ex post facto criminal laws—against punishing people for things they did before those things were crimes—is an important principle of justice. Rather, we must make new and clear laws against imposing certain dangers on workers and citizens generally, and then hold people to those laws no matter what their class standing. Crime in the suites should be prosecuted and punished as vigorously as crime in the streets.

The law must be drawn carefully so that individuals are not punished for harm they could not foresee or could not have avoided, or that others have freely consented to risk. Moreover, this is not a matter of punishing people for any and everything they do that might lead to harm. The pursuit of security must not swamp the legitimate claims of liberty and progress. Some risks are the inevitable companions of freedom, and some are part of modern life. For every mile of highway we build, we can predict the number of people who will be killed in accidents on it. This does not justify treating the highway engineer as a murderer. Rather, we must have an open and ongoing discussion about risk and decide together which risks are worth taking, and what level of risk is reasonable to impose on workers or citizens generally. Within this framework, we must rid the law of the distinction between *one-on-one* harm and *indirect* harm and *treat all harm-producing acts in proportion to the actual harm they produce. We must enact and implement punishments that fit the harmfulness of the crime without respect to the class of the criminal.* There is, for instance, general agreement that incarceration functions as an effective deterrent to corporate crime where the threat of imprisonment is believed.[2] To be believed, it must be used.

Because responsibility for corporate actions tends to get spread or even blurred in large organizations, we need legal requirements that make corporations identify in advance the individuals legally responsible for specific acts. Kip Schlegel recommends that a standard of "reckless supervision" be built into sentencing guidelines for corporate offenses, so that individuals with supervisory authority be held responsible for failure to exercise that authority when there is substantial risk of harm.[3]

But this is only the beginning. There is much more that can and should be done. In his book, *Corporate Crime and Violence,* Russell Mokhiber sets out a "50-Point Law-and Order Program to Curb Corporate Crime."[4] Mokhiber's suggestions are quite realistic and many fit well within the framework just outlined. Among them are recommendations for new laws that would require corporate executives to report activities that may cause death or injury, that would make it a criminal offense to willfully or recklessly fail to oversee an assigned activity that results in criminal conduct, that would enable federal prosecutors to bring federal homicide charges against companies that have caused death on a national scale (such as Manville or the tobacco companies), that would hold corporations responsible for how they respond to wrongful acts (do they cover up or take measures to prevent repetition, etc.?), that would facilitate class action suits against corporations, that would require convicted companies to notify their victims and to make restitution to them, that would better protect whistle blowers from reprisal, that would increase the penalties for convicted corporate executives, that would make it a crime for a corporation to have a faulty system for ensuring compliance with the law, and that would—for serious or repeated offenses—"execute" corporations (by stripping them of their corporate charters). Such laws, duly applied, would begin to make the criminal justice system's response proportionate to the real dangers in our society.

The other side of the coin is the decriminalization of "victimless crimes," acts like prostitution, homosexuality, gambling, vagrancy, drunkenness, and, of course, drug use. As long as these acts involve only persons who have freely chosen to participate, they are no threat to the liberty of any citizen. This also means that there is generally no complainant for these crimes, no person who feels harmed by these acts and who is ready and able to press charges and testify against the wrongdoers. Therefore, police have to use a variety of shady tactics involving deception and bordering on entrapment, which undermine the public's respect for the police and the police officers' respect for themselves. In any event, the use of such low-visibility tactics increases the likelihood of corruption and arbitrariness in the enforcement of the law. Beyond this, because these acts produce no tangible harm to others, laws against them make criminals out of people who have no intention to harm or take advantage of others. In short, such laws fill our prisons with people who aren't dangerous, while leaving truly dangerous people on the streets. To make good on its claim to protect society, the criminal justice system must not only treat the dangerous acts of business executives as crimes but also decriminalize those acts that are not clearly dangerous.[5]

More than 100 years ago, John Stuart Mill formulated a guiding principle, still relevant to our time, for the design of legislation in a society committed to personal liberty:

> *That principle is, that the sole end for which mankind are warranted, individually or collectively, in interfering with the liberty of action of any of their number, is self-protection. That the only purpose for which power can be rightfully exercised over any member of a civilized community, against his will, is to prevent harm to others.*[6]

Although the principle has had to be modified in recognition of the ways in which individuals can cause future harm to themselves because of present injudicious choices, particularly in a complex modern society where people must deal with machines and chemicals beyond their understanding,[7] the heart of the principle is still widely accepted. This is the notion that a necessary condition of any justifiable legal prohibition is that it prohibit an act that does harm to someone other than the actor himself. Because priority should be give to freedom of action, this harm should be *demonstrable* (i.e., verifiable by some widely agreed upon means, say, those used by medical science), and it should be of sufficient gravity to outweigh the value of the freedom that is to be legally prohibited.[8]

This principle should not only guide legislators and those engaged in revising and codifying criminal law but it should be raised to the level of an implicit constitutional principle. The U.S. Supreme Court recognizes certain traditional principles of legality as constitutional requirements even though they are not explicitly written into the Constitution. For instance, some laws have been held unconstitutional because of their vagueness[9] and others because they penalized a condition (like being a drunk or an addict), rather than an action (like drinking or using drugs).[10] The entire tenor of the Bill of Rights is to enshrine and protect individual liberty from the encroachment of the state, and thus Mill's principle is arguably already implicitly there.

Whether as a legislative or a judicial criterion, however, Mill's principle would undoubtedly rid our law of the residues of our puritan moralism. And it would eliminate the forced induction into criminality of the individuals, mainly those of the lower class, who get arrested for "victimless crimes." It would eliminate the pressure toward secondary crime (the need of the prostitute for a pimp to provide protection, theft by drug addicts to support their habits, violent turf wars between drug gangs, and so on). And it would free up resources for the fight against the really dangerous crimes. Before all, then,

We must legalize the production and sale of "illicit drugs" and treat addiction as a medical problem.

When drug addicts cannot obtain their fix legally, they will obtain it illegally. Because those who sell it illegally have a captive market, they will charge high prices to make their own risks worthwhile. To pay the high prices, addicts must, will, and do resort to crime. Thus, every day in which we keep the acquisition of drugs a crime, we are using the law to protect the high profits of drug black marketeers, *and* we are creating a situation in which large numbers of individuals are virtually physically compelled to commit theft. There can be little doubt that our present "cure" for narcotics use is more criminal (and criminogenic) than the narcotics themselves. Kurt Schmoke, mayor of Baltimore, says that, of 335 homicides committed in Baltimore in 1992, 48 percent were drug-related.[11] Another observer says that it is the drug war—not the drugs—that is shattering our inner cities. One of its effects is that a quarter of all black American men between the ages of 20 and 29 are behind bars, on parole or probation—which in turn makes them even less likely to find decent employment, and this locks them further into poverty.[12] And while we lock up so many young black men , we wonder why there are so many single black mothers and we don't notice the connection.

Ethan Nadelmann, of the Woodrow Wilson School of Public and International Affairs, points out that "there is no single legalization option. Legalization can mean a free market, or one closely regulated by the government, or even a government monopoly. . . .Legalization under almost any regime, however, does promise many advantages over the current approach. Government expenditures on drug-law enforcement would drop dramatically. So would organized crime revenues."[13] I will not enter into debate about the various ways in which drugs can be legalized. Although most observers seem to agree that the British system of dispensing heroin to registered addicts is superior to our own punitive system, a number of experts have gone even further. Norval Morris and Gordon Hawkins urge that narcotics use be decriminalized and the drugs be sold in pharmacies by prescription. Arnold Trebach urges that doctors be permitted to prescribe heroin for the treatment of addicts and as a powerful painkiller. Kurt Schmoke, mayor of Baltimore, has called for permitting health professionals to give drugs to addicts as part of a treatment and detoxification plan. Phillip Baridon recommends that pure heroin—clearly labeled as to contents, recommended dosage, and addictive potential—be sold at a low fixed price in pharmacies, without prescription, to anyone aged 18 or over.[14] Jerry Wilson, former Washington, D.C., police chief, has suggested the possibility of selling and taxing marijuana in the way that tobacco is currently sold and taxed, treating opiates and cocaine derivatives the way alcohol currently is treated, while keeping some psychoactive drugs available only at pharmacies with a doctor's prescription.[15]

Any reasonable plan of legalization will start by decriminalizing marijuana, which is virtually harmless. On the other hand, there may be some drugs that are so addictive or so likely to stimulate people to violence that we must keep them illegal. This may be the case with "crack" and with PCP, also known as "angel dust." If this turns out to be true (and the government has so exaggerated the dangers of illicit drugs over the years that healthy skepticism is warranted about these recent claims), it may be necessary to exclude these from the general program of decriminalization. With less dangerous drugs decriminalized, however, many users of crack or PCP might switch to the less dangerous ones, and, in any event, already overstretched law enforcement resources would be freed up to concentrate on the really dangerous drugs and on the crucial problem of keeping illicit drugs away from youngsters. 

Ending poverty, criminalizing the really dangerous acts of the well off, and decriminalizing victimless crimes will reduce crime, protect society, and free up our police and prisons for the fight against the criminals who really threaten our lives and limbs. For these, however,

We must develop correctional programs that promote rather than undermine personal responsibility, and we must offer ex-offenders real preparation and a real opportunity to make it as law-abiding citizens.

The scandal of our prisons has been amply documented. Like our drug policy, our prisons seem more calculated to produce than reduce crime. The enforced childhood of imprisonment may be the painful penalty offenders deserve, but if it undermines their capacity to go straight after release, we are cutting off our noses to spite our faces. People cannot learn to control themselves responsibly if they have spent years having every aspect of their lives—the hour they wake, the number of minutes they wash, the time and content of eating and working and exercising, the hour at which lights go out—regulated by someone else. Add to this the fact that convicts usually emerge with no marketable skill and little chance of getting a decent job with the stigma of a prison sentence hanging over them. The result is a system in which we never let criminals finish paying their debt to society and give them every incentive to return to crime.

If we are going to continue to punish people by depriving them of their liberty, we must do it in a way that prepares them for the life they will lead when their liberty is returned. Anything less than this is a violation of the Constitution's Eighth Amendment guarantee against "cruel and unusual punishment." Depriving a person of his or her liberty may be an acceptable punishment, but *depriving people of their dignity and a chance to live a law-abiding life when their punishment is supposed to be over is cruel and* (should be but sadly is not) *unusual!*

If, as I think, depriving people of a chance to live a law-abiding life after prison is cruel and unusual punishment, then pursuant to the guarantee of the Eighth Amendment, every imprisoned person should have a right to training at a marketable skill as well as a right to compete equally with nonex-convicts for a job once the punishment is over. This might require making it illegal to discriminate against ex-convicts in hiring and illegal to require job applicants to state whether they had ever been arrested, convicted, and/or imprisoned for a crime. This requirement might have to be modified for particularly sensitive occupations, although on the whole I think it would be fairer and more effective in rehabilitating ex-cons to enact it across the board and to have the government finance or subsidize a fund to insure losses incurred as a result of ex-convicts. My hunch is that this would be much less costly than paying to support ex-cons in prison and their families on welfare when they return to crime for lack of a job. Beyond this, prison industries should pay inmates at prevailing wages; this money then could be used for restitution to victims and to purchase privileges and possibly increased privacy or freedom for the prisoners—all of which might tend to give them greater practice at controlling their own lives so that they will be prepared to do so after release.

To release them back into a safer and more peaceful society,

We must enact and vigorously enforce stringent gun controls.

Americans are armed to the teeth. The handgun is the most easily concealed, the most effective, and the deadliest weapon there is. Its ubiquity is a constant temptation to would-be crooks who lack the courage or skill to commit crime without weapons or to chance hand-to-hand combat. Its ubiquity also means that any dispute may be transformed into a fatal conflict beyond the desires or expectations of the disputants. And the handgun is only part of the story. In recent years, it has become relatively easy to obtain rapid-firing assault rifles. Trying to fight crime while allowing such easy access to guns is like trying to teach a child to walk and tripping him each time he stands up. In its most charitable light, it is hypocrisy. Less charitably, it is complicity in murder.[16]

These changes, taken together, would be likely to reduce dangerous crime and to bring us a legal order that actually punished (and, it is hoped, deterred) all and only those acts that really threaten our lives, limbs, and possessions, and punished them in proportion to the harm they really produce. Such a legal system could be truly said to protect society.

Promoting Justice

The changes recommended above would, in part, make the criminal justice system more just, because people would be punished in proportion to the seriousness of their antisocial acts, and the number of innocent persons victimized by those acts would be reduced. At the same time, however, we have seen that the criminal justice system is biased against the poor, and until poverty is eliminated, much must be done to assure justice for the poor people who get caught up in the criminal justice system.

A criminal justice system should arrest, charge, convict, and sentence individuals with an eye only to their crime, not to their class. Any evidence of more frequent arrest or harsher penalties for poor persons than for others accused of the same crime is a grave injustice that tends to undermine the legitimacy of the criminal justice system. Because many of the decisions that work to the disadvantage of the poor—police decisions to arrest, prosecutors' decisions to charge, and judges' decisions on how long to sentence—are exercises of discretion often out of public view, they are particularly resistant to control. Because, unlike prosecutors' or judges' decisions, the police officer's decision *not* to arrest is *not* a matter of record, it is the least visible exercise of discretion and the most difficult to control. Our best hope to make arrests by police more just lies in increased citizen awareness and education of police officers so that they at least become aware of the operation and impact of their own biases and are held more directly accountable to, and by, the public they serve and sometimes arrest.

As for prosecutorial and judicial discretion, two approaches seem potentially fruitful. First, lawmakers ought to spell out the acceptable criteria that prosecutors may use in deciding whether or what to charge and the criteria that judges may use in deciding whether or what to sentence. The practice of multiple charging (e.g., charging an accused burglar with "the lesser included crimes" of breaking and entering, possession of burglar's tools, and so on) should be eliminated. It is used by prosecutors to "coax" accused persons into pleading guilty to one charge by threatening to press *all* charges. Of all the dubious features of our system of bargain justice, this seems most clearly without justification because it works to coerce a plea of guilty that should be uncoerced if it is to be legally valid.[17] The law should also set out more specific sentencing ranges because the present system leads to individuals receiving widely varying sentences for the same crimes—a practice that can be viewed only as arbitrary and capricious, that violates the principle that citizens should know in advance what is in store for them if they break a law, and that produces in convicts disrespect for the law rather than remorse for their violations. In addition to, and in conjunction with, these legislative changes, we ought to require prosecutors and judges to put in writing the reasons they have charged or sentenced in one way rather than another. They should be required to give an account of their policies and practices to some truly representative body to show that they are fair and reasonable.

The recently developed federal sentencing guidelines (followed by the inception of sentencing guidelines in many states) are an important step in this direction.[18] But they are only a step. They have not eliminated discrimination. D'Alession and Stolzenberg found that lower socioeconomic–status offenders were likely to receive harsher sentences for nonproperty and morals offenses than higher socioeconomic–status offenders, and that sentencing guidelines did not appear to reduce these disparities.[19] And as I pointed out in Chapter 3, for similar charges white defendants are more likely to get sentences below the guideline minimums than blacks. It appears that such guidelines have not so much eliminated discretion as shifted it from judges to prosecutors (who decide what to charge), and because prosecutors are less insulated from political pressures than judges, that is a step backwards. Thus, sentencing guidelines must be matched with charging guidelines.[20] Neither sort of guidelines need be so rigid as to leave no room for the expert judgment of judges or prosecutors. Rather, we need rules that hold those officials accountable for their judgments by requiring them to explain and justify their decisions.

Moreover, the sentencing guidelines that we have arose during the Reagan era, with its emphasis on extreme punitiveness. They often either include or are accompanied by very draconian mandatory minimum sentences for small crimes, particularly anything to do with drugs. In response to this, an advocacy group was recently formed called Families Against Mandatory Minimums, whose "files bulge with cases of citizens serving drug sentences of 5, 10 and 20 years without parole chances for first and often minor offenses."[21] Because this very punitive approach has dramatically expanded our prison populations without seriously reducing crime, it is time to separate the task of assuring evenhanded sentencing from that of hard-fisted sentencing. However we achieve it, it is clear that to make the criminal justice system function justly:

We must narrow the range in which police officers, prosecutors, and judges exercise discretion, and we must develop procedures to hold them accountable to the public for the fairness and reasonableness of their decisions.

All these changes still leave standing what is probably the largest source of injustice to the poor in the system: *unequal access to quality legal counsel.* We know that, by and large, privately retained counsel will have more incentive to put in the time and effort to get their clients off the hook, and we know that this results in a situation in which *for equal crimes* those who can retain their own counsel are more likely to be acquitted than those who cannot. The present system of allocating assigned counsel or public defenders to the poor and privately retained lawyers to the affluent is little more than a parody of the constitutional guarantee of *equal protection under the law.*

There are simply no two ways about this. In our system, even though lawyers are assigned to the poor, justice has a price. Those who pay get the choicest cut—those who cannot, get the scraps. Little over a century ago, before there were public police forces in every town and city, people got "police protection" by hiring private police officers or bodyguards if they could afford it. Protection was available for a price, and so those who had more money were better protected under the law. Today, we regard it as every citizen's right to have police protection, and we would find it outrageous if police protection were allocated to citizens on a fee-for-service basis. *This is precisely where we stand with respect to the legal protection provided by lawyers!*

Legal protection is not only provided by the police. Attorneys are necessary to protect individuals from losing their freedom at the hands of the laws before they have exhausted the legal defenses that are theirs by right. Both police officers and lawyers are essential to the individual's legal protection. It is sheer hypocrisy to acknowledge everyone's right to equal protection under the law by the police and then to allocate protection under the law by lawyers on the basis of what individuals can pay. As long as this continues, we cannot claim that there is anything like equal treatment before the law in the criminal justice system.

We must transform the equal right to counsel into the right to equal counsel as far as it is possible.

Although this would appear to be a clear requirement of the "equal protection" and "due process" clauses of the Constitution, the Supreme Court has avoided it, perhaps because it poses massive practical problems—and surely it does. However, the creation of public police forces to protect everyone posed many practical problems in its time as well.

Certainly it would not be appropriate to use the police as a model for resolving the problem of equal counsel. To establish a government legal service for all—in effect, to nationalize the legal profession—might make equal legal representation available to all. It would, however, undermine the adversary system by undercutting the independence of defense attorneys from the state. Some form of national legal insurance to enable all individuals to hire private attorneys of their own choice, however, could bring us closer to equal legal protection without compromising the adversarial relationship.

Such insurance would undoubtedly have to be subsidized by the government, as are the police, the courts, and prisons; but it would not necessarily have to be totally paid for out of taxes. People can rightly be expected to pay their legal bills up to some fraction of their income, if they have one. The rest would be paid for by a government subsidy that would pay the difference between what the accused could afford and the going rate for high-quality legal counsel. Nothing in the system need interfere with the freedom of the accused to select the lawyer of his or her choice (an option closer to the hearts of free enterprisers than the present public defender system allows) or interfere with the independence of the lawyer.

Undoubtedly, such a system would be costly. Our commitment to equal justice, however, remains a sham until we are willing to pay this price. Americans have paid dearly to protect the value of liberty enshrined in the Constitution. Is it too much to ask that they pay to realize the ideal of justice enshrined there too?

One final recommendation remains to be made. I have already argued that the criminal justice system, by its very nature, embodies the prevailing economic relations in its laws. This means that it is an error to think of the criminal justice system as an entity that can be reformed in isolation from the larger social order. A criminal justice system is a means to protect that social order, and it can be no more just than the order it protects. A law against theft may be enforced with an even and just hand. But if it protects an unjust distribution of wealth and property, the result is *injustice evenly enforced*. A criminal justice system cannot hold individuals guilty of the injustice of breaking the law if the law itself supports and defends an unjust social order. 

Without economic and social justice, the police officer in the ghetto is indeed an occupying soldier with no more legitimacy than his or her gun provides. Without economic and social justice, the criminal justice system is the defender of injustice and is thus morally indistinguishable from the criminal. A *criminal justice system can be no more just than the society its laws protect*. Along with the other recommendations I have made in this chapter, the achievement of economic and social justice is a necessary condition for establishing the criminal justice system's moral superiority to crime.

We must establish a more just distribution of wealth and income and make equal opportunity a reality for all Americans.

This is not merely a matter of throwing money in the direction of poor people. It is a call for investment in our most important resource: people; and for targeting that investment where it is most urgently needed and morally required: to rebuild our squalid inner cities, to educate our young, to offer real opportunity to poor people to lift themselves out of poverty without lowering themselves into dependency. This would amount to a redistribution of wealth and income in the direction of greater social and economic justice. Because it would also reduce the temptations to crime produced by poverty, it brings us full circle to the first recommendation that I made for protecting society. *Here the requirements of safety and justice converge.*

Summary

Every step toward reducing poverty and its debilitating effects, toward criminalization of the dangerous acts of the affluent and vigorous prosecution of "white-collar" crime, toward decriminalization of "illicit drugs" and "victimless crimes," and toward domestic disarmament; every step toward creating a correctional system that promotes human dignity, toward giving ex-offenders a real opportunity to go straight, toward making the exercise of power by police officers, prosecutors, and judges more reasonable and more just, toward giving all individuals accused of crime equal access to high-quality legal expertise in their defense; and every step toward establishing economic and social justice is a step that moves us from a system of *criminal* justice to a system of criminal *justice*. The refusal to take those steps is a move in the opposite direction.

Study Questions

1. What do the three quotations at the beginning of this chapter mean? How do they apply to the American criminal justice system?
2. Do you support gun control legislation? Why or why not?
3. What is meant by "victimless crimes"? Should they be kept criminal?
4. Would you be willing to have your taxes go to pay for equal-quality legal counsel for the poor?
5. Is the distribution of wealth and income in America just? How is this related to the justice of the criminal justice system?
6. Are the recommendations made in this chapter likely to be instituted? What does your answer imply about your view of the American legal system?

Additional Readings

MILLER, JEROME. *Last One Over the Wall: The Massachusetts Experiment in Closing Reform Schools.* Columbus: Ohio State University Press, 1992.

PEPINSKY, HAROLD AND RICHARD QUINNEY. *Criminology as Peacemaking.* Bloomington: Indiana University Press, 1991.

SCHLEGEL, KIP. *Just Deserts for Corporate Criminals.* Boston: Northeastern University Press, 1990.

TREBACH, ARNOLD AND JAMES INCIARDI. *Legalize It? Debating American Drug Policy.* Washington D.C.: American University Press, 1993.

Notes to Conclusion

1. Although I think this way of looking at the legal system, at justice, and at the moral legitimacy of the law is common to most moral and legal philosophers, it should be acknowledged that my own formulation bears a heavy debt to the conceptions of justice and morality developed by John Rawls, Kurt Baier, and Herbert Morris. See John Rawls, *A Theory of Justice* (Cambridge, Mass.: Harvard University Press, 1971); Kurt Baier, *The Moral Point of View: A Rational Basis of Ethics* (New York: Random Hose, 1965); and Herbert Morris, "Persons and Punishment," in *Human Rights,* ed., A. I. Melden (Belmont, Calif.: Wadsworth, 1970), pp. 111–134. On the issue of the legitimacy of states (i.e., political-legal systems), see Robert Paul Wolff, *In Defense of Anarchism* (New

York: Harper and Row, 1976), Jeffrey H. Reiman, *In Defense of Political Philosophy* (New York: Harper and Row, 1972), Reiman, "Autonomy, Authority, and Universalizability," The Personalist (January 1978), pp. 85–92; and Reiman "Anarchism and Nominalism: Wolff's Latest Obituary for Political Philosophy," Ethics (October 1978). On the issue of the legitimacy and moral justification of police authority in particular, see Jeffrey H. Reiman, "Police Autonomy vs. Police Authority: A Philosophical Perspective,: in The Police Community, eds., Jack Goldsmith and Sharon S. Goldsmith (Pacific Palisades, Calif.: Palisades Publishers, 1974), pp. 225–233; and Roger Wertheimer, "Are the Police Necessary?" in *The Police in Society,* eds., Emilio C. Viano and Jeffrey H. Reiman (Lexington, Mass.: Lexington Books, 1975), pp. 49–60. See also Jeffrey Reiman, Justice and Modern Moral Philosophy (New Haven: Yale University Press, 1990).

2. These are the words of a former director of the fraud division of the Department of Justice:

> *No one in direct contact with the living reality of business conduct in the United States is unaware of the effect the imprisonment of seven high officials in the Electrical Machinery Industry in 1960 had on the conspiratorial price fixing in many areas of our economy; similar sentences in a few cases each decade would almost completely cleanse our economy of the cancer of collusive price fixing and the mere prospect of such sentences is itself the strongest available deterrent to such activities.*

Gordon B. Spivak, "Antitrust Enforcement in the United States: A Primer," *Connecticut Bar Journal* 37 (September 1963), p. 382.

3. Kip Schlegel, *Just Deserts for Corporate Criminals* (Boston: Northeastern University Press, 1990), p. 137. This book contains a very extensive and valuable analysis of the jurisprudential and philosophical issues involved in assessing the guilt of both individual corporate officers and corporations themselves.

4. Russell Mokhiber, *Corporate Crime and Violence: Big Business Power and the Abuse of Public Trust* (San Francisco: Sierra Club, 1988), pp. 38–65.

5. See chap. 1, "The Overreach of the Criminal Law," in Morris and Hawkins, *The Honest Politician's Guide to Crime Control,* pp. 1–28; Herbert Packer, *The Limits of the Criminal Sanction* (Stanford, Calif.: Stanford University Press, 1968); and Jeffrey H. Reiman, "Can We Avoid the Legislation of Morality?" in *Legality, Morality and Ethics in Criminal Justice,* eds., Nicholas N. Kittrie and Jackwell Susman (New York: Praeger, 1979), pp. 130–41.

6. John Stuart Mill, *On Liberty* (1859) (New York: Appleton-Century-Crofts, 1973), p. 9.

7. See, for example, Gerald Dworkin, "Paternalism," in Morality and the Law, ed., Richard Wasserstrom (Belmont, Calif. : Wadsworth, 1971), pp. 107–26; and Joel Feinberg, "Legal Paternalism," in *Today's Moral Problems,* ed., Richard Wasserstrom (New York: Macmillan, 1975), pp. 33–50.

8. See, for instance, the excellent discussion of the principle in Peter T. Manicas, *The Death of the State* (New York: Putnam, 1974), chap. 5: "The Liberal Moral Ideal," pp. 194–241; and H. L. A. Hart, *Law, Liberty and Morality* (New York: Vintage, 1963).

9. The standard laid down in *Conally v. General Constr. Co., 269 U.S. 385, 391, 70 L. Ed. 322, 46 S. Ct. 126 (1926)* is "whether or not the vagueness is of such a character , 'that men of common intelligence must necessarily guess at its meaning'." *See also Lanzetta et al. v. State of New Jersey,* 306, U.S. 451, 83 L. Ed. 888, 59 S. Ct. 618 (1939), where the Supreme Court struck down a New Jersey statute that made it a felony for anyone not engaged in any lawful occupation to be a member of a gang because the terms of the statute were "vague, indefinite and uncertain" and thus "repugnant to the due process clause of the Fourteenth Amendment." Both cases are cited and discussed in Jerome Hall, *General Principles of Criminal Law,* 2d ed. (New York: Bobbs-Merrill, 1960), pp. 36–48. For a constitutional and philosophical argument for treating Mills's harm principle as an implied constitutional principle, see David A. J. Richards, *Sex, Drugs, Death, and the Law: An Essay on Human Rights and Overcriminalization* (Totowa, N.J.: Rowman and Littlefield, 1982), pp. 1–34, inter alia.

10. See *Robinson v. California,* 370 U.S. 66 (1962), where the court held that a state law penalizing a person for a "status" such as addiction constitutes "cruel and unusual punishment" in violation of the Eighth Amendment. Cited and discussed in Nicholas N. Kittrie, *The Right to Be Different: Deviance and Enforced Therapy* (Baltimore: Johns Hopkins University Press, 1971), pp. 35–36, inter alia.

11. Kurt Schmoke, "It's Time to Get Real About Guns and Drugs," *Washington Post Outlook,* October 3, 1993. p. C4.

12. Jonathan Marshall, "How Our War on Drugs Shattered the Cities," *Washington Post Outlook,* May 17, 1992, pp. C1, C2.

13. Ethan Nadelmann, "U.S. Drug Policy: A Bad Export," in Robert Lang, ed., *Drugs in America* (New York: Wilson, 1993), p. 232.

14. Norval Morris and Gordon Hawkins, *The Honest Politician's Guide to Crime Control* (Chicago: University of Chicago Press, 1970), pp. 3, 8–10; Arnold S. Trebach, *The Heroin Solution* (New Haven, Conn.: Yale University Press, 1982), pp. 267–70; Phillip C. Baridon, *Addiction, Crime, and Social Policy* (Lexington, Mass.: Lexington Books, 1976), p. 88; Schmoke, "It's Time to Get Real About Guns and Drugs," pp. C1, C4.

15. Jerry V. Wilson, "Our Wasteful War on Drugs, " *Washington Post,* January 18, 1994, p. A20.

16. See the thoughtful recommendations for gun control and their rationale in Morris and Hawkins, *The Honest Politician's Guide to Crime Control,* pp. 63–71.

17. I have already pointed out that the vast majority of persons convicted of crimes in the United States are not convicted by juries. They plead guilty as the result of a "bargain" with the prosecutor (underwrtten by the judge), in which the prosecutor agrees to drop other charges in return for the guilty plea. Kenneth Kipnis argues that the entire system of bargain justice is a violation of the ideal of justice because it amounts to coercing a guilty plea and often to punishing an offender for a crime other that the one he or she has committed. It is an argument worth considering. See Kenneth Kipnis, "Criminal Justice and the Negotiated Plea," *Ethics* 86. no. 2 (January 1976), pp. 93–106.

18. "Justices Uphold Disputed System of U.S. Sentencing," *New York Times*, January 19, 1989, p. A1.

19. Stewart D'Alessio and Lisa Stolzenberg, "Socioeconomic Status and the Sentencing of the Traditional Offender," *Journal of Criminal Justice* 21 (1993), pp. 71, 73, 74.

20. This proposal is also made in Note, "Developments in the Law: Race and the Criminal Process," *Harvard Law Review* 101 (1988), pp. 1550–51. The authors of this article recommend that charging guidelines be supplemented with an "impact-inference standard." Under this standard, a defendant who believes that he or she has been discriminatorily charged would have to show that (1) he or she is the member of an identifiable class, (2) there is statistical evidence of discriminatory impact of prosecutorial decisions in the jurisdiction, and (3) the prosecutor's office lacked internal guidelines and procedures adequate to prevent abuse. If a defendant succeeded in showing these three elements, the burden of proof would shift to the government to explain its actions. Ibid., pp. 1552–53.

21. Colman McCarthy, "Justice Mocked: The Farce of Mandatory Minimum Sentences," *Washington Post*, February 27, 1993, p. A23.

Appendix: The Marxian Critique of Criminal Justice[1]

Here in the Appendix I shall try to present the reader with an overview of Marxian theory that goes from Marxism's theory of capitalism to its theory of law and from there to criminal justice. This addresses some of the same aspects of criminal justice we discussed in the main text of this book, but it sets them in a theoretical framework different from (although not incompatible with) the Pyrrhic defeat theory, with its historical inertia explanation of the failure of criminal justice. I shall close with comments on the ethical implications of the Marxian analysis.

Criminal justice has a concrete reality comprising police, prisons, courts, guns, and the rest. What is most important for our purposes, however, is the particular shape that this concrete reality takes in capitalism. This shape is governed according to certain principles that spell out what shall count as violations, what shall be done to violators, and so on. (For simplicity's sake, I shall use the term *criminal justice* as shorthand for the principles that normally govern criminal justice practices and practitioners in capitalism, and use the term *criminal justice system* as shorthand for the concrete reality of the practices and practitioners so governed.) Marxian analysis is in the first instance directed toward these governing principles. It aims to show that these principles are "economic reflexes," that is, they reflect and thus support the existing economic arrangements—in our case, the capitalist mode of production.

Criminal justice plays an ideological role in support of capitalism because people do not recognize that the principles governing criminal justice are reflections of capitalism. The principles of criminal justice appear instead to be the result of pure reason, and thus a system that supports capitalism is (mistakenly) seen as an expression of rationality itself! Engels—Marx's lifelong collaborator—writes that "the jurist imagines he is operating with *a pri-*

ori [i.e., purely rational] principles, whereas they are really only economic reflexes; so everything is upside-down. And it seems to me obvious that this inversion . . . , so long as it remains unrecognized, forms what we call *ideological conception.*"[2] As a consequence of this "inversion," criminal justice embodies and conveys a misleading and partisan view of the reality of the whole capitalist system. Because capitalism requires laws that give individual capitalists the right to own factories and resources, a view of these laws that makes them appear to be purely rational makes capitalism appear purely rational as well.

Before proceeding, a few words about the nature of Marxian theory are in order. First of all, Marx's theory of capitalism is separate from his advocacy of socialism and communism. Marx might be right about how capitalism works or about capitalism's unjust nature, even if socialism or communism would in fact be worse or even if they are just utopian dreams that cannot be made real. This is important because of the tendency to think that the collapse of communism in eastern Europe and the former Soviet Union (as well as the unpalatable features of that communism before it collapsed) refutes Marxian theory generally. This is quite untrue. What the collapse of eastern European and Soviet communism refutes is, if anything, the theories of Lenin and Stalin about how to establish communism. Marx himself said very little about such things, and what he does say generally favors a much more democratic kind of socialism and communism than what Lenin and Stalin managed to bring about. Accordingly, it is still useful to look at what Marx thought about capitalism, even if one is convinced by recent events of the undesirability of actual communism or the impossibility of ideal communism.

Second, when we turn to Marx's theory of capitalism, we see that Marx portrays capitalism in pure form. He does so not to claim that that is how it actually exists anywhere, but rather to show the shape to which it tends everywhere. Actual systems will be a product of the force of that tendency versus the force of local factors, traditions, talent, innovation, luck, resources, the success or failure of particular human actions, and so on. Likewise, a Marxian analysis of criminal justice will indicate the pure form toward which criminal justice systems tend insofar as they support the functioning of capitalism. Actual criminal justice systems will be approximations of this tendency. Actual criminal justice systems will also clearly be shaped by human actions—often substantially so. No Marxist need deny that criminal justice in the capitalist United States is quite a different thing from criminal justice in, say, capitalist Chile. What she must claim, rather, is that as capitalism develops in both, their criminal justice systems will increasingly tend to take on the shape that the theory implies.

I shall try to show how Marxism leads to a theory of the structure that criminal justice systems tend to have under capitalism, while at the same time recognizing that any existing criminal justice system is only an approximation of this structure. To give the reader as complete a picture as possible (in this short space) of the whole of Marxian theory—from general theory of capitalism to particular theory of criminal justice, and from there to ethical evaluation—I will have to sacrifice a lot of detail. I shall largely ignore the differences that individual actions may make in determining the shape of actual systems. I hope I have said enough to suggest that this in no way implies that human actions are irrelevant to actual historical outcomes.

I proceed in the following way. In the first section, "Marxism and Capitalism," I sketch out enough of Marx's theory of the capitalist mode of production as is necessary to lay the foundation for a Marxian theory of law. Because law is, for Marxism, a form of ideology, we shall have to see how ideology works in capitalism. I take this up in the next section, "Capitalism and Ideology." In "Ideology and Law," I develop the Marxian theory of law and from it the Marxian theory of criminal justice. Then in the final section, "Law and Ethics," I consider the characteristic Marxian moral judgments about criminal justice—particularly about guilt and punishment—that are appropriate in light of the Marxian account.

Marxism and Capitalism

Marx says that capitalism is a system of "forced labour—no matter how much it may seem to result from free contractual agreement."[3] Here is both the truth that Marx asserts about capitalism and the legal ideology that shrouds that truth. To understand precisely how this works, we must consider the nature of the coercion that Marx discovered in capitalism.

For Marx, the value of any commodity is equivalent to the average amount of labor-time necessary to produce it.[4] Under capitalism, the worker's ability to labor—Marx calls this *labor-power*—is sold to the capitalist in return for a wage. Because labor-power is also a commodity, its value is also equivalent to the average amount of labor-time necessary to produce it. "Producing labor-power" means producing the goods needed to maintain a functioning worker. The value of labor-power then is equivalent to the labor-time that on the average goes into producing the goods (food, clothing, shelter, and so on) necessary to maintain a functioning worker at the prevailing standard of living, which Marx understood to differ among countries depending on their respective histories (*Capital,* vol. 1, p. 171). The worker receives this in the form of a wage, that is, in the form of the money necessary to purchase these goods.

The capitalist obtains the money she pays as a wage by selling what the worker produces during the time for which he is employed. If the worker produced an amount of value equivalent only to his wage, there would be nothing left over for the capitalist and no reason for her to hire the worker in the first place. Labor-power, however, has the unique capacity to produce more value than its own value (*Capital,* vol. 1, pp. 193–94). The worker can work longer than the labor-time equivalent of the value of the wage he receives. The amount of labor-time that the worker works to produce value equivalent to his wage Marx calls *necessary labor.* The additional labor-time that the worker works beyond this Marx calls *surplus labor,* and the value it produces he calls *surplus value.* The surplus value, of course, belongs to the capitalist and is the source of her profit (*Capital,* vol. 1, pp. 184-186); that is, when the capitalist sells the product made by the worker, the capitalist gives some of the money she gets back to the worker as a wage (this corresponds to the value that the worker put into the product during his necessary labor-time), and the capitalist keeps the rest as profit (this corresponds to the surplus labor-time that the worker puts in after his necessary labor-time).

Profit, then, rests on the extraction of unpaid surplus labor from the worker. To see this, one need only recall that although all products in the economy are produced by labor, only a portion of those products are wage-goods that the workers get paid with (they get them for the money they receive as wages). The remainder belongs to their bosses and is effectively uncompensated. The wage-goods are not compensation because the workers produce these goods themselves. What they produce beyond this goes to the capitalist gratis. Thus, writes Marx, "The secret of the self-expansion of capital [that is, the secret of profit] resolves itself into having the disposal of a definite quality of other people's unpaid labour" (*Capital,* vol. 1, p. 534).

For Marx, however, capitalism is not only a system in which unpaid labor is extracted from workers, it is a system in which workers are *forced* to provide this unpaid labor. Workers are not merely shortchanged, they are enslaved. Capitalism is "a coercive relation" (*Capital,* vol. 1, p. 309). The coercion, however, is not of the direct sort that characterized slavery or feudal serfdom. It is, rather, an indirect force built into the very fact that capitalists own the means of production and laborers do not. Means of production are things like factories and machines and land and resources—things that are necessary for productive labor. Lacking ownership of means of production, workers lack their own access to the means of producing a livelihood. *By this very fact* workers are compelled to sell their labor to capitalists for a wage because the alternative is (depending on conditions) either painful or fatal: relative pauperization or absolute starvation.

This compulsion is not in conflict with the fact that the terms upon which the worker works for the capitalist are the result of free contractual agreements. Indeed, the compulsion works *through* free agreements. Because the agreements are free, each side must offer the other a reason for agreeing. If workers offered capitalists only as much labor as went into the wage-goods they will get back in return from the capitalists, the capitalists would have no reason to purchase their labor. It follows that, no matter how free the wage contract is, as long as it occurs in a context in which a few own all the means of production, those who do not own means of production will be compelled to give up some of their labor without compensation to those who do. Thus, Marx describes the wage-worker as a "man who is compelled to sell himself of his own free will" (*Capital,* vol. 1, p. 766). The compulsion of the worker operates through the structure of property relations: "The dull compulsion of economic relations completes the subjection of the labourer to the capitalist. Direct force, outside economic conditions, is of course still used, but only exceptionally" (*Capital,* vol. 1, p. 737).

The very existence of the social roles of capitalist and worker—defined by ownership and nonownership of means of production, respectively—is what coerces the worker to work without compensation. It coerces in the same way that a social structure that allotted to one group ownership and thus control of all the available oxygen would coerce. Beyond what was necessary to defend this group against challenges to its ownership of the oxygen, no additional force would be necessary for the coercion to operate. Indeed, it would operate quite effectively by means of bargains freely struck in which the nonoxygen-owners had to offer something to the owners to get the chance to breathe. They, too, would be compelled to sell themselves of their own free will. The same can be said of capitalism. Once its structure of social roles is in place, all that is necessary is that individuals choose, from among the alternatives available to them in their roles, the course of action that best serves their self-interest, and the extraction of unpaid surplus labor is enforced without further need for overt force except in unusual circumstances.

As with the oxygen-owning society, so too with capitalism: Overt force is used or threatened to defend owners against challenges to their ownership. That is just another way of saying that, in capitalism, the state uses overt force to protect private property. And this force is used to protect both the property of the capitalist (her factories and resources) and the property of the worker (his labor-power). This differs crucially from the way in which overt force is exercised in social relations like slavery. In slavery, the use of overt force is part of the normal exercise of the master's power. In capitalism, overt force is used to defend all against forceful interference with their right to dispose of whatever property they happen to own, be it means of production or labor-power. Accordingly, such force is not part of the capitalist's power but left to a third party that is neutral toward all owners—the state.

With both capitalists and workers protected in their capacity to dispose of what they own, the process by which workers are forced to work gratis can proceed apace. This effect can be achieved with the state functioning neutrally. Although the state normally favors the interests of capitalists over workers,[5] it can serve the process of forced extraction of unpaid labor by protecting both capitalists and workers alike in their freedom to dispose of what they happen to own. Thus the state can treat capitalists and workers as having the same or "equal" property rights over what they own. It just turns out that what capitalists happen to own is means of production, and what workers happen to own is the muscles in their arms. Capitalism, then, naturally appears as a system of free exchanges between people with equal rights (over unequal amounts of property). This brings us to the phenomenon of ideology.

Capitalism and Ideology

Of the study of social revolutions, Marx writes:

> *In considering such transformations a distinction should always be made between the material transformation of the economic conditions of production, which can be determined with the precision of natural science, and the legal, political, religious, aesthetic or philosophic—in short, ideological forms in which men become conscious of this conflict and fight it out.*[6]

The legal, then, is an ideological form. This is not to say that it is merely mental. It has a material reality in the form of police and prisons and guns and courts and legislators and law books and the rest. What is crucial is how this material reality is shaped, and for that we must understand how ideology is shaped.

As its etymology suggests, *ideology* means the science of ideas, where science can be taken in the ordinary sense as the study of causal connections. (Recall the discussion of ideology in Chapter 4.) In the context of Marxian theory, ideology comes to mean the ideas caused by the mode of production (in our case, the capitalist mode of production), and, equally important for Marxism, the caused ideas are in some important way false. Thus understood, for Marxism, the study of ideology denotes the study of how the mode of production gives rise to people's false beliefs about society. In *The German Ideology,* Marx writes

> *If in all ideology men and their circumstances appear upside down as in a camera obscura, this phenomenon arises just as much from their historical life-process as the inversion of objects on the retina does from their physical life-process.*

> *. . . The phantoms formed in the human brain are also, necessarily, sublimates of their material life-process, which is empirically verifiable and bound to material premises.*[7]

As this statement makes clear, the study of ideology requires that both the existence and the falsity of ideological beliefs be given a *materialist* explanation.

To understand this requirement, consider that Marxian materialism is the conjunction of two distinct claims, an ontological claim and a social scientific one. The *ontological* claim is that what exists is material, that is, physical objects in space. Mind or spirit in any immaterial sense are chimera. ("From the start the 'spirit' is afflicted with the curse of being 'burdened' with matter, which here makes its appearance in the form of agitated layers of air, sounds, in short, of language" [*German Ideology,* p. 19]). The *social scientific* claim is that the way in which a society is organized for the production of the material conditions of its existence and reproduction ("the mode of production") plays the chief (though by no means the only) causal role in determining the nature and occurrence of social events. ("The mode of production of material life conditions the social, political and intellectual life process in general."[8]) According to this social scientific claim, the belief that societies are shaped primarily by their members' attitudes, or that history is shaped by the progressive development of knowledge or ideals, is false. Rather, it is primarily the organization of production that shapes people's attitudes, and the progressive development of modes of production that shapes history. ("That is to say, we do not set out from what men say, imagine, conceive, nor from men as narrated, thought of, conceived, in order to arrive at men in the flesh. We set out from real, active men, and on the basis of their real life-process we demonstrate the development of the ideological reflexes and echoes of this life-process" [*German Ideology,* p. 14]; "it is not the consciousness of men that determines their being, but, on the contrary, their social being that determines their consciousness."[9])

Of these two claims, the social scientific is more restrictive than the ontological. The ontological claim requires only that we attribute ideology to material realities, be they brains or agitated layers of air or modes of production. The social scientific claim requires that among these material realities, priority be given to the mode of production as the primary cause of ideological beliefs. This means that the *main* source of false ideology is to be looked for not in the perceiving subject but in the perceived objects. It is not a "subjective illusion," the result of erroneous perception by individuals of their material conditions, but an "objective illusion," the result of more or less accurate perception of those conditions.[10] Viewing ideology this way has the added benefit of leaving the door open just wide enough so that the theory of ideology does not exclude the possibility of all true beliefs—and thus of the very science upon which it is based. A materialist theory of ideology, then, must show that false ideology is an *objective illusion* arising primarily from more or less accurate perception of the organization of material production, rather than from some subjective error.[11] Bear in mind that this is a matter of placing primary emphasis on objective factors, not of absolutely excluding subjective ones.

We can fix the idea of an "objective illusion" by considering a very common example of one, namely, the illusion that the sun goes around the earth. Any illusion, any erroneous belief that an individual holds, can be *stated* as a subjective error—but not every erroneous belief arises primarily *because* of a subjective error. A person who believes that the sun rises above a stationary horizon in the morning makes a mistake. However, this sort of mistake differs crucially from, say, the mistake that a colorblind person might make of believing that the light is green when it is red, or the mistake a person balancing her checkbook might make of believing that a number is 4 when it is 2. In these latter cases, the mistaken beliefs are not merely held by the individuals; they arise in the individuals primarily as the result of a defective perceptual faculty or misuse of a sound one. These are subjective illusions. In these cases, correcting the defect in or the use of the perceptual faculty should undo the mistake. The mistaken belief that the sun goes around the earth, by contrast, arises as a result of a sound perceptual faculty properly exercised. This is an objective illusion. Neither healthier vision nor looking more carefully is likely to enable an individual to correct this mistake and see that what occurs at dawn is not the sun rising above the horizon, but the horizon tipping down before the sun.

The ideology of capitalism is the illusion that capitalism is uncoercive. This illusion is a mistake of the same type as the illusion that the sun goes around the earth. What corresponds in capitalism to the movement of the sun seen from the earth is the free exchange of wages and labor-power between capitalists and workers. That the sphere of exchange is the objective basis of ideology is recognized in effect by Marx, when he writes that this sphere,

> *within whose boundaries the sale and purchase of labour-power goes on, is in fact a very Eden of the innate rights of man. There alone rule Freedom, Equality, Property. Freedom, because both buyer and seller of a commodity, say of labour-power, are constrained only by their free will [Capital, vol. 1, p.176].*

The normal perception of what goes on in exchange gives rise to the ideological illusion that capitalism is uncoercive. This is not because the freedom in exchange is an illusion. The fact is that, for Marx, capitalism works only because the moment of exchange, through which the circuit of capital continually passes, is truly free.

> *For the conversion of his money into capital, therefore, the owner of money must meet in the market with the free labourer, free in the double sense, that as a free man he can dispose of his labour-power as his own commodity, and that on the other hand, he has no other commodity for sale, is short of everything necessary for the realization of his labour-power [Capital, vol. 1, p. 169].*

That the second of these senses of freedom is the worker's "freedom from" ownership of means of production does not deny the reality of the first sense, without which we would have slavery or serfdom rather than capitalism.

In exchange, the power that capitalists have over workers recedes from view. If we distinguish two sorts of power—the power to withhold one's commodity until offered something preferable and the power to command obedience and back this up with violent force—then it is clear that, in the sphere of exchange, the latter power is suspended and all that remains is the former power. This former power is a power that all parties to the exchange have equally. Thus, the unequal power of capitalist and worker appears as their equal power to withhold from exchange what they happen to own, and their social inequality appears as the difference between the things that they happen to own. To use the celebrated words of Marx's analysis of the fetishism of commodities, a "social relation between men assumes, in their eyes, the fantastic form of a relation between things" (*Capital,* vol. 1, p. 72).

If this accurate perception of what goes on in exchange is to explain how capitalism appears uncoercive, we need to understand how the sphere of exchange—which is only part of capitalism—should be the source of beliefs about the whole of capitalism. Why should the experience of freedom in exchange, rather than, say, the experience of taking orders on the production line, determine the beliefs that members of capitalist societies come naturally to have? How is the representation of exchange *generalized* into a view of capitalism as a whole?

Marx offers a clue to the answer to this question when he says that the fetishism of commodities results because "the producers do not come into contact with each other until they exchange" (*Capital,* vol. 1, p. 73). Exchange transactions are the salient points of social contact for economic actors in capitalism. They literally punctuate capitalist social relations. Every social interaction between individuals playing roles in the capitalist mode of production begins with such a transaction (say, the signing of a wage contract, exchanging labor-power for money) and can be ended with such a transaction (say, the dissolution of the wage contract). Each of these beginnings and endings is characterized by the absence of either party's having the power to command the other's obedience and use violence to get it. Each party knows that he can enter or withdraw from any capitalist social interaction without being subject to the command or the overt force of the other. What constraint either feels seems to be only a matter of what he happens to own, which naturally appears as a feature of his own good or bad fortune rather than a condition coercively imposed by the other. Thus, *all* capitalist social interactions, *not just the exchanges themselves,* appear as voluntary undertakings between equal people who happen to own different things.

Exchange accurately perceived and then generalized is what leads workers in capitalist societies to believe that they are free, although they take orders most of their waking lives. Thus, ideologically false beliefs about capitalism result from accurate perception of exchange, when the rest of capitalism is, by default, assumed to be more of the same. The law follows suit.

Ideology and Law

"Law," wrote Marx in *The Poverty of Philosophy,* "is only the official recognition of fact."[12] For capitalist law, the fact is exchange. Law in capitalism is the official recognition of the fact of the economic relations in which the exchangers stand to one another. This insight—which will guide the materialist explanation of criminal law that I shall develop in this section—must be credited to the work of the Soviet legal theorist Evgeny Pashukanis, whose *General Theory of Law and Marxism* was published in Russian in 1924.[13] Among the things for which Pashukanis argued was that law was a product of capitalism and consequently had no legitimate place in socialism. As Stalin took firm control of the Soviet Union and saw fit to use the law to shore up that control, Pashukanis came eventually into disfavor. He recanted his views to some extent, but it was too late. By 1937, he had been declared an enemy of the people and shortly thereafter "disappeared." Recently rediscovered by Western Marxists, Pashukanis's work was first the object of lavish praise and subsequently the target of harsh criticism. I do not intend to endorse or defend the whole of Pashukanis's theory. He aimed at a general theory of law and made only a few observations about criminal law, which is my main concern here. I shall try to show that his basic insight about the relation between law and exchange can be developed into an explanation of the content of the criminal law and of the constitutional protections relevant to criminal justice.

Marx writes that parties to an exchange

> *must behave in such a way that each does not appropriate the commodity of the other, and part with his own, except by means of an act done by mutual consent. They must, therefore, mutually recognize in each other the rights of private proprietors. This juridical relation, which thus expresses itself in a contract, whether such contract be part of a developed legal system or not, is a relation between two wills, and is but the reflex of the real economic relation between the two [Capital, vol. 1, pp. 88-89].*

Exchangers must in fact refrain from forcing those with whom they would trade to part with their goods or services or money. Official recognition of this fact takes the form of granting to exchangers "the rights of private proprietors." Because this recognition is related to the ideological failure to perceive the coerciveness reproduced in exchanges between proprietors of capital and proprietors of labor, exchanges are understood legally as acts of the free will of the parties as long as no overt violence is used or threatened. Consequently, exchangers treat one another as *free subjects* whose freedom is expressed in their *right to dispose of their property without interference from others*.

It is the difference between what capitalists own and what workers own that, for Marx, makes it possible to reproduce a coercive relation through free exchange. If the law follows ideology in representing the relation between exchangers as noncoercive, then the law must abstract from this difference in what is owned and treat each party as having the same right to dispose of his property irrespective of what that property is. The law reflects this in its formality. The legal right of property is an empty form to be filled in with different content, depending on what an individual owns. Capitalists and workers have the same right of property; they just happen to own different things. It just happens that what some people own are factories and what others own are their bodies, but their property rights in these things are the same. Their freedom to dispose of their property also is the same.[14] Thus, exchangers treat each other as *equal* free subjects with equal property rights—that is to say, as legal *persons*.[15]

We saw in the previous section that ideology is not to be understood as merely an illusion. Ideology reflects the real way in which capitalism appears to its participants. By the same token, the ideological nature of law reflects the real relations in which exchangers stand to one another. The written law, even the institutions of law (from lawmakers to law enforcers), are not the source of law. They reflect real, objective relations between members of a capitalist society, relations that exist, so to speak, on the ground first and only later on the page or in the courts for that matter. It is here that the "inversion" of which Engels wrote does its ideological work. Although the law is a reflection of the relations of exchangers on the ground, it appears that the law is an expression of rationality itself, with the consequence that the relations among exchangers seem so as well.

Here, however, a problem arises for the Marxian materialist: If law is the reflection of the actual practice of economic exchange, how does law come to function as a norm? A simple reflection would represent whatever occurs, and thus could not identify some actions as infractions. How can the materialist account for the normative dimension of law that arises as a reflection of economic relations?

The answer to this is that law is not a simple reflection of economic relations but an *idealized* reflection. As exchanges occur over and over, people naturally tend to average out the peculiarities of individual cases and discern an "essential core." In time, when individual cases diverge enough from this essential core, they are seen as deviant and thus as violations. The legal reflex of economic relations, then, is not an exact replica but the result of a natural sifting out of arbitrariness and idiosyncrasy such that what emerges is an idealized "average" that stands in a normative relation to particular instances. This tendency to go from what happens "on average" to what is normative is a common feature of human social existence. People tend to take what usually happens as what should happen. This tendency of the statistical norm (what people can generally be expected to do) to become the moral norm (what is expected of people) is visible in early civilization (where, for example, natural and moral law are not distinguished from each other) and in advanced civilization (where, for example, existing business practice is often taken by courts as creating legally enforceable obligations).

This brings us to a second question. It would seem that law that reflects (even the idealized "average" core of) exchanges would include not only the criminal law but also what we currently understand as contract or civil law. How can the theory that traces law to exchange account for the nature of the criminal law per se, with its special content and its unique remedies?

To answer this, note first that there is considerable overlap in the content of criminal and civil law; criminal acts, such as theft or battery, also can be causes of civil action. This overlap, however, is largely asymmetrical: Virtually any criminal act can be a cause of civil action, but only some civil causes are subject to criminal prosecution. This suggests that the criminal law is more distinctive in its remedies than in its content. In general, criminal prosecution seeks punishment of the guilty, and civil action seeks recovery of damages from the one responsible for a loss. Now on the materialist theory, both sorts of law—criminal and civil—represent the "essential core" of normal exchange and aim to rectify violations of or deviations from that core. Thus, to explain the nature of the criminal law per se, we must show why some class of deviations from normal exchange is singled out for the distinctive "criminal" remedy, namely, punishment. Because punishment is generally a graver matter than recovery of damages, we should expect the criminal law to be addressed to the most serious violations of normal exchange, whereas the civil law can be addressed to all violations.

Violations of normal exchange can be distinguished in the following way: Some threaten the very possibility of free exchange by depriving people of the ability to dispose of their property. Other violations threaten not the possibility of free exchange but its success in meeting the wishes of the exchangers. What threatens the very possibility of exchange are acts of violence that overtly block the capacity of individuals to exercise their wills, acts of theft that overtly bypass the capacity of individuals to choose how their property is disposed of, and acts of deception that have the same effect, so to speak, behind the backs of their victims. These are so serious that they must be prevented in advance—and that requires a standing threat of punishment. Accordingly, the criminal law is primarily aimed at acts of violence, theft, and fraud.[16]

Less serious violations are compatible with the existence of exchange but cause exchanges in some way to fall short of the wishes of the exchangers. These violations are mainly failures to live up to the terms of explicit or implied contracts. They can be remedied by requiring performance or payment from the one responsible. These are suitable targets for the civil law, although nothing is lost by allowing the civil law to apply to recovery of losses due to the more serious violations as well.

Actual exchanges will be characterized by the full range of violations and deviations, from failure to meet agreed-upon deadlines to gross expropriation with the threat or use of violence. All such violations undermine the likelihood of the same parties exchanging again. Because it is generally in people's long-term interest that stable trading relationships be maintained, it will generally be in people's interest to eliminate such violations. Accordingly, over time the vast majority of exchanges, particularly those between people in continuing exchange relationships, will tend to be free of violations. Thus, an average core of exchange, characterized by absence of violence and fraud as well as by dependable fulfillment of agreements, will emerge as the norm. The law in general will represent this norm.

However, of the violations, there is a class that stands out in the extremity of the threat it poses to the possibility of exchange. This is the class of threats and acts of violence, theft, and fraud because all of these directly attack the ability of people to dispose of what they own according to their own free will. Consequently, the maintenance of stable exchange relations will require establishing a secure peace, free of violence, theft, and fraud.[17] Because these violations are so serious as to threaten the very possibility of ongoing exchange relations, they must be prevented in advance by the standing threat of punishment, rather than remedying them afterward. They are appropriately the subject of the criminal law.

On the whole, then, although the entire law in capitalism reflects the conditions of normal exchange, the content of the criminal law—the acts it identifies as "crimes"—are those that threaten the very possibility of normal exchange. Moreover, because the normal relations of exchange are not only idealized but (as we saw in the previous section) generalized to the whole of capitalism, they will shape people's normative expectations beyond exchange. Thus, they determine the limits that will be imposed on officials taxed with the job of finding and prosecuting criminals, the shape of court proceedings, the relation of punishment to offense, and the emphasis on the free will of the offender. Accordingly, by tracing law to its source in exchange, we can account for at least the general content of criminal law and the general shape of the criminal justice system and of the constitutional limits within which that system operates. Here, briefly sketched and numbered for ease of identification, are the main ways in which this works:

1. Normal exchange presupposes that people are treated as having property rights in whatever they are to trade, and that must mean not only goods but their bodies as well, because bodily actions are what workers trade with capitalists for their wage. Crime, then, is any violation by one individual of the property rights of another in whatever he owns, including his body. This explains why the criminal law is primarily directed against acts of violence, theft, and fraud. Moreover, because criminal law protects an individual's body because he owns it (and not, say, because it is the earthly vessel of his immortal soul), the law will be primarily concerned with injuries done to people's bodies against their will—otherwise such injuries do not violate the individual's ownership of his body. This accounts for the liberal principle, *volenti non fit injuria* (no injury to one who has consented) and thus, via generalization, for the tendency in capitalism to decriminalize (or reduce in importance) "victimless crimes" or "morals offenses."

2. This account also tells us what we are not likely to see as crime in capitalist society, namely, exercises of the power inherent in the ownership of property itself. Thus, we will not generally find that death due to preventable dangers in the workplace will be taken as murder because that would assume that the worker was somehow forced into the workplace by the power inherent in his boss's private ownership of the means of production. Because that is just the power that is invisible in capitalism, the worker is taken as freely consenting to his job and thus freely accepting its risks. Accordingly, when the criminal law is used against employers to get them to eliminate occupational hazards, it is never with the understanding that employers who do not eliminate such hazards are violent criminals. If the criminal law is used in these cases at all, it is as a regulatory mechanism applied to employers because this is the most efficient way to reduce the social costs of occupational injury and disease. The treatment of guilty employers is generally light-handed, even though far more people lose their lives due to preventable occupational hazards than as a result of what the law currently treats as murder. In capitalism, subjection to one person is seen as arbitrary and thus unlawful coercion, but subjection to the capitalist class is not seen at all. (Here is how the

Marxian theory understands the phenomena we discussed in the main text of this book and accounted for with the historical inertia explanation.)

3. The other side of criminal law—the limits placed on legal officials in their pursuit of suspected criminals (for example, in the Bill of Rights)—likewise reflects the generalized conception of people as owners of their bodies and other property. Accordingly, we find protections against official invasions of suspects' property (for example, the Fourth Amendment protections against unreasonable search and seizure) and against penetration of suspects' bodies or minds (for example, the Fifth Amendment protection against self-incrimination). Moreover, this explains why corporal punishment, which was the norm in feudalism and slavery, tends to be eliminated in capitalism. The bodies of slaves are literally owned by their masters, and lords have natural (that is, parentlike) authority over their serfs. In these cases corporal punishment fits the existing social relations. In capitalism, employer and employee meet as owners of their respective bodies, and thus corporal punishment looks increasingly out of place.

   The existence of these various limitations on what can be done to enforce the law is evidence that the Marxian view of law includes recognition of the way law functions not only to control the working class but as a limit on the behavior of the ruling class. Indeed, the Marxian view can be taken as claiming that it is precisely as a system that protects everyone alike in her property (including the body) by limiting both what citizens and law enforcers can do to the bodies (and other property) of other citizens, that the law most effectively serves the purpose of keeping the working class selling its labor-power to owners of means of production—both classes safe in the knowledge that no one can interfere with their right to dispose of what they happen to own.

4. As crime is a violation of normal exchange, so punishment is thought of on the same model of equivalence as exists in exchange. "Punishment emerges as an equivalent which compensates the damage sustained by the injured party."[18] The commercial model doesn't end here. The adversary system reproduces it in court. "The public prosecutor demands a "high" price, that is to say a severe sentence. The offender pleads for leniency, a "discount," and the court passes sentence in equity."[19] Crime deforms exchange by taking with force rather than payment. Punishment restores exchange by using force to pay the criminal back for his force. This is the tribute in retribution. The court is the extraordinary market where this extraordinary exchange is negotiated. The scales in Justice's hands are the same as those used by the merchant.

5. Because exchange normally brings payment to an individual only when she freely chooses to offer up her goods or services for it, so then the payment of punishment comes due only when the offender has freely chosen to commit the offense for which the punishment is payment. Accordingly, liability for punishment is subject to conditions of the same sort as apply to liability to contractual obligations. One is not bound by a contract that she has not signed freely, or that she signed while insane, or in ignorance of its contents, and so on. Likewise, the offender is liable to punishment, and thus is truly a criminal, only if he has committed his violation freely, sanely, and with knowledge of what he was doing. By the same logic, the law generally prohibits ex post facto attribution of criminal liability because a person cannot choose freely to violate a law before it has been passed.

Here, then, we read off the face of exchange, albeit idealized and generalized, the main contours of criminal justice as it develops in capitalism. As I suggested at the outset, this is no more than a skeleton. It does not aim to account for the full rich detail of any particular criminal justice system. Actual criminal justice systems exist in societies with other modes of production present alongside capitalism and are affected by the complex interplay of human actions, and so on, so that each actual system—like each actual face—will have a distinct physiognomy while sharing in the basic structure. Some criminal justice systems will be slower in eliminating "morals offenses," some will be stricter on occupational hazards, some will abolish the death penalty while others will retain it, and so on.[20] These specific outcomes will be a function of the strength of various social groupings (such as religious organizations, labor unions, academia, the press, and the like) come to have in the specific history of specific countries, and of all the largely unpredictable features that determine the outcome of particular battles over the content of the law and the funding of the legal apparatus. This notwithstanding, the Marxian claim is that criminal justice will tend toward the shape sketched out above.

Law and Ethics

We reach now the question of the moral stance toward capitalist criminal justice that is appropriate if the Marxian account is correct. Marxism describes capitalism as an exploitative system, meaning one in which workers are forced to work for capitalists without compensation. Marxists characteristically regard exploitation, and consequently capitalism, as unjust or immoral. Broadly speaking, they reach this condemnation by one of three routes. One is to view capitalist exploitation as wrong because it promotes antagonistic or alienated relations between human beings.[21] The second way is to view capitalist exploitation as wrong because it is a form of forced servitude or slavery.[22] The third way is to view capitalist exploitation as wrong because it is based on an unjust distribution of wealth, namely, the unjustifiable exclusive ownership by a few of the means of production.[23] I shall call these three views, respectively, "the alienation charge," "the slavery charge," and "the maldistribution charge." Each of these has moral implications for capitalist criminal justice. The task of identifying these implications is simplified by the fact that the second and third charges incorporate each other. The slavery charge accepts that private ownership of means of production is a case of unjust maldistribution (because it is a means of forcing servitude), and the maldistribution charge accepts that private ownership of means of production is a means of enslavement (because it is a power wrongly monopolized by a few). For our purposes, then, the charges against capitalism can be reduced to two: the alienation charge and the slavery-maldistribution charge.

Those who raise the alienation charge point out that capitalism is a system in which each person's well-being is in conflict with that of others. Capitalism pits class against class (competing over the division of the economic product into wages versus profit), worker against worker (competing for jobs), and capitalist against capitalist (competing for market shares). Moreover, proponents of this charge hold that antagonism of interests is neither a necessary feature of human life nor a desirable condition. It is caused by capitalism. It was less marked in feudalism, and might be eliminated in the future if a more cooperative arrangement, such as socialism, could be established. Criminal justice as it emerges in capitalism is understood as a means to regulate this antagonism of interests. Because it assumes that this antagonism is inevitable, criminal justice serves to confer permanent validity on capitalism. Moreover, criminal justice promotes this antagonism by teaching people that the rights of each are in conflict with the rights of others rather than mutually supportive, that freedom is *freedom from* invasion by others rather than freedom to develop with others, that what people owe each other is noninterference rather than a helping hand.

Also important is the fact that a society based on antagonism of interests is one in which people earn their daily bread only as long as someone else can profit as a result. When that changes, workers may find themselves in need and with little in the way of help from the rest of society. On this view, then, the large crime rates characteristic of capitalism are due to the fact that people in capitalism are taught to see their interests as in conflict with others' and thus they are trained to have limited altruism and fellow feeling, and to the fact that a society based on antagonism of interests is one in which economic need and insecurity are endemic. When limited fellow feeling meets economic need and insecurity, the result is crime. (Recall the views of Bonger and Gordon, discussed in Chapter 4.) The same system that calls criminals individually guilty, then, is responsible for the antagonism of interests that breeds crime in the first place. The upshot of this charge is that criminals are not—or at least not wholly—guilty of the crimes they commit. On this charge, criminals are in large measure unjustly punished for actions caused by the very system that punishes them.

On the slavery-maldistribution charge, the emphasis is on the wrongness and coerciveness of private ownership of means of production. Capitalism promotes a system of criminal justice based on protecting the freedom of individuals to dispose of what they rightly own; but the system itself is based on the wrongful appropriation of means of production, and with it the power to coerce others to labor without compensation. On this view, socialism would cure capitalism not so much by replacing antagonism of interest with harmony but by replacing private ownership of means of production by a few with social ownership by everyone.

To understand the moral implications for criminal justice of this charge, imagine for a moment that we see someone take a sheep from the field owned by another. In response, suppose that we make the normal judgment that a theft, an unjust expropriation, has occurred. Now suppose further that we learn that the field owner had himself stolen the sheep from the sheep taker some time before. According to these new facts, we shall change our views about the moral status of the sheep taking. Now we are likely to say that the one we saw take the sheep was not, morally speaking, a criminal but the opposite, a victim responding justifiably to an earlier crime. Likewise, if we come to see ownership of means of production as itself a violation of justice (because it is unjustly maldistributive or unjustifiably coercive), we will see the things that people do in response to it as more just than they appeared when we didn't question the justice of ownership of means of production. Recall the discussion in Chapter 4 of how a judgment that an individual is guilty of a crime presupposes that the social context in which his act occurred was just. By the same logic, judgment that the social context is unjust weakens the judgment that the individual is guilty.

On the slavery-maldistribution view, then, the individuals normally labeled "criminal" are seen as the victims of a prior "crime" to which they are responding. That criminals may not (and usually do not) see themselves as doing this only reflects the fact that they are taken in by capitalist ideology no less than law-abiding folks are. The "criminal" then is not a doer of injustice but the reverse. He is a victim of injustice trying to improve his situation by means that have been made necessary by the fact that capitalism leaves him few alternatives. The upshot of this charge is that criminals are not really morally guilty. They are in large measure unjustly punished for *re*acting against crimes perpetrated by the very system that punishes them.

In sum, the Marxist critique of criminal justice does lead to a moral condemnation of criminal justice under capitalism. This moral condemnation comes in two forms, both of which share the claim that capitalist criminal justice wrongly punishes people who do not deserve to be punished. In the first form, the alienation charge, criminals are thought not to deserve punishment because their acts are caused by socially conditioned antagonism to their fellows in conjunction with limited and unstable opportunities to satisfy their needs and desires. In the second form, the slavery-maldistribution charge, criminals are thought not to deserve punishment because their apparent crimes are reactions against conditions that are themselves, morally speaking, criminal. Needless to say, it is possible for the same person to endorse both forms of condemnation.

Several things that apply to both charges are worth noting. First of all, in both cases, the features of capitalist criminal justice that come in for ethical condemnation reflect the failure to see the way criminal justice reflects the mode of production—mentioned at the outset. In the case of the alienation charge, the failure is that of not seeing that capitalist criminal justice emerges to regulate the antagonistic relations between human beings that capitalism produces. Seeing capitalist criminal justice as the product of independent reason, it sees those antagonistic relations as a natural feature of human life that always must be so regulated. Then, capitalist criminal justice, rather than protecting the interests of capitalists, appears merely to be the necessary condition of any peaceful social coexistence.

In the case of the slavery-maldistribution charge, the failure is of not seeing how property in capitalism is an expression of a particular and morally questionable constellation of social forces. Seeing capitalist criminal justice as the product of independent reason, it sees the property criminal justice protects as a natural feature of human life that is always in need of such protection. Then, capitalist criminal justice, rather than protecting the interests of capitalists, appears merely to be protecting everyone's interest.

What's more, it follows that the continued and heavily publicized activities of criminal justice serve to reinforce ideological blindness, on the first view, blindness to capitalism's role in causing the alienated and antisocial attitudes and conditions that lead to crime and, on the second view, blindness to the moral dubiousness of capitalist property relations.

It also must be borne in mind that the ethical implications of both charges are general propositions that will fit actual criminal cases in varying degrees. For example, while the alienation charge suggests that criminals are not culpable because shaped by an antagonistic society, in actual cases, the degree to which individual lawbreakers have been so shaped will vary. There may be some who have largely escaped the deleterious influences and yet, out of selfishness or greed, commit crimes. Marxism naturally claims that the number of criminals of this sort is small compared with the number of criminals all told. Marxism, however, need not deny that there are some criminals like this and thus that they deserve punishment. Likewise, on the slavery-maldistribution charge, whereas criminals are generally taken to be victims of the prior injustice of private ownership of means of production, actual criminals differ in the degree to which they are so victimized and in the degree to which their actual crimes can be thought of as reactions thereto. Relatively privileged persons, or others whose crimes bear little relation to their class position (some rapists, for example), may well be more culpable than the general run of criminals. It seems to me appropriate for Marxists to view responsibility—and thus guilt—as existing in varying degrees, relative to the actual impact of the social structure on a given individual's criminal act.

Finally, note that on neither of the two views we have discussed does the criminal emerge as any kind of "proto-revolutionary," as is sometimes asserted of Marxism. On the alienation charge, the criminal is at best relieved of responsibility because he has been shaped by the social system to have antisocial attitudes and fated by that system to experience need and insecurity that, together with those attitudes, lead to crime. On the slavery-maldistribution charge, the criminal is at best a victim because he is the object of the unjust coercion or expropriation characteristic of private ownership of means of production. His crime, rather than being a kind of rebellion against what victimizes him, is most often a narrowly self-interested striking out against whatever he can get his hands on. On both charges, Marxism does imply reduced or no blame for (most) criminals; but it does not imply any celebration of their acts. This is particularly so in light of the fact that most victims of crime are other exploited people, members or would-be members of the working class. Crime and criminality must on the whole be placed by Marxism among the costs of capitalism, lined up alongside poverty, unemployment, pollution, and the rest.

Notes to the Appendix

1. This essay is a revised and shortened version of an article that appeared in *Criminal Justice Ethics* 6, no. 1 (Winter/Spring 1987). Peter Darvas assisted me with the research for that article.
2. Frederick Engels, "Letter to Conrad Schmidt (October 27, 1890)", in Karl Marx, *Selected Works*, ed., V. Adoratsky (Moscow: Cooperative Publishing Society of Foreign Workers in the USSR, 1935), vol. 1, p. 386.

3. Karl Marx, *Capital* (New York: International Publishers, 1967), vol. 3, p. 819.

4. Note that Marx does not hold that the value of a commodity is equivalent to the actual amount of labor-time that goes into producing it. On that view, commodities would increase in value the more inefficiently they were produced. Instead, recognizing that a commodity will command a price no higher than that for which commodities like it are selling, Marx takes the commodity's value to be determined by the average or socially necessary labor-time it takes to produce commodities of its kind. See *Capital*, vol. 1, p. 189. Furthermore, although Marx claims that value is equivalent to average labor-time, he only assumes that values and market prices coincide for the purposes of the argument of volume 1 of Capital about the fundamental nature of capitalism. In the subsequent volumes, Marx shows at length the mechanisms in capitalism that lead prices to diverge from values. Even after these common misinterpretations of the theory are eliminated, it must be admitted that Marx's labor theory of value has come in for so much criticism in recent years that many, even many Marxists, have given it up for dead.

5. See, for example, G. William Domhoff, *Who Rules America?* (Englewood Cliffs, N.J.: Prentice-Hall, 1967); M. Green, J. Fallows, and D. Zwick, *Who Runs Congress?* (The Ralph Nader Congress Project) (New York: Grossman, 1972); Edward S. Greenberg, *Serving the Few: Corporate Capitalism and the Bias of Government Policy* (New York: Wiley, 1974); and Ralph Miliband, *The State in Capitalist Society* (New York: Basic Books, 1969).

6. Karl Marx, "Preface to A Contribution to a Critique of Political Economy," in *The Marx-Engels Reader*, 2d ed., ed., Robert Tucker (New York: Norton, 1978), p. 5.

7. Karl Marx and Friedrich Engels, *The German Ideology*, parts 1 and 3 (New York: International Publishers, 1947), p. 14.

8. Marx, "Preface to A Contribution to a Critique of Political Economy," p. 4.

9. Ibid.

10. "It is not the subject who deceives himself, but reality which deceives him," Maurice Godelier, "Structure and Contradiction in Capital," in *Ideology in Social Science*, ed., Robin Blackburn (Glasgow: Fontana/Collins, 1977), p. 337.

11. Examples of theories of ideology that trace its distortions to subjective illusions are the attempt by some members of the Frankfurt School to explain the affection of German laborers for fascism by means of a Freudian account of the persistence of irrational authoritarian attitudes and the attempt of some sociologists to trace ideology to an existential need to reify a mythic worldview as protection against the terrors of meaninglessness. For the former, see Martin Jay, *The Dialectical Imagination: A History of the Frankfurt School and the Institute for Social Research, 1923-1950* (Boston: Little, Brown, 1973). For the latter, see Peter Berger and Thomas Luckmann, *The Social Construction of Reality* (New York: Doubleday, 1966).

12. Karl Marx, *The Poverty of Philosophy* (Moscow: Progress Publishers, 1955), p. 75.

13. Evgeny B. Pashukanis, *Law and Marxism: A General Theory*, trans. by B. Einhorn, ed., C. Arthur (London: Ink Links, 1978).

14. "The labor contract is to be freely entered into by both parties. But it is considered to have been freely entered into as soon as the law makes both parties equal on paper. The power conferred on the one party by the difference of class position, the pressure thereby brought to bear on the other party—the real economic position of both—that is not the law's business." Frederick Engels, *The Origin of the Family, Private Property, and the State* (New York: International Publishers, 1942), p. 64.

15. Pashukanis, *Law and Marxism*, pp. 112-13, inter alia.

16. Pashukanis approvingly attributes to Aristotle "the definition of crime as an involuntarily concluded contract" (ibid., p. 169).

17. Pashukanis observes that the exchange contract or pactum derives from pax or peace (ibid., p. 167).

18. Ibid., p. 169; see also Alan Norrie, "Pashukanis and 'the Commodity Form Theory': A Reply to Warrington," *International Journal of the Sociology of Law 10* (1982), pp. 431-34.

19. Pashukanis, *Law and Marxism*, p. 177.

20. See Georg Rusch and Otto Kirchheimer, *Punishment and Social Structure* (New York: Russell & Russell, 1968), for a classic Marxian-inspired historical study of the relationship between penal policy and the supply and demand for labor.

21. This is the view of, for example, Allen Buchanan in *Marx and Justice* (Totowa, N.J.: Rowman and Littlefield, 1982).

22. This is essentially the view argued for by, for example, Allen Wood, in "The Marxian Critique of Justice," *Philosophy & Public Affairs 1*, no. 3 (Spring 1972), pp. 244-82.

23. This is the view of, for example, G. A. Cohen in "Freedom, Justice and Capitalism," *New Left Review* 126 (March/April 1981), pp. 3-16. There is, by the way, a substantial literature on the question of whether Marxism holds that capitalism is wrong because it is unjust or that justice is part of what's wrong with capitalism. See articles in M. Cohen, T. Nagel, and T. Scanlon, eds., *Marx, Justice, and History* (Princeton, N.J.: Princeton University Press, 1980); K. Nielsen and S. Patten, eds., *Marx and Morality* (*Canadian Journal of Philosophy*, supplemental vol. 7, 1981), and J. Pennock and J. Chapman, eds., *Nomos XXVI: Marxism* (New York: New York University Press, 1983); as well as Norman Geras's review of the whole discussion, "The Controversy About Marx and Justice," *New Left Review* 150 (March/April 1985), pp. 47-85. My own views are presented in "The Possibility of a Marxian Theory of Justice," in *Marx and Morality*, eds., Nielsen and Patten, pp. 307-22.

About the Author

Jeffrey Reiman is William Fraser McDowell Professor of Philosophy at The American University in Washington D.C. He was born in Brooklyn, New York, in 1942. He received his B.A. in Philosophy from Queens College in 1963, and his Ph.D. in Philosophy from the Pennsylvania State University in 1968. He was a Fulbright Scholar in India during 1966-67. He joined The American University faculty in 1970, in the Center for the Administration of Justice (now called the Department of Justice, Law and Society of the School of Public Affairs). After several years of holding a joint appointment in the Justice program and the Department of Philosophy and Religion, Dr. Reiman joined the Department of Philosophy and Religion full-time in 1988, becoming Director of the Master's Program in Philosophy and Social Policy. He was named William Fraser McDowell Professor of Philosophy in 1990. He is a member of the Phi Beta Kappa and the Phi Kappa Phi honor societies. In addition to *The Rich Get Richer and the Poor Get Prison: Ideology, Class, and Criminal Justice,* Dr. Reiman is the author of *In Defense of Political Philosophy, Justice and Modern Moral Philosophy,* and numerous articles in philosophy and criminal justice journals and anthologies.

Index